Joseph Edwin Crawford

The constitution of Canada

Joseph Edwin Crawford

The constitution of Canada

ISBN/EAN: 9783337208431

Printed in Europe, USA, Canada, Australia, Japan

Cover: Foto ©Suzi / pixelio.de

More available books at **www.hansebooks.com**

THE CONSTITUTION

OF

CANADA.

BY

J. E. C. MUNRO,

OF THE MIDDLE TEMPLE, BARRISTER AT LAW, PROFESSOR OF LAW
OWENS COLLEGE, VICTORIA UNIVERSITY.

CAMBRIDGE:
AT THE UNIVERSITY PRESS.

1889

Cambridge:

PRINTED BY C. J. CLAY, M.A. AND SONS,

AT THE UNIVERSITY PRESS.

PREFACE.

SOME years ago I began to collect materials for a survey of the legal aspects of the constitution of the empire, but my purpose as regards the constitution of Great Britain and Ireland was anticipated by the publication of Sir William Anson's valuable work on the Law and Custom of the Constitution, and I therefore restricted myself to the constitutions of our colonies. Of these it is not possible to take a general survey without examining each in detail. Our colonies exclusive of the Indian dependencies fall into four groups: (1) the North American group, (2) the Australian group, (3) the South African group and (4) the Crown colonies. I have selected Canada for treatment first, not merely because a special interest has of recent years been taken in its constitution, but for the further reason that some recent Canadian statutes have given a completeness to the Dominion system of government it did not previously possess.

I have not attempted to criticise the working of the constitutions described or to investigate the development of purely local government—any adequate treatment of such subjects would require a greater personal knowledge of Canada than I can claim to possess: they are therefore reserved for consideration at some subsequent time. Constitutional customs are dealt with briefly, as Mr Todd in his

M.   b work on Parliamentary Government in the Colonies has discussed such matters at full length. In the chapter on the Dominion Parliament I have availed myself of the very valuable work of Mr Bourinot on Parliamentary Procedure in Canada.

In the last session of the Canadian Parliament several Acts were passed that modify some of the statements in the text. By the 51 Vic. c. 11 the Dominion Elections Act has been amended as regards the nomination of candidates, the method of voting, and the definition of corrupt practices; by the 51 Vic. c: 17, the organisation of the Department of Public Printing has been modified; and by the 51 Vic. c. 43 appeals in criminal cases to the Judicial Committee of the Privy Council have been forbidden.

The most important change introduced into the constitution has been the formation of a Legislative Assembly for the North West Territories. By chapter 50 of the Revised Statutes of Canada the Council of the North West Territories, as soon as its number reached twenty-one, was to give way to a Legislative Assembly[1]. The new Assembly is to consist of twenty-two elected members and three legal experts, the former to be elected by such male British subjects, other than unenfranchised Indians, as have been resident in the Territories for twelve months, and in their electoral districts for three months, preceding the election; the latter to be nominated by the Governor-General in Council.

The legal experts have the same privileges as elected members, except that they are not allowed to vote: on a dissolution taking place they vacate their offices.

The Lieutenant-Governor is authorised to nominate four members of the Assembly to act as an "advisory council" on

[1] See *post*, p. 36.

matters of finance. At meetings of this council the Lieutenant-Governor is to preside, and he is allowed a vote as well as a casting vote. Before being introduced all money bills must be recommended by him to the Assembly.

Notwithstanding the existence of this Assembly the constitution of the North West Territories differs in several important respects from that found in the provinces. The Territories do not constitute "a Province," and the Assembly has therefore only such legislative powers as the Dominion Parliament confers on it. The Lieutenant-Governor exercises the chief executive power and is not to the same extent as in the Provinces bound to defer to his advisers. No doubt in time the more settled districts in the Territories will be formed into a new province.

I am much indebted to Mr J. G. Colmar, secretary to the High Commissioner for Canada, for valuable assistance during the progress of the work; to Mr J. S. O'Halloran, secretary of the Royal Colonial Institute, and to the Librarian of the Colonial Office for permission to consult their libraries; and to my friends Professor T. N. Toller and Mr R. T. Wright for their kind aid in revising proofs.

J. E. C. M.

7, NEW SQUARE,
  LINCOLN'S INN.

CONTENTS.

CHAPTER I.

INTRODUCTION.

CHAPTER II.

CONSTITUTIONAL HISTORY OF THE PROVINCES.

CHAPTER III.

SOURCES OF THE LAW AND CUSTOMS OF THE CONSTITUTION.

CHAPTER IV.

PROVINCIAL LEGISLATURES.

CHAPTER V.

THE PROVINCIAL ASSEMBLIES.

CHAPTER VI.

PROVINCIAL LEGISLATIVE COUNCILS.

CHAPTER VII.

METHOD OF LEGISLATION.

CHAPTER VIII.

THE LIEUTENANT-GOVERNOR.

CHAPTER IX.

THE PROVINCIAL ADMINISTRATION.

CHAPTER X.

THE PROVINCIAL JUDICATURE.

CHAPTER XI.

THE DOMINION PARLIAMENT.

CHAPTER XII.

The House of Commons.

CHAPTER XIII.

The Senate.

CHAPTER XIV.

The Method of Legislation.

CHAPTER XV.

The Governor-General.

CHAPTER XVI.

THE PRIVY COUNCIL.

CHAPTER XVII.

DOMINION ADMINISTRATION.

CHAPTER XVIII.

THE DOMINION JUDICATURE.

CHAPTER XIX.

DIVISION OF LEGISLATIVE POWER.

CHAPTER XX.

Dominion Control of the Provinces.

CHAPTER XXI.

Imperial Control of the Dominion.

APPENDIX.

TABLE OF CASES.

TABLE OF STATUTES.

I. IMPERIAL ACTS.

II. CANADIAN ACTS PRIOR TO CONFEDERATION.

III. DOMINION ACTS.

IV. PROVINCIAL ACTS.

i. BRITISH COLUMBIA.

ORDINANCES.

STATUTES.

CONSOLIDATED STATUTES, 1877 (40 Vic.).

CANADIAN REPORTS REFERRED TO.

Can. S. C. R. ......Supreme Court of Canada.
Cart. ....Cartwright's cases decided on the B. N. A. Act, 1867.
Dor. App. ....Dorion's Quebec Appeals—Queen's Bench, Quebec,
         Appeal Side.
Grant ....Grant's Chancery Reports, Ontario.
Hannay ....Hannay's Reports of the Supreme Court of New
         Brunswick.
L. C. J. ....Lower Canada Jurist.
L. N. ....Legal News, Quebec.
Ont. App. ....Reports of the Court of Appeal of Ontario.
Ont. Rep. ....Reports of the High Court of Justice, Ontario.
Pug.................Pugsley's Reports of the Supreme Court of New
         Brunswick.
Pug. and B. ......Pugsley's and Burbidge's Reports of the Supreme
         Court of New Brunswick.
Q. L. R. ....Quebec Law Reports.
R. and C. ....Russell and Chesley's Reports of the Supreme
         Court of Nova Scotia.
R. and G. ....Russell and Geldert's Reports of the Supreme
         Court of Nova Scotia.
U. C. C. P. ....Reports of the Court of Common Pleas, Ontario.
U. C. Q. B..........Reports of the Court of Queen's Bench, Ontario.
Steph. Dig.........Stephen's Digest of Quebec Reports.

ABBREVIATIONS.

N. B. ....New Brunswick.
N. S. ....Nova Scotia.
N. S. Rev. Stat............The Revised Statutes of Nova Scotia, 1884.
N. W. T.....................North West Territories.
O...............................Ontario.
O. R. S. ....The Revised Statutes of Ontario, 1887.
P. E. I. .. ..Prince Edwards Island.
P. E. I. Rev. Stat.........The Revised Statutes of Prince Edward's Island,
                              1856.
P. C............................Privy Council.
Q...............................Quebec.
R. S. C. ....The Revised Statutes of Canada, 1886.
S. O..........................Standing Orders.

CHAPTER I.

INTRODUCTION.

ON the 1st day of July in the present year (1888) the Canadian federation attained its majority; twenty-one years having elapsed since by an Order in Council the Provinces of Ontario, Quebec, Nova Scotia and New Brunswick were formed into the Dominion. Twenty-one years is not a long period in the life of a State, and it is not to be expected that the Constitution of Canada will prove as instructive a subject of study as that of the United States with its hundred years of growth and development. But in many respects the Canadian Constitution offers a special field for the inquirer. It is a successful effort to solve the problem of uniting distinct states or provinces under a central government. A similar task had already presented itself to an English speaking people, but the conditions of the problem solved in Canada differed in many respects from the conditions that faced Washington and his associates. While the American States had to create not merely a central government but a government which, within the limits laid down, should be supreme, the Canadian Provinces had to organize a Union subject to a supreme Executive, Legislature and Judicature all of which already existed. The executive supremacy of the Queen, the legislative power of the Imperial Parliament, and the judicial functions of the Privy Council remained unaffected by the Union, and this to some extent simplified the work to be done.

Differences between Canada and U. S.

It has been more than once stated that the Canadian Constitution is a mere copy of the American. Such a statement is very far from the truth. That the framers of the Quebec resolutions adopted portions of the American system is undoubted, but every care was taken to avoid those weak points in that system which the experience of years had brought to light. "We can now," said Sir John Macdonald when moving in the Legislative Assembly of Canada the resolution in favour of the Union, "take advantage of the experience of the last seventy-eight years during which the (U. S.) Constitution has existed, and I am strongly of belief that we have in a great measure avoided in this system which we propose for the adoption of the people of Canada the defects which time and events have shewn to exist in the American Constitution." The election of a President for a term of four years, the independence of the President during this period both of his ministers and of Congress, and the delegation to the central Government of definite specified powers leaving the balance of legislative power in the States, are three of the most important characteristics of the United States Constitution. But not one of these principles was adopted in Canada. The Executive authority was vested in the Crown, represented in Canada by a Governor-General (appointed by the Crown), who is required to act by the advice of a ministry responsible to the Canadian Parliament. Specified powers only are given to the Provinces, the balance of legislative power being lodged in the Dominion or in the British Parliament, for the belief prevailed in Canada that the exceptional powers of the American States and the doctrine of state rights had been leading factors in bringing about the great Civil War. Further differences between the two Constitutions will be referred to later on.

The English Constitution and the Constitution of the different North American Colonies at the time furnished many suggestions which were embodied in the Act of Union. The House of Lords was taken as the type of the Senate or Upper House, nomination for life being substituted for the hereditary principle. The practice of introducing money bills in the House of Commons on the advice of a minister was adopted, and the procedure of the British Parliament was followed as to the manner and method of passing bills. No important change was introduced in the constitution of the executive or legislative bodies of the provinces, except that the province of Canada was divided into the provinces of Ontario and Quebec, and a separate constitution was given to each. *Influence of British Constitution.*

During the years immediately succeeding the Union the Dominion was chiefly engaged in the work of organization. Different departments of state had to be created and appropriate duties assigned to each minister. From 1870 to 1873 arrangements were concluded that resulted in the admission of British Columbia, Prince Edward's Island, and the North West Territories into the Union, in the formation of the province of Manitoba, and in the organization of a government for the Territories. Under the term North West Territories was included all territory not within the jurisdiction of a province, and it embraced not only lands bordering on the Arctic Seas, but lands between the Eastern boundary of Ontario and the Western boundary of British Columbia, and extending as far south as the boundary of the United States. The acquisition of the Territories gave the Dominion jurisdiction from the Atlantic to the Pacific, and rendered possible the physical union of the provinces by means of the Canadian Pacific Railway. *Legislative activity of Dominion.*

In 1875 the Dominion established a Supreme Court, but such Court, it should be remembered, is not "supreme" in the American sense of the term, as an appeal may lie, if

not of right yet by special permission of the Crown, from
such Court to the Judicial Committee of the Privy Council.
Subsequent years saw further results of activity on the part
of the Canadian legislature in the establishment of a uniform
election law throughout the Dominion (1885) and in the
revision and consolidation of all the statutes passed since
1867, a work not yet fully completed.

In surveying a Constitution it seems desirable for many
reasons to work upwards rather than downwards, that is to
say, to begin with the local institutions and end with the
central government. In the case of Canada this method is
specially appropriate, as the legislative powers of the Dominion
cannot be understood without reference to the powers of
the Provinces. It also seems desirable before referring to
the executive which administers laws or the judicature
which enforces laws to deal with the legislature which enacts
laws. In this work the Province comes under consideration
before the Dominion and the legislature before the executive.

General
scheme of
Constitu-
tion.
The general scheme of the Canadian Constitution may
be described as follows. The Legislative power, subject always to the supremacy of the Imperial Parliament, is divided
between a central legislature and the provincial legislatures.
The Executive power in theory is lodged in the Queen, but
in practice it is exercised by three executive bodies, viz.
the Lieutenant-Governor with his Provincial Council, the
Governor-General with his Privy Council, and the Queen
with the English Ministry. The sphere of executive power
in each case corresponds with the sphere of legislative
power; the supremacy of the Crown preventing or determining any executive conflict between the Dominion and a
province. Each province establishes its own courts of judicature, but a Supreme Court, constituted by the Dominion,
acts as a Court of Appeal, from which a further appeal may,

under certain circumstances, lie to the Judicial Committee of the Privy Council.

It follows from what has been said that a citizen of Canada is subject to three distinct legislatures, the provincial Legislature, the Dominion Parliament, and the Imperial Parliament, and to three distinct executive bodies, the Provincial Executive, the Dominion Privy Council, and the English Cabinet. If he thinks that in legislating on any matter affecting his rights the Dominion or the Provincial legislature has overstepped the limits of its powers, he may challenge the legality of the statute in a court of law, but as regards a statute of the British Parliament he has no legal redress. The decision of a Dominion court is as binding on him as the decision of a court of his province, and as the Sheriff and other officials who execute provincial judgments are *ex officio* officials of the Dominion, the Courts of the Central Government have the requisite machinery for exacting obedience to their decrees. *Three legislatures.*

Each province has the right of determining whether its legislature shall consist of one or two houses. In Ontario, Manitoba and British Columbia the legislature consists of one house only. The qualifications of voters and of members is, as a rule, determined by the province. The legislative powers of a province are fixed by Imperial Statutes, and as far as possible are specifically enumerated. A province may legislate on property and civil rights, provincial lands, the borrowing of money for provincial purposes, direct taxation, public institutions, tavern licences, the incorporation of provincial companies, and the solemnization of marriage. All local works and undertakings as well as municipal institutions and "all matters of a merely local or private nature in the province" are within its jurisdiction. In order to secure a uniform criminal law throughout the Dominion, criminal law and procedure have been placed under the Dominion, *Powers of Provinces.*

otherwise the province has full jurisdiction in regard to the administration of justice, and may by fine or imprisonment enforce any law relating to any subject within its jurisdiction.

All laws require the assent of the Lieutenant-Governor of the province, and power is given to the Governor-General to disallow any provincial law.

Provincial Executive. At the head of the Provincial Executive is the Lieutenant-Governor, a Dominion officer, appointed by the Governor-General. An Executive Council, selected by him on the same principles that govern the selection of the members of the English Cabinet, assists and advises him in administering public affairs. The Council holds office so long as it retains the confidence of the legislature; if such confidence be lost the members resign, and those who enjoy the support of the majority in the legislature take their places.

The Lieutenant-Governor summons, prorogues and dissolves the provincial legislature, and discharges other important duties conferred on him by statute.

Dominion Legislature. In framing the constitution of the central legislature the House of Lords seems to have been taken as the type of an Upper House, and the United States Assembly as the type of a Lower House. Some difference of opinion prevailed as to whether members of the Upper House should be elected or nominated, but it was finally decided that the nominative principle should be followed, and that as an hereditary body was unsuited to Canada all appointments should be for life. A property qualification of 4000 dollars was imposed, and all senators were required to be not less than 30 years of age.

The Senate. The number of senators was fixed at 72, and as it was found that the provinces in favour of union fell into three groups, viz. Upper Canada or Ontario, with its agricultural population and agricultural interests, Lower Canada or Quebec, with its special institutions and laws, and the maritime provinces, with their commercial interests, it was resolved that each division should be equally represented in the Senate by 24 members. On the formation of the province of Manitoba and the admission of British Columbia three members were assigned to each of these two provinces, and subsequently provision was made for the representation of the North West Territories by two senators, so that the normal number of the Senate is now 80.

In the formation of the House of Commons it was deemed desirable to make provision for the adjustment of representa- House of Commons. tion to population, and for this purpose a simple and ingenious plan was adopted. The Province of Quebec or Lower Canada, which enjoyed a population of a permanent character, was taken as the starting point, and the fixed number of 65 members was assigned to it. To the remaining provinces were assigned as many representatives in proportion to their population as 65 bore to the population of Quebec. Adjustments of the representation took place after the census of 1871 and the census of 1881, and in 1886 representation was conceded to the North West Territories. The total number of members of the House of Commons is now 215. Taking the total population of Canada as 4,324,810 we have one representative for every 20,115 people as compared with one representative for every 155,465 in the United States.

No attempt was made in 1867 to introduce a uniform franchise throughout the Dominion, but the precedent of the Franchise. Canada Union Act of 1841 was followed, and a vote for the Dominion House of Commons was given to every man who in his own province was qualified to vote for his own provincial assembly. It was not until 1885 that the Dominion Parliament exercised its power of providing a general franchise for the whole Dominion. The franchise is now based on either ownership, or occupation, or income. The ownership or occupation of premises of the value of $300 in cities, $200 in towns, and $150 in other places confers the right to vote,

provided that in the case of occupation the occupation has
lasted for one year. An income of $300 a year, or an annuity
of $100 a year, if accompanied by residence of one year,
also gives a vote. A son if resident with his father may become qualified through his father's ownership or occupation,
and a fisherman can be placed on the register if he owns
land, boats, or fishing tackle of the value of $300. Special
provision is made for giving the franchise to Indians.

Duration of Parliament. The duration of Parliament was fixed, subject to the power
of the Crown to dissolve it at any time, at five years. Previous
to the Union the average duration of the legislature in the
old province of Canada had been three and a half years.
Since the Union there have been five parliaments, the first
continued practically for five years, the second was dissolved
within a year, the third had an existence of four years and
five months, the fourth did not quite complete its fourth year,
whilst the fifth, which met in Feb. 1883, was not dissolved
until 1887.

Dominion Executive. In the constitution of the Executive the English Constitution has been followed. The executive power is vested in the
Sovereign, who carries on the work of administration through
a Governor-General, assisted by a body of ministers known as
the Canadian Privy Council. The Governor-General is appointed by the Crown, and the ministers are appointed by the
Governor-General. But in accordance with the principle of
"responsible government" the Governor-General is by constitutional practice required to select as his ministers those
members whose policy obtains the confidence of the House of
Commons. The position of a minister is therefore similar to
that of a member of the Cabinet; but whilst the English
Cabinet is "unknown to the law," the Union Act makes
express provision for the constitution of the Canadian Privy
Council.

Governor-General. In all matters not directly affecting Imperial interests the
Governor-General is required to act by the advice of his

ministers. His power is therefore of a much more limited nature than that enjoyed by the President of the United States. The President during his term of office may act independently of his ministers, who are to be regarded rather as heads of departments than as advisers of the Chief of the State.

The Canadian Parliament has full power to legislate on all matters not assigned to the Provinces, and not directly or indirectly reserved to the Imperial Parliament. Twenty-nine classes of subjects are enumerated in the Union Act of 1867 as within the legislative competence of the Dominion, but it is expressly declared that such enumeration shall not restrict the general power given "to make laws for the peace, order and good government of Canada in relation to all matters not coming within the classes of subjects assigned exclusively to the legislatures of the Provinces." The enumeration of specific subjects is therefore to be taken by way of illustration, or as throwing light on the specific powers assigned to the provinces. *Powers of Legislation.*

The Dominion legislature is restricted not merely by the provincial powers but by the express and implied reservations in favour of the Imperial Parliament. No duties as between the different provinces can be imposed by the Dominion, nor can the Dominion alter the leading principles of its Constitution. In such matters the Imperial Parliament alone can take action, and when, for example, it was thought desirable to provide for the representation of the North West Territories in parliament, an Imperial Act had to be obtained giving the requisite power to pass the necessary legislation.

Comparing the powers of the Dominion Parliament with those of the United States Congress the chief differences are as follows: *Dominion Parliament and U. S. Congress.*

1. The only portion of Criminal Law delegated to Congress relates to counterfeiting securities and current coin of the *1. Criminal Law.*

United States, and to the definition and punishment of piracies and felonies committed on the high seas, and of offences against the law of nations; whereas in Canada the whole Criminal Law, except the constitution of Courts of Criminal Jurisdiction, is practically within the jurisdiction of the Dominion. This course was adopted not from any distrust of the provinces, but from the desire to secure a uniform criminal code throughout the Dominion, so that a citizen in whatever part of the Confederation he might be would always know what was his position in regard to the Criminal Law[1].

2. War.   2. Congress can declare war, a power that in Canada belongs to the Crown.

3. State powers.   3. In the United States the powers not specifically delegated to the United States are within the jurisdiction of each State: in Canada the powers not specifically given to the Provinces are reserved to the Dominion. The Canadian principle was adopted with the express object of strengthening the central government, and of preventing any question arising as to "state rights" or to the sovereignty of a province. The exercise of the power of the Governor-General to veto a Provincial bill, on the ground of its infringing the settled policy of the Dominion, has however brought about a conflict between Manitoba and the Dominion, though such conflict tends to be peacefully settled.

Restrictions.   4. Certain restrictions exist on the legislative powers of Congress that are not found in Canada. That direct taxes should be in proportion to the census, or that no *ex post facto* law or bill of attainder should be passed, are principles binding on Congress but not on the Dominion Parliament.

    5. There is another class of restrictions imposed on the legislative power of Congress which though they embody principles that have been incorporated into the law do not apply to Canada. Canada respects freedom of speech, freedom of

---

[1] Debates on Confederation, p. 41.

the press, the right of the people to assemble or to petition the Government; but whilst Congress cannot pass a law infringing these rights, the Canadian, like the British, Parliament may do so.

6. Congress with the assent of three-fourths of the States *Amendment of* may amend its Constitution; the Dominion Parliament has *Constitution.* no similar power. The Dominion may alter the franchise or legislate on matters relating to the election of members of the House of Commons, but so far as substantial changes in the Constitution are concerned recourse must be had to the Imperial Parliament.

It is naturally to be expected that difference of opinion *Conflict between* would occasionally arise as to the limits of the Dominion and *Provinces* the Provincial powers respectively. The only serious conflict *and Dominion.* that has arisen is due to the exercise of the right of the Governor-General to veto a Provincial Act. In this respect the Governor-General by statute possesses a power that does not belong to the Crown. The Crown may veto an Act of the Dominion, but cannot veto an Act of a Provincial legislature. The number of Provincial Acts vetoed by the Governor-General is comparatively small, but the mere fact that the Governor-General, acting on the advice of his ministers, may find himself obliged to veto a Provincial Act on the ground that it is contrary to the "policy of the Dominion," may give rise to a serious conflict of Provincial *versus* Dominion policy.

In Canada, as in the States, the judiciary (including *Judiciary.* under this term the Judicial Committee of the Privy Council) tends to occupy the most prominent place as the arbiter between Provincial and Dominion rights. The decisions of the Courts as to the limits of the legislative power of the Dominion and of the Provinces have been loyally accepted in Canada as in the States, and as time goes on there seems every reason to expect that the importance and power of the judicature will be one of the most striking developments of the Constitution. The judges of the superior, district, and county courts of each province are appointed by the Governor-General. The independence of the judges is secured by making their office tenable only during good behaviour, by charging their salaries on the civil list, and by the provision that they can be removed only by the Governor-General on address to the Senate and the House of Commons.

Unexpected developments. Some unexpected constitutional developments have occurred in Canada as in the United States. In the States there is no more characteristic feature than the growth of the power of the Senate as compared with the decreased influence of the House of Representatives. In Canada, on the other hand, the influence of the House of Commons has grown at the expense of the Senate. Two reasons may be assigned for this. In the first place the Canadian senators are nominated by the Governor-General as the representative of the Crown, whereas the American senators are elected by the State legislatures, and an elected body tends to become more powerful than a nominated body. The system of nomination is indeed sufficient of itself to explain the decadence of the Canadian Senate; but the election of senators by the State legislatures is not sufficient to account for the power of the American Upper House. Such a method of election is not far removed from the method of nomination. The real cause of the predominance of the latter body seems to lie in the fact that all ministers and officials are appointed by the Senate though nominated by the President. No such power has been given to the Canadian Senate. All ministers and officials are appointed by the Governor-General as representing the Crown, though such appointments, when not the result of examination, are made on the advice of the Privy Council.

A second unexpected result has been the conflict between

at least one of the Provinces and the Dominion. When the framers of the Constitution provided that all powers not specifically delegated to the Provinces should remain with the Dominion, it was thought that all danger of conflict between the central authority and the province had been removed. The exercise of the Governor-General's right of veto in the case of the Manitoba Railway Acts shewed that this was not the case, and that where the veto is exercised, not on the ground that the province has exceeded its legislative powers, but on grounds of "general policy," a conflict may arise. It should be added that the Dominion is fully alive to the necessity of rarely interfering with provincial legislation, except where clearly illegal[1].

[1] See post, chap. xv.

CHAPTER II.

CONSTITUTIONAL HISTORY OF THE PROVINCES.

THE Dominion of Canada as now constituted comprises seven organized Provinces, one organized District, and a vast extent of territory, sparsely inhabited, known as the North West Territories.

Area and population. The area and population of Canada is as follows:

	Area, square miles.	Population.
Ontario	101,733	1,923,228
Quebec	188,688	1,359,027
Nova-Scotia	20,909	440,587
New Brunswick	27,174	321,129
Manitoba	123,200	65,954
British Columbia	341,305	49,459
Prince Edward's Island	2,133	108,928
Keewatin North-West Territory and Islands	3,000,352	56,446
	3,805,494	4,324,758

Union of the Provinces. Originally the Dominion was composed of the Provinces of Ontario and Quebec (previously known as Upper and Lower Canada respectively), Nova Scotia and New Brunswick. By an Imperial Order in Council[1] dated the 23rd June 1870 the North West Territories were ceded to the Dominion as from the 15th July 1870, and a Canadian Act (33 Vic. c. 3) formed out of these territories the new Province of Manitoba. British Columbia was admitted into the Dominion as from the 20th July 1871 by an Order in

[1] See Appendix.

Council[1] dated the 16th May 1871, and Prince Edward's Island was admitted as from the 1st July 1873 by an Order in Council[1] dated the 26th July 1873. In 1876 the District of Keewatin was carved out of the North West Territories, and received a special form of government under the direction of the Lieutenant-Governor of Manitoba. By the British North American Act 1867 provision was made for the admission of Newfoundland, but it still remains a separate colony, though there is at present a movement in progress in the island in favour of Union.

The following brief outline of the Constitutional history of the various Provinces may prove useful to the student.

1. ONTARIO AND QUEBEC.

After the conquest of Canada and its cession to England by the capitulations of Montreal in 1760, confirmed by the treaty of the 10th Feb. 1763, the Crown by Letters patent constituted the Province of Quebec. General Murray was appointed Governor, and he was ordered to execute his office according to his commission and the accompanying instructions and such other instructions as he should receive, and according to all laws made with the advice and consent of the Council and Assembly. Power was given to him, with the consent of the Council and as soon as the circumstances would permit, to call an assembly of the free-holders and planters, and until this was done the Governor and Council were invested with "authority to make such rules and regulations as should appear to be necessary for the peace, order and good government of the Province." *Constitution of the Province of Quebec.*

The Instructions required members of the proposed assembly to take in addition to the oaths of allegiance and supremacy a declaration against transubstantiation, but the French population who were Catholics refused to take such *No assembly met.*

_____
[1] See Appendix.

tests, and the assembly though formally summoned never met[1]. The government therefore remained in the hands of the Governor and the Council.

The Council.

The Council consisted of the Lieutenant-Governors of Montreal and Three Rivers, the Chief Justice, and eight others chosen from the residents in the Province[2]. It possessed legislative as well as executive powers: the Crown retaining the right to disallow all laws.

Uncertainty of laws.

Great uncertainty prevailed as to what laws were actually in force in the Province. Some thought that the effect of the conquest and of the proclamation of the 7th Oct. 1763 was to establish the law of England in all its branches, the French settlers maintained that the old Canadian laws remained unrepealed, whilst some of the leading lawyers held that the result of the proclamation was to introduce the Criminal Law of England and to confirm the Civil Law of Canada.

The Government of Quebec retained the above form until 1774 when the English Parliament gave a new Constitution to the Province by an Act known as the Quebec

Report of Thurlow and Wedderburne.

Act[3]. Previous to the passing of this Act the Crown by Order in Council had directed Attorney-General Thurlow and Solicitor-General Wedderburne " to take into consideration several reports and papers relative to the laws and courts of judicature of Quebec and to the present defective mode of government in that Province and to prepare a plan of Civil and Criminal Law for the said Province and to make their several reports thereon." On the reports made in pursuance of these orders the Quebec Act was based[4].

The new constitution recognised the religion of the French population by relieving Catholics from the necessity of taking the test oath, and enacts that the English Criminal

[1] Christie, I. p. 50. [2] Garneau, II. p. 87.
[3] 14 Geo. III. (i) c. 83. [4] Christie, I. p. 27.

law was to prevail in criminal matters, but as regards property and civil rights recourse was to be had to the laws of Canada which were based on the customs that the French settlers had brought with them. The legislative power was placed in the hands of a Council appointed by the Crown, consisting of not more than 23 and not less than 17 persons. No ordinance was to be passed unless a majority of the Council were present, and every ordinance was to be transmitted, within six months after its enactment, for His Majesty's approbation, and if disallowed was to be null and void from the time the disallowance was promulgated at Quebec. *The Legislative Council.*

Shortly after the passing of the Quebec Act war broke out between England and her American Colonies. One result of the war was the immigration of a large number of British subjects into the Province. The new settlers located themselves chiefly in the west, along the banks of the St Lawrence, and in the neighbourhood' of the lakes Ontario and Erie[1]. Serious complaints were made by the new British settlers of the state of affairs in the Province, and a demand was made for a constitution resembling that to which they had been accustomed. *Results of war with Colonies.*

In 1791 a bill was introduced by Pitt dividing the Province into Upper and Lower Canada, the line of division being so drawn as to give a great majority to the British element in Upper Canada and a great majority to the French settlers in Lower Canada. The measure was strongly opposed by Fox, who urged that the separation of the English and French inhabitants was most undesirable, and that general and political expediency required that the French and English should coalesce into one body, so that the different distinctions of the people might be extinguished for ever. Many Canadians were opposed to the principle of the bill, and their *Bill introduced by Pitt.*

---

[1] Christie, I. p. 68.

agent, Mr Adam Lymburner, a merchant of Quebec, was heard at the bar of the House of Commons.

The Act was passed, and is known as the Constitutional Act of 1791[1].

The Constitutional Act, 1791. — The Act divided Quebec into two provinces, Upper Canada and Lower Canada. In each province the legislature was to consist of the Governor, a Legislative Council and a Legislative Assembly.

The Governor. — The Governor had power to give or withhold the royal assent to bills, or to reserve them for consideration by the Crown. He could summon, prorogue, or dissolve the legislature, but was required to convene the legislature at least once a year.

The Legislative Council. — The Legislative Council in Upper Canada consisted of not less than 7, and in Lower Canada of not less than 15 members, chosen by the King for life, the Speaker being appointed by the Governor-General.

The Legislative Assembly was in counties elected by 40s. freeholders, and in towns by owners of houses of £5 yearly value and by resident inhabitants paying £10 yearly rent. The number and limits of electoral districts were fixed by the Governor-General. Lower Canada had 50 members, Upper Canada 16 members, assigned to their respective legislatures.

Non-success of the Constitution Act. — The new Constitution did not prove a success. Serious differences arose between the Legislative Council and the Legislative Assembly in regard to the control of the revenue and supplies, differences which were aggravated by the conflict that still went on between the French and English races. The state of Canada was brought before the House of Commons, but the House rejected the proposal to make any radical changes. The discontent resulted in the rebellion of 1837—8, and an Act was passed suspending the Constitution of Lower Canada[2], and under its provisions a special

---

[1] 31 Geo. III. (i) c. 31.   [2] 1 & 2 Vic. (i) c. 9.

Council was appointed to administer the province. Lord Durham was appointed Governor-General, and was intrusted with large powers as high Commissioner for adjusting the relations and government of the two provinces. On his arrival he dissolved the special Council and appointed a new executive, and then proceeded to examine into the causes of the failure of the Constitution of 1791. The result of his inquiries was embodied in the famous Durham report presented to Parliament in 1839, in which he recommended the union of the two provinces and the introduction of responsible government. Lord John Russell brought forward a bill to carry out the former of these recommendations, and the bill became law on July 23rd, 1840[1].

This Act united the two provinces and established a Legislative Council of not less than 20 members, appointed for life by the Governor, and a legislative Assembly of 84 members, consisting of an equal number from Upper and Lower Canada. Toronto, Montreal and Quebec were to return two members each, certain other towns and the county constituencies one member each, power being given to the Governor to fix the limits of the constituencies. The number of representatives was not to be changed without the concurrence of two-thirds of the members of each House. A real property qualification to the amount of £500 was required of all members of the Assembly. As regards the revenue and expenditure certain fixed charges, amounting to about £75,000, were thrown on the consolidated fund, and all other expenditure was placed within the control of the Assembly.

The Union Act, 1840.

It only remained for the home Government to give effect to that portion of the Durham report which recommended the introduction of responsible government, and in a Despatch

Responsible government.

---

[1] 3 & 4 Vic. (i) c. 35.

dated the 5th Feb. 1841 Lord John Russell instructed the Governor-General to call to his Councils "those persons who by their position and character have obtained the general confidence and esteem of the inhabitants of the province," and "only to oppose the wishes of the Assembly when the honour of the Crown or the interest of the Empire are deeply concerned." For some years difficulties arose between the governors and the people as to how the principle of responsible government was to be carried into effect. At length Lord Elgin in 1847 was expressly instructed "to act generally on the advice of the Executive Council and to receive as members of that body those persons who might be pointed out to him as entitled to do so by their possessing the confidence of the Assembly."

Changes in the Constitution. The Constitution of 1840 remained unchanged until 1853, when, by a vote of two-thirds of the Legislature, the number of representatives was increased from 84 to 130, and the elective franchise was extended.

Changes in Legislative Council. In the following year an Imperial Act was passed[1] empowering the legislature to alter the constitution of the Legislative Council, and a Canadian Act was passed in 1856[2] making the members elective. The existing members were allowed to retain their seats, 48 elected members were added to the Council, and these elected members were to retain their seats for eight years. British subjects of the age of thirty years and owning real estate of the value of £2000 were eligible for election, and the qualification of electors was made the same as that required in the case of electors of the Assembly.

Further powers of self government. Control of the civil list was surrendered to Canada in 1847[3], and of the Post Office in 1849[4]. In the former year

---

[1] 17 & 18 Vic. (i) c. 118.   [2] 19 & 20 Vic. c. 140.
[3] 10 & 11 Vic. (i) c. 71.   [4] 12 & 13 Vic. (i) c. 66.

the St Lawrence was freed from the Navigation Laws[1], and the Colony obtained full power to reduce or repeal duties imposed by Imperial Acts on goods imported into Canada[2].

At the time of the Union of 1840 Lower Canada possessed Federation. the larger population, but in a short time immigration into Upper Canada gave that province an excess in population of 250,000 over its neighbour. A demand soon arose in Upper Canada for a redistribution of the representation, and "representation in proportion to population " became the important political question of the day. Parties at length became so balanced that from the 21st May, 1862, to the end of June, 1864, there were no less than five different ministries in office[3], and the efficient conduct of public business became impossible. In 1864 the maritime provinces began to entertain the idea of a union, and on the defeat of the Taché-Macdonald ministry in June of that year overtures were made by the opposition to the Hon. John A. Macdonald which resulted in the formation of a coalition ministry pledged to the adoption of a federal union of all the provinces.

Permission was asked to attend the Conference of the Charlottetown and delegates of the Maritime Conference at Charlottetown, and Quebec delegates on behalf of Canada were also present at the ad-Conferences. journed Conference held at Quebec. Little difficulty was found in obtaining the adhesion of the legislature to the proposed scheme of confederation : the legislative Council by 45 votes to 15, and the Assembly by 91 votes to 33, adopted the address to Her Majesty praying her to submit an Act to the Imperial Parliament for the union of all the provinces[4].

In reading the list[5] of Governors of Ontario and Quebec List of it must be remembered that the Governor of the Province Governors. of Canada was also Governor-General until the federation :

---

[1] 12 & 13 Vic. (i) c. 29.   [2] 9 & 10 Vic. (i) c. 94.   [3] Burinot, p. 40.
[4] Debates in the Parliament of Canada on Confederation, Quebec, 1865.
[6] See Appendix.

that in 1791 Upper Canada was made a separate province under a governor or administrator: and that in 1840 the provinces of Upper and Lower Canada were re-united, only to be separated in 1867.

2. Nova Scotia.

The province of Nova Scotia and the surrounding territory, including the present provinces of New Brunswick and Prince Edward's Island, though claimed by England on the ground of the discoveries of Cabot in the 15th century, were ceded to France by the treaty of St Germains in 1632. By the treaty of Utrecht the province was restored to England, but it was not until the year 1749 that any adequate attempt was made at colonization or the introduction of a settled form of government. A scheme for encouraging officers and privates then lately dismissed from the army and navy to settle in the province proved successful, and was carried into effect by the Honourable Edward Cornwallis, who was appointed Governor. On his arrival the new Governor formed a Council, and this Council exercised both legislative and executive functions[1].

Council formed by Cornwallis.

Courts.

One of the instructions to the Governor was to establish Courts of Judicature, and after consultation with the Council he erected three courts, (1) a Court of Sessions, (2) a County Court for the whole province, which sat monthly and was invested with all powers of the Courts of King's Bench (except criminal matters), Common Pleas and Court of Exchequer, from which there was an appeal to the General Court, and (3) the General Court, which was a Court of Assize and general gaol delivery, and a Court of Appeal from the County Court, and in which the Governor and Council sat with the Judges.

In 1752 the County Court was transformed into a Court

[1] Haliburton's *Nova Scotia*, i. p. 140.

of Common Pleas, and in 1754 a Supreme Court was substituted for the General Court.

No formal constitution was conferred on Nova Scotia or on Cape Breton when that island was a separate province. The early constitution of the province is to be found in the commissions issued to successive Governors, in the Royal Instructions accompanying such commissions as modified from time to time by despatches from Secretaries of State, and in the Acts of the Legislature.

From 1713 to 1758 the government consisted of the Government from Governor or Lieutenant-Governor and a Council, and or- 1713 to dinances were from time to time passed by such Council. In 1758. 1755 Chief Justice Belcher pointed out that the Government Commissions and the Instructions required all laws to be passed with the consent of an Assembly, and that therefore the ordinances of the Lieutenant-Governor and Council had not the force of law. This view was confirmed by the law officers of the Crown in England, and the Lords of Plantations required the Lieutenant-Governor to summon an Assembly after consultation with the Chief Justice.

The following plan for an Assembly was eventually adopted Plan for by the Council after receiving the approval of the Crown: calling Assembly

The Assembly to consist of 22 members, 16 to be elected by the Province at large, two by the township of Lunenburg, and four by the township of Halifax. Whenever 50 qualified electors had settled in any district which was erected into a township, such township to elect two members. The qualification for voting at an election or for sitting in the legislature to be, possession in the person's own right of a freehold estate within the district in which he voted or for which he should be elected. No person to be qualified to vote or to be elected who was a popish recusant or who was under the age of 21. Members absent from the province for two months to be liable to have their seats declared vacant by the Governor[1].

---

[1] Haliburton, I. p. 209. Can. Sess. Papers, 1883, No. 70, pp. 14—16.

First Assembly.

The elections were held, and on the 2nd Oct. 1758 the Assembly met.

On the dissolution of the second Assembly by the death of the King in 1760, the Council altered the distribution of seats, allotting two members to each of four counties and to each of six townships, and giving Halifax four members. The representation was again altered in 1765 by the Governor and Council, the county of Halifax receiving four members, the town of Halifax two members, the other counties two each, and the other townships one each[1].

Legis-
lative
Council.

The Council continued to exercise both executive and legislative functions until 1838. In that year the Assembly passed a series of resolutions (afterwards rescinded) in which amongst other things they expressed the view that a separation should be made between the legislative and the executive functions of the Council, similar to that effected in the Canadas in 1791 and in New Brunswick in 1832. The suggestion was adopted by the home Government, and in 1838 Instructions[2] were issued to Earl Durham, the Lieutenant-Governor, to appoint an Executive Council, not exceeding nine in number, and a Legislative Council, not exceeding 15. By the Commission given to Lord Monck[3] power was given to extend the number of the Legislative Council to 21.

Cape
Breton.

As regards Cape Breton, which was annexed to Nova Scotia in 1763, the island was included in all the Commissions issued to the Government of Nova Scotia until 1784, when it was made a separate Government, but subordinate to Nova Scotia[4]. Major Desbarres was appointed Lieutenant-Governor, and he was assisted by a Council possess-

[1] Haliburton, I. p. 244.
[2] The Instructions are printed in Can. Sess. Papers, 1883, No. 20, p. 39.
[3] Ass. Jour., N. S., 1862, No. 34.
[4] See Despatch from Lord Sydney to Governor Parr, Ass. Jour., N. S., 1841, App.

ing executive and legislative functions. Power was given to summon an assembly, but such assembly was never called. In 1820 the island was re-annexed to Nova Scotia[1].

The constitution of Nova Scotia, save as expressly altered by the B. N. A. Act, 1867, remains practically as it was at the time of the union.

Though Nova Scotia was the first province to propose confederation, the Government, deterred by the unfavourable result of the elections in New Brunswick in March, 1865, took no step to bring the Quebec resolutions before the Legislature until 1866, when a resolution in favour of confederation was carried by 31 to 15.

Confederation.

3. NEW BRUNSWICK.

The present province of New Brunswick was originally part of Nova Scotia. In 1784 it was made a separate province, and in the following year the government was entrusted to a Governor and a Council possessing legislative and executive functions with power to call an Assembly of the freeholders[2].

The first Governor was Colonel Thomas Carleton, who remained in office until 1803. After he retired the government was carried on by the President of the Executive Council, who during the war with the United States was a military and not a civil officer. In 1818 a regular Governor was appointed. The Council continued to possess legislative power until 1832, when a separate legislative Council was appointed. The executive occupied a very independent position, as the territorial revenue of the Crown was sufficient to defray the expenses of the civil list. The refusal of the executive to give the Assembly any return of the receipts and expenditure of the revenues from the Crown lands led

Governor Carleton.

Legislative Council.

[1] See Despatch of Earl Bathurst and Proclamation of Sir James Kempt, *Ass. Jour.*, N. S., 1841, App.

[2] See Commission of Gov. Carleton, Can. Sess. Papers, 1883, No. 70, p. 47.

to a deputation being sent to England to request that the control of the public revenues be vested in the Assembly.

Control of finance. The Colonial Secretary complied with the request, and issued instructions to the Governor and Executive Council to surrender the territorial revenues in consideration of the grant by the Assembly of a liberal permanent civil list.

Responsible government. The next step taken by the Assembly was to establish the responsibility of the ministers to the Assembly. In 1847 Earl Grey as Colonial Secretary forwarded a despatch to the Governor of Nova Scotia defining the theory of responsible government as applicable to the provinces. He laid down the principle that the executive councillors who directed the policy of the government should hold office only while they retained the confidence of the House, and that all government officials should be excluded from both branches of the legislature. In the following year a resolution asserting the application of the above principles was introduced and passed by a large majority of the Assembly, and from that time the responsibility of ministers was fully recognised.

Federation. The Quebec resolutions for effecting a Confederation of the Provinces were brought before the people at the general election held in March, 1865, but a majority of the new Assembly proved hostile to the scheme. In the following year the Legislative Council passed a resolution favourable to the Union, and the ministry thereupon resigned. A general election immediately followed, and on the 30th of June a resolution in favour of confederation was carried in the Assembly by 31 votes to 8. A similar resolution was passed by the Legislative Council.

4. MANITOBA.

By section 146 of the British North American Act, 1867, power was given to Her Majesty in Council, on address from the Houses of Parliament of Canada, to admit Rupert's Land and the North West Territory, or either of them, into the Union on such terms and conditions in each case as should be expressed in such addresses and as Her Majesty should approve, subject to the provisions of the Act, and it was further declared that any Order in Council in that behalf should have the force of an Act of Parliament.

In 1867 the Canadian Houses of Parliament adopted a joint address to Her Majesty praying for the admission of the above two territories into the Union : but it was found that the then existing charter of the Hudson's Bay Company which owned and enjoyed certain rights over a portion of the territory in question, would prevent full powers of government and legislation over Rupert's Land and the North West Territory being transferred to the Canadian Parliament. To remedy this state of things the "Rupert's Land Act, 1868[1]," was passed, enabling the Hudson's Bay Company to surrender to Her Majesty and Her Majesty to accept a surrender of all their lands and rights enjoyed under their Letters Patent, provided that the terms and conditions on which Rupert's Land was to be admitted into the Dominion should be approved by Her Majesty and embodied in an address from both Houses of the Dominion Parliament. *Admission of N. W. Territories.* *Rupert's Land Act, 1868.*

The details of the surrender being settled a second address was presented to Her Majesty in 1869, and on the 24th June, 1870, it was by Order in Council[2] declared that from the 15th day of July, 1870, the North West Territory and Rupert's Land were to be admitted into and become part of the Dominion.

The admission was made subject to the terms and conditions contained in the addresses, but on looking at the addresses it will be found that the first address relating to the North West Territory contains only two clauses of importance, viz. (1) "the Government and Parliament of Canada will be ready to provide that the legal rights of any corporation, com- *Conditions.*

[1] 31 & 32 Vic. (i) c. 105.   [2] See Appendix.

pany or individual within the same shall be respected and placed under the protection of courts of competent jurisdiction."

(2) "That the claims of the Indian tribes to compensation for land required for purposes of the settlement will be considered and settled in conformity with the equitable principles which have uniformly governed the British Crown in its dealings with the aborigines."

The second address relating to Rupert's Land dealt mainly with the rights reserved to the Hudson's Bay Company, but stipulated that claims of Indians to compensation for land required for purposes of settlement should be disposed of by the Canadian Government in communication with the Imperial Government.

Legislative power over the Territories From the date of the admission the Canadian Parliament acquired legislative power over the newly admitted territories. By the Order in Council it was declared as regards the North West Territory that "the Parliament of Canada should from the day aforesaid have full power and authority to legislate for the future welfare and good government of the said territory," and such Order in Council has by the British North American Act, 1867, the force of an Act of Parliament.

and Rupert's Land. As regards Rupert's Land the Order in Council was silent as to legislative power, but by the Rupert's Land Act, 1868[1], it was enacted as regards all territories belonging to the Hudson's Bay Company that

"it shall be lawful for the Parliament of Canada from the date aforesaid (i.e. of admission) to make ordain and establish within the land and territory so admitted as aforesaid all such laws institutions and ordinances and to constitute such courts and officers as may be necessary for the peace order and good government of Her Majesty's subjects and others therein."

Provision for government Previous to the surrender of the North West Territories an Act was passed by the Dominion Parliament providing

[1] 31 & 32 Vic. (i) c. 105, s. 5.

for their temporary government, and the first Lieutenant- of the N. W. Ter-
Governor was appointed in 1869. The outbreak of the in- ritories.
surrection among the half-breeds prevented the Lieutenant-
Governor exercising any of his functions, and immediately
after the rebellion was over an Act was passed to establish
a new province carved out of the North West Territories,
under the name of Manitoba. A constitution, similar to Manitoba.
that existing in the other provinces, was conferred on the
new province, and the first legislature was elected in 1871.
The province is divided into four counties, and these are
subdivided into twenty-four districts or divisions for legislative, judicial and electoral purposes.

5. BRITISH COLUMBIA.

British Columbia, the largest of the Canadian provinces,
cannot be said to have had any existence as a colony until
1858. Previous to that year provision had been made by a
series of Acts for extending the Civil and Criminal Laws of
the Courts of Lower and Upper Canada over territories not
within any province, but otherwise the territory was used as
a hunting ground of the Hudson's Bay Company. The disputes and difficulties that arose from the influx of miners
owing to the gold discoveries in 1856, resulted in the revo-
cation of the licence of the Hudson's Bay Company and the
passing of the Imperial Act 21 & 22 Vic. c. 99 to provide
for the government of British Columbia. Power was given to Constitu-
Her Majesty by Order in Council to appoint a Governor of tion of the Province.
the Colony, to make provision for the administration of justice
therein, and to establish all laws and institutions necessary
for the peace, order and good government of persons therein.
Her Majesty was also authorised by Order in Council to
empower the Governor to constitute a Legislature, consisting
of the Governor and a Council, or a Council and an Assembly,
to be composed of such persons as Her Majesty might deem

fit. Power was given to annex Vancouver's Island on receiving an address from the two Houses of the Legislature of that Island.

Sir James Douglas was appointed Governor and by his commission he was authorised to make laws, institutions and ordinances for the peace, order and good government of British Columbia, by proclamation issued under the public seal of the colony. The first proclamation issued was one for indemnifying the Governor and other officers for all acts done previous to the date of the proclamation, whilst by a subsequent proclamation the English Civil and Criminal law as it existed on the date of the proclamation of the 21 & 22 Vic. c. 99, i.e. 19 Nov. 1858, was declared to be in force in the colony[1]. The Governor continued to legislate by proclamation until 1864, when his proclamations gave way to Ordinances passed by the Governor with the advice and consent of the Legislative Council. The Legislative Council consisted of five officials, five magistrates, and five other members selected from the inhabitants.

Up to this time the Governor of British Columbia was also Governor of the neighbouring island of Vancouver.

Vancouver's Island. Vancouver's Island is historically an older colony than British Columbia. Though discovered in 1592 it remained practically unknown to Europeans for two centuries, and it was not until 1849, when the island was granted to the Hudson's Bay Company, that a Governor was appointed. The first Governor called a legislative Council of nine members, and his successor constituted an Assembly of seven members under the direction of the Secretary of the Colonies. Freeholders of twenty acres, being British subjects, were qualified to vote, and members of the legislature were required to possess real property of the value of £300.

[1] But the effect of this proclamation was modified by the Ordinance of the 6th March, 1867, which enacted that the English law as it existed on the 19 Nov. 1858 should apply "so far as the same are not from local circumstances inapplicable."

The seat of government in British Columbia had been fixed by the 21 & 22 Vic. (i) c. 99 at New Westminster, but Victoria in Vancouver's Island was fixed as the Governor's residence. The complaints of the inhabitants of the mainland regarding the continual absence of the Governor from the seat of government led to the passing of the 26 & 27 Vic. (i) c. 83 establishing separate governments at Victoria and New Westminster.

In 1865 the legislature of the island adopted a series of resolutions in favour of union with British Columbia, and by the Imperial Act 29 & 30 Vic. (i) c. 67 the two colonies were united. The power and authority of the executive government and of the legislature of British Columbia was extended over the island, and the number of Councillors was increased from 15 to 23 in order to provide for the representation of the island in the legislature. No other alteration was made in the constitution of the legislature, which until the admission of the colony into the union continued to consist of the Governor and a Council.

Though British Columbia was not represented at the Quebec Conference, the legislative Council on the 18th March, 1868, unanimously adopted a resolution expressing the desire that the province should be admitted into the union. Negotiations were entered into with the Dominion and resolutions embodying the terms and conditions agreed upon were adopted by the Dominion Parliament on the 31st March, 1871, and by the legislature of British Columbia.

By an Order in Council dated the 16th day of May, 1871[1], British Columbia was declared to be a province of the Dominion from the 20th July, 1871.

Admission to the Dominion.

----

[1] See Appendix.

6. Prince Edward's Island.

Prince Edward's Island, the smallest province of the Dominion, originally called St John's Island, until **1770** formed part of Nova Scotia. The first Governor was Walter Patterson, and by his commission[1] he was required to execute the duties of his office in accordance with his commission, the royal instructions, and such laws as might be passed by the Council and the Assembly. The Council possessed both executive and legislative functions, and the Governor and the Council were empowered to call an Assembly of the freeholders and the planters. After the first Assembly was summoned all laws were to be passed by the Governor, the Council and the Assembly, a power of disallowance being reserved to the Crown. The Governor was authorized by and with the consent of the Council to constitute Courts of Justice "for the hearing and determining of all causes as well criminal as civil according to law and equity," and full power was given to appoint judges, commissioners, justices of the peace, sheriffs, and other officers and ministers for the administration of justice[2]. The Governor had also the right of pardoning criminals and presenting to benefices: of levying forces for the defence of the island and of erecting castles and forts: of disbursing public money for the support of the government and of granting Crown lands.

Early Constitution.

The first Assembly met in **1773** and consisted of 18 members.

In **1839** the Executive Council was separated from the Legislative Council, and in **1862** an Act was passed making the Legislative Council elective.

Introduction of responsible government.

In **1847** the Assembly adopted an address to the Crown, representing that the Lieutenant-Governor alone should be responsible to the Crown and Imperial Parliament for his

---

[1] Can. Sess. Papers, 1883, No. 70.   [2] Ib. p. 4.

acts and that the Executive Council should be deemed the constitutional advisers of Her Majesty's representative.

Earl Grey in a despatch to the Lieutenant-Governor in January 1849 pointed out, that the introduction of responsible government in a colony depended on the increase of the community in wealth, numbers and importance, and expressed the view that the conditions which would warrant the introduction of responsible government into Prince Edward's Island were wanting.

In a subsequent despatch Earl Grey intimated that if the other expenses of government were defrayed by the Island the home Government would provide the salary of the Governor. The Assembly offered to accept the suggestion provided the Crown surrendered all claim to the quit rents and Crown lands and conceded responsible government. The latter condition Earl Grey refused to grant and the Assembly thereupon adopted the expedient of refusing supplies. This course proved successful and in 1851 the concession was made.

The proposal to unite all the provinces in one Confedera- Federa-tion was not received with favour in Prince Edward's Island. tion. After the Quebec Conference public meetings were held to protest against the Island joining the Union and in the Assembly only five members were in its favour. In the following session (1866) the Assembly resolved that "this House cannot admit that a federal union of the North American Provinces and Colonies which would include Prince Edward's Island could ever be accomplished on terms that would prove advantageous to the interests and well-being of the people of this island, separated as it is and must ever remain, from the neighbouring provinces by an immoveable barrier of ice for many months in the year." The question continued to be discussed in the following years, and at length in 1873 the Executive Council adopted a minute that, if liberal terms of union were offered, the Government would dissolve the Assembly in order to give the people an opportunity of deciding the question. Delegates were appointed to meet the Dominion Government and certain terms and conditions were agreed to. The Assembly was dissolved but the new House passed a resolution to the effect that the terms and conditions proposed did not secure to the Island a sum sufficient to defray the requirements of its local government. A compromise was ultimately arrived at, and the House unanimously resolved to present an address to Her Majesty to unite the island with the Dominion. The necessary Order in Council was issued on the 26th of June 1873[1], and the Island was declared to be a province of the Dominion from the 1st day of July of the same year.

The principal terms and conditions were :—

Conditions of the Union.

(1) That the Island not having incurred a debt equal to 50 dollars a head of its population, i.e. of 4,701,050 dollars, should receive from the Dominion interest at 5 per cent. per annum on the difference between the actual amount of its indebtedness and the above amount.

(2) That as the Government of the Island held no lands from the Crown and therefore enjoyed no revenue from that source for the construction and maintenance of public works, the Dominion Government should pay by yearly instalments to the Government of the Island 45,000 dollars yearly less 5 per cent. on any sum not exceeding 800,000 dollars which the Dominion might advance to the Island for the purchase of land held by large proprietors.

(3) That in consideration of the transfer to Canada of the powers of taxation mentioned in the B.N.A. Act, 1867, the Dominion was to pay the Government of the Island 30,000 dollars and an annual grant equal to 80 cents per head of its population as shewn by the census of 1871, such grant to increase as the population increased until it reached 400,000.

(4) That the Dominion should assume the following

[1] See Appendix.

charges, the salaries of the Lieutenant-Governor and the judges, the charges in respect of customs, post-office, protection of fisheries, militia, lighthouses, shipwrecked crews, quarantine, marine hospitals, the geological survey, and the penitentiary.

(5) That the Dominion Government should assume the railway then being built.

7.   District of Keewatin.

In 1876 an act was passed by the Dominion Parliament erecting into a separate government under the name of the District of Keewatin the portion of the North West Territories lying to the north of Manitoba.   The district contains about 395,000 acres, and is principally occupied by Icelandic colonists.

The Lieutenant-Governor of Manitoba is *ex officio* Lieu- Administenant-Governor of Keewatin.   He is assisted in the adminis- tration. tration of the district by a council of not more than ten and not less than five members appointed by the Governor-General in Council.   The Lieutenant-Governor in Council has such legislative powers as are conferred by the Governor-General in Council, and the Governor-General in Council has the balance of legislative power, but no law can be passed either by the Governor-General in Council or by the Lieutenant-Governor in Council which

(a) is inconsistent with any Dominion Act applying to the District,

(b) imposes any tax or any duty of customs or excise or any penalty exceeding 100 dollars,

(c) alters or repeals the punishment provided in any Act in force in the District, or

(d) appropriates any public money, lands or property of Canada without the authority of Parliament.

Copies of all laws passed by the Lieutenant-Governor in

Council require to be transmitted to the Governor in Council who may disallow any law within two years of its passing[1].

8. THE NORTH WEST TERRITORIES.

The North West Territories comprise all lands not within the limits of any province or of the District of Keewatin. The area of the Territories is about 3,000,000 square miles or four times as great as the area of all the provinces together. The Territories were ceded to Canada by an Order in Council dated the 24th June 1870[2] under the authority of the 146th section of the B. N. A. Act, 1867. The southern portion of the territories between Manitoba and British Columbia has been formed into four provisional districts, viz. Assiniboia, Saskatchewan, Alberta and Athabasca. By the Dominion Act 38 Vic. c. 49 executive and legislative powers were conferred on a Lieutenant-Governor and a Council of five members subject to instructions given by Order in Council or by the Canadian Secretary of State. Provision was made for the election of representatives to the Council by districts having a population of 1000 adults, and owing to the increase in population there are now 14 elected members. When the number of elected members reaches 21, the Council is to cease and the members are to constitute a legislative Assembly. The Acts relating to the government of the Territories have been consolidated and form c. 50 of the Revised Statutes of Canada.

9. THE UNION OF THE PROVINCES.

Steps towards a federal union.

A federal union of the British North American Colonies had been a favourite scheme with many Colonial statesmen and on several occasions was discussed by some of the legislatures.

---

[1] See The Keewatin Act, R. S. C., 49 Vic. c. 53.
[2] See Appendix.

The honour of taking a decided step towards such a union belongs to the legislature of Nova Scotia. In 1861 a resolution favourable to a union was passed by that legislature and transmitted to the Duke of Newcastle, then Colonial Secretary, who in turn forwarded it to the Governor-General and the Lieutenant-Governors of the provinces. The Lieutenant-Governors brought the subject before their respective legislatures; and the legislatures of the maritime provinces passed a resolution authorizing the respective Lieutenant-Governors to appoint delegates not exceeding five to confer with delegates of the other provinces "for the purpose of discussing the expediency of a union of the three provinces under one government and legislature." Delegates were appointed and it was arranged that the conference should meet on the 1st September at Charlottetown. *Initiative of Nova Scotia.*

Before the Conference met a coalition government was formed in the Province of Canada pledged to a union of the provinces, and the Government at once asked for and obtained permission to send delegates to the Charlottetown Conference, who however were not authorized to consider the question of a *legislative* union. The proposal to unite the maritime provinces was deemed impracticable, but the delegates were unanimously of opinion that a union on a wider basis was possible and the Canadian delegates proposed that with the consent of the provinces a further conference should be held at Quebec. The proposal was adopted and the Conference ended. *Charlottetown Conference.*

The Quebec Conference met on the 10th October. Twelve delegates were present from Canada, seven from New Brunswick, five from Nova Scotia, seven from Prince Edward's Island and two from Newfoundland. *Quebec Conference.*

The Conference sat for eighteen days and the result of its deliberations was the celebrated "Seventy-two" resolutions on which the Act of Union was afterwards based. Each delegation undertook to submit the resolutions to its own government, and pledged itself to use every legitimate means to ensure the adoption of the scheme by its legislature.

Canada. The Canadian legislature met in January 1865, and after a debate of a fortnight's duration the resolutions were adopted in the Council by a vote of 45 to 15. The debate in the Assembly lasted for five weeks, but the resolutions were adopted by 91 to 33.

New Brunswick. In New Brunswick the general election of 1865 resulted in the return of an Assembly hostile to the scheme: but in the following year the Legislative Council declared for the Union. The Ministry resigned, a general election followed, and the new Assembly on the 30th June declared in favour of confederation.

Nova Scotia. In Nova Scotia the Quebec Resolutions were brought before the Assembly in 1866 and were approved by a vote of 31 to 15.

Newfoundland. In Newfoundland the Governor introduced the subject in the legislature at the opening of the session in January 1866. On the 8th March the Assembly after sitting in committee for several days adopted the following resolution:

"That whilst duly regardful of the momentous character of the subject and of the promise to his Excellency to give it attention, yet, as no information has been received demanding its immediate reconsideration, the House does not deem it expedient to enter upon its discussion with a view to any decision thereon."

Prince Edward's Island. In Prince Edward's Island the scheme was not received with favour and several years elapsed after the Union was accomplished before the Island joined the Dominion.

A sufficient number of provinces, viz. Canada, New Brunswick and Nova Scotia, had by 1866 declared for union and in that year delegates were appointed to settle the details and to determine the precise character of the Imperial Act necessary to carry the union into effect. The delegates met in London in December 1866, under the presidency of Hon. John A. Macdonald, and on the 7th February 1867 Lord Carnarvon introduced the Bill "for the Union of Canada, Nova Scotia and New Brunswick and the government thereof: and for purposes connected therewith." The measure received the support of all parties and was read a third time in the House of Lords on the 26th of February. On the 8th March it passed through the House of Commons and on the 29th of that month received the Royal assent. *Union Act of 1867.*

The Act authorized Her Majesty in Council to declare by proclamation that on and after a certain day the provinces of Canada, Nova Scotia and New Brunswick should form one Dominion under the name of Canada. The necessary proclamation was issued on the 22nd of May and the 1st of July was fixed as the day from which the Union should take effect.

CHAPTER III.

THE SOURCES OF THE LAW AND CUSTOM OF THE CONSTITUTION.

THE legal rules and constitutional customs that form the "Constitutional Law and Custom" of Canada are derived from seven sources:—(1) Imperial Acts, (2) Dominion Acts, (3) Provincial Acts, (4) Orders in Council issued under Imperial, Dominion or Provincial authority, (5) Orders and rules of the Dominion Parliament and of Provincial Legislatures, (6) Usages, and (7) The Letters Patent, Commission and Instructions issued to the Governor-General.

1. *Imperial Acts.* Though the Union Act of 1867 contains the general scheme of the Constitution it has been supplemented by several subsequent and important statutes.

The 34 & 35 Vic. (i) c. 28 conferred on the Dominion power to establish new provinces and to provide for the government of any territory not within the limits of a province.

The 38 & 39 Vic. (i) c. 38 repealed the 18th section of the Act of 1867 relating to the privileges of the Dominion Parliament and more clearly defined the powers of the legislature to determine its own privileges, and the 49 & 50 Vic. (i) c. 35 authorized the Canadian Parliament to make provision for the representation of new provinces in the Senate and House of Commons.

2. *Dominion Acts.* Many important statutes have been passed by the Parliament of Canada relating to its constitution. Immediately after the Union Act of 1867 came into force a series of statutes had to be passed for the organization of the different departments of State. As regards the Legislature it was not until 1885 that a general election law[1] was carried regulating the election of members of the House of Commons, and several subsequent statutes have been passed on the same subject.

By the 38 Vic. c. 11 a Supreme Court was established for the Dominion, and on the admission of Rupert's Land and the North West Territories, Acts were passed forming the new province of Manitoba (33 Vic.c.3) and providing for the government of the North West Territories[2]. These as well as other Acts will be found in the recently issued edition of the Consolidated Statutes of Canada.

3. *Provincial Acts.* The main features of the constitutions of Ontario and Quebec are contained in the Union Act of 1867, but as regards the other provinces, though that Act governs the division of legislative power and contains certain general provisions relating to all the provinces, recourse must be had to the respective Provincial Acts for the details of the Provincial Constitutions. It is from these Acts that the functions of the different provincial departments of State, the qualifications of members of, and electors to, the legislative Assemblies, and the organization of the Provincial Judicature are to be learned. The custom that prevails in all the provinces, except in Prince Edward's Island, of revising the Statutes at intervals, and consolidating the law on one subject in one statute, makes the provincial statute book very accessible to students.

4. *Orders in Council.* The most important Orders in Council relating to Canada that have been issued under Imperial Statute are those admitting the North West Terri-

---

[1] 49 Vic. c. 3.   [2] 32 & 33 Vic. c. 3.

tories[1], British Columbia[2], and Prince Edward's Island[3] into the Dominion. Several Orders in Council have been issued disallowing Acts of the Dominion Parliament.

Orders in Council are often issued under the authority of Statute by the Governor and Privy Council of Canada. The Lieutenant-Governor of the North West Territories for instance carries on the government and administration of these Territories partly under the provision of the Statute Law partly under Orders of the Dominion Privy Council.

5. *Orders of the Dominion Parliament and Provincial Legislatures.* The Dominion Parliament and the Provincial Legislatures conduct their proceedings partly under the authority of statutes, partly under standing and other orders, and partly under customs and usages. Each House has its own standing orders and resolutions, based mainly on the practice that prevails in the English House of Commons. The written rules of the Dominion House of Commons and of the Quebec Legislative Assembly are much more detailed than those drawn up by the other legislative bodies, but all the Legislative Assemblies agree in adopting as a standing order that "in all unprovided cases the rules, usages and forms of the House of Commons of the United Kingdom of Great Britain and Ireland shall be followed."

6. *Usages.* The constitutional usages that always tend to come into existence cannot be neglected, whether the effect be to supply the absence of a necessary legal rule or to modify the administration of a law. The Hon. J. S. C. Wurtele, Speaker of the Legislative Assembly of Quebec, has compiled a body of such usages in force in that assembly[4], and Mr Bourinot, in his valuable work on *Parliamentary Practice*, refers to many similar usages followed by the Dominion Parliament.

7. *Letters Patent and Instructions relating to the office of the Governor-General.* The Letters Patent constituting the

---

[1] 30th June, 1870.   [2] 16th May, 1871.   [3] 26th June, 1873.
[4] *Manual of the Legislative Assembly of Quebec.*

office of Governor-General and the Instructions issued to the Governor-General were revised in 1878[1]. By these instruments he is authorized to exercise several important executive and prerogative powers vested in Her Majesty, as for instance the summoning, proroguing and dissolving parliament, the pardoning of criminals and the appointment of judges, ministers and other officers.

It is not usual on the appointment of the Lieutenant-Governor of a province to issue instructions to him, but such a course has been occasionally adopted.

[1] See Appendix.

CHAPTER IV.

PROVINCIAL LEGISLATURES.

1. *Parties to Legislation.*

IN the Provinces of British Columbia and Manitoba the legislature consists of a Lieutenant-Governor and a Legislative Assembly, whilst in Quebec, New Brunswick, Prince Edward's Island and Nova Scotia it consists of a Lieutenant-Governor, a Legislative Council, and a Legislative Assembly.

North West Territories. Provision has been made by the Dominion for the government of the North West Territories, but as yet these territories have not been formed into a province. The Lieutenant-Governor in Council may make ordinances within certain limits for the government of the Territories.

2. *How summoned.*

Provisions of the Union Act. It is remarkable that the British North America Act, 1869, contains no general provision relating to the summoning of the local legislatures. By section 81 power is given to the Lieutenant-Governors of Ontario and of Quebec to summon in the Queen's name by instrument under the Great Seal of the Province the Legislative Assemblies of these provinces, but no reference is made to the other provinces. Up to 1878 the Instructions. Instructions given to the Governor-General contained a clause referring to the Lieutenant-Governors, and authorizing them to exercise from time to time all powers necessary in respect of the assembling, proroguing and dissolving of Legislative

Councils or the Legislative or General Assemblies of the provinces respectively.

This clause was omitted in the revised instructions of 1878 in deference to the contention of the Dominion that the Lieutenant-Governor of the provinces other than those expressly referred to in the Union Act had implied powers for the above purposes.

"Any powers," said Mr Blake, the Dominion Minister of Justice, "which may be thought necessary should have been conferred upon the Lieutenant-Governor by the British North America Act, and it appears to me they must be taken to be expressly or impliedly so conferred. The provision giving these powers to the Lieutenant-Governor by the Governor-General's Commission appears somewhat objectionable, and it might perhaps be advisable to leave these matters to be dealt with by those officers under the B. N. A. Act, the 82nd section of which in terms confers on the Lieutenant-Governor of the new provinces of Ontario and Quebec the power in the Queen's name to summon the local bodies, a power which no doubt was assumed to be continued to the Governors of the other provinces[1]." *Contention of the Dominion.*

The provincial legislatures are summoned by the Lieutenant-Governor, in some provinces, as for instance in British Columbia in his own name, and in other provinces in the name of the Queen. The following form is the one in use in Quebec: *Form of Summons.*

Canada }
Province of Quebec }   L. R. MASSON

L. S.

Victoria by the Grace of God of the United Kingdom of Great Britain and Ireland, Queen, Defender of the Faith, &c. &c.

To our beloved and faithful the Legislature Councillors of the Province of Quebec and the Members elected to serve in

[1] Can. Sess. Paper, 1877, No. 13, p. 7.

the Legislative Assembly of our said province and summoned and called to a meeting of the Legislature of our said province at our City of Quebec on the 15th day of the month of March instant to have been commenced and held, and to every of you

GREETING :

A PROCLAMATION.

WHEREAS the meeting of the Legislature of the Province of Quebec stands prorogued to the 15th day of the month of March instant. Nevertheless for certain causes and considerations We have thought fit to prorogue the same to the eighth day of the month of April next so that neither you nor any of you on the said fifteenth day of March instant at our city of Quebec to appear are to be held and constrained for We do will that you and each of you and all others in this behalf interested on Thursday the eighth day of the month of April next at our said city of Quebec personally you be and appear for the despatch of business to treat do act and conclude upon those things which in our said Legislature of the Province of Quebec by the Common Council of our said Province may by the favour of God be ordained.

In testimony whereof We have caused these our Letters to be made Patent and the Great Seal of our said Province of Quebec to be hereto affixed. Witness our truly and well-beloved the Honorable Louis-François-Rodrigue Masson, Lieutenant-Governor of Quebec, Member of our Privy Council for Canada. At our Government House in our city of Quebec in our said province of Quebec this twelfth day of March in the year of our Lord 1886 and in the 49th year of our reign.

By Command,

C. H. Huot,

Clerk of the Crown in Chancery,

Quebec.

When a dissolution takes place, a proclamation is issued **Meeting after a dissolution.** dissolving the Assembly. This is followed by a second proclamation announcing that orders have been given for issuing writs for holding a new election and directing the writs to bear a certain date, and to be returnable on a certain date, and fixing the day on which nominations are to be held.

A further proclamation directs the legislature to meet on a given day.

3. *The opening of the Legislature.*

The method of opening a provincial legislature is similar **English practice followed.** to that followed at the opening of the Imperial Parliament[1]. The proceedings in Quebec for instance at the opening of the new parliament in 1882 were as follows:

On the first day of the meeting appointed for the despatch **Swearing in members.** of business pursuant to the Proclamation of the Lieutenant-Governor, the Commissioners appointed to administer the oath of allegiance to the members—usually the clerk and the clerk's assistant—attended at the table of the House at the hour of ten in the morning, and proceeded to swear in members who subscribed the roll containing the oath. At three o'clock in the afternoon the members who had taken the oath assembled and took their seats in the House and awaited a message from the Lieutenant-Governor.

On receiving a message through the Usher of the Black Rod to the effect that "His Honour the Lieutenant-Governor desires the immediate attendance of the members of this Hon. Assembly in the Legislative Council Chamber" the members proceeded to the Council Chamber. The Clerk of the Legislative Council then addressed them as follows:

"Honourable Gentlemen and Gentlemen of the Legislative Assembly.

---

[1] All the Provincial Assemblies have a standing order to the effect that in unprovided cases the rules, usages and forms of the Imperial House of Commons as in force at the time shall be followed.

Election of Speaker.

"His Honour the Lieutenant-Governor does not see fit to declare the causes of his summoning the present Provincial Legislature until a Speaker of the Legislative Assembly shall have been chosen according to law, but that to-morrow at the hour of three o'clock His Honour will declare the causes of his calling the present Legislature."

The members of the Assembly returned to their own Chamber and a member addressing the Clerk proposed a member as Speaker. The question was put by the Clerk, and after the Speaker was elected and had been congratulated the mace was placed on the table and the House adjourned.

On the following day the members again assembled, and on receipt of a message from the Lieutenant-Governor they, preceded by the Speaker, proceeded to the Council Chamber.

The Speaker in the Legislative Council.

The Speaker then spoke as follows:

"May it please Your Honour,

"The Legislative Assembly have elected me as their Speaker, though I am but little able to fulfil the important duties thus assigned to me.

"If in the performance of these duties I should at any time fall into error I pray that the fault may be imputed to me and not to the Assembly whose servant I am and who through me, the better to enable them to discharge their duty to their Queen and Country, humbly claim all their undoubted rights and privileges, especially that they may have freedom of speech in their debates, access to Your Honour's person at all seasonable times and that their proceedings may receive from Your Honour the most favourable interpretation."

Then the Honourable the Speaker of the Legislative Council said:

"Mr Speaker,

"I am commanded by His Honour the Lieutenant-Governor to declare to you that he freely confides in the duty and attachment of the Assembly to Her Majesty's person and government, not doubting that their proceedings will be conducted with wisdom, temper and prudence, he grants and upon all occasions will recognize and allow their constitutional privileges.

"I am commanded also to assure you that the Assembly shall have ready access to His Honour upon all seasonable occasions, and that their proceedings as well as your words and actions will constantly receive from him the most favourable construction."

The members retired as before, and the Speaker informed the House of what had occurred. Leave was then given to bring in a bill, which was read a first time. In the afternoon the House was summoned to the Legislative Council to hear the speech read, and on its return the Speaker reported that the Lieutenant-Governor had been pleased to make a speech to both Houses of which he had obtained a copy. The speech was ordered to be taken into consideration on the following day, and the House proceeded to appoint Committees and to transact other business.

The Speech.

4. Adjournment.

"An adjournment of either House," says Sir Wm. Anson in his *Law and Custom of the Constitution*[1], "takes place at its own discretion unaffected by the proceedings of the other House. Business pending at the time of the adjournment is taken up at the point at which it dropped when the House meets again." This rule is followed in Canada. Each House usually adjourns from day to day, but on Fridays the adjournment is usually until Monday morning.

Adjournment.

5. Prorogation and Dissolution.

Express powers of dissolving the Legislature were given to the Lieutenant-Governors of Ontario and Quebec by s. 85 of the B. N. A. Act, but no reference was made to prorogation or to dissolution in the other provinces[2]. Some of

Prorogation.

---

[1] p. 63.   [2] See *ante*, p. 44.

the Provinces have expressly conferred on the Lieutenant-Governor power to prorogue or to dissolve the Legislature[1].

Manner of prorogation. The Legislature may be prorogued by the Lieutenant-Governor either in person or by proclamation. Prorogation at the end of a session is usually effected in person. For instance, after the usual speech had been delivered in the Quebec Legislative Council on the 21st June, 1886, the Speaker of the Legislative Council said:

"Honourable Gentlemen of the Legislative Council and Gentlemen of the Legislative Assembly:

"It is His Honour the Lieutenant-Governor's will and pleasure, that this Provincial Legislature be prorogued until Monday the ninth day of August next to be then here holden and this Provincial Legislature is accordingly prorogued until Monday the ninth day of August next."

Prorogation during recess. When it is desired to prorogue the Legislature during the recess, a proclamation is issued. Leaving out the formal parts[2] the following form is used in Quebec:

A PROCLAMATION.

WHEREAS the meeting of the Legislature of the Province of Quebec stands prorogued to   at which time at our City of Quebec you were held and constrained to appear. Now know ye that for divers causes and considerations and taking into consideration the ease and convenience of our loving subjects, we have thought fit by and with the advice of our Executive Council of the Province of Quebec to relieve you and each of you of your attendance at the time aforesaid hereby convoking you and by these presents requiring you and each of you that on   you meet us in our Legislature of the said Province at our City of Quebec and therein to do as may seem necessary. Herein fail not.

Dissolution. A dissolution of the Provincial Assembly takes place either

[1] O. R. S. 1887, c. 11, s. 3.   Q. 44 & 45 Vic. c. 7, s. 2.   B. C. 34 Vic. c. 42, s. 31.   [2] See *ante*, p. 45.

by act of the Crown or by lapse of time: the demise of the Crown having no such effect. The Lieutenant-Governor as representing the Crown may dissolve the Legislature in person or by proclamation, the latter being the usual course.

The form of proclamation used in Quebec in 1882 was as follows:

Form of Proclamation.

Canada
Province of   THÉODORE ROBITAILLE
Quebec
   L. S.

Victoria by the Grace of God of the United Kingdom of Great Britain and Ireland, Queen, &c. &c.

To our beloved and faithful the Legislative Councillors of the Province of Quebec and the citizens and burgesses elected to serve in the Legislative Assembly of our said Province and to all whom it may concern

GREETING

A PROCLAMATION

WHEREAS it has pleased us by our proclamation dated the 11th of October last to convoke the Legislature of our Province of Quebec for the fifteenth day of the month of November instant and WHEREAS We have thought fit by and with the advice and consent of our Executive Council of our Province of Quebec to dissolve the Legislative Assembly of our said Province Now know ye that by this our royal proclamation We dissolve the said Legislative Assembly: Accordingly We exempt the Legislative Councillors and the citizens and burgesses of the Legislative Assembly of the obligation of meeting and attendance on the said fifteenth day of November instant.

In testimony whereof &c.

A Provincial Assembly lasts for four years except in the Province of Quebec, where it lasts for five years subject to the

Lapse of time.

4—2

right of the Lieutenant-Governor to dissolve it at any time. In Quebec, New Brunswick, British Columbia, Manitoba, and Prince Edward's Island the period begins to run from the day of the return of the writs: but in Ontario the period begins to run from the 55th day, and in Nova Scotia from the expiration of the 40th day after the date of the issue of the writs for holding the election[1].

In the North West Territories the elected members hold their seats for two years[2].

6. *Annual Sessions.*

In England there is no statutory authority requiring Parliament to meet every year. The 16 Car. II., c. 1[3] required Parliament not to be intermitted above three years at the most, and the 6 Will. & Mary, c. 2 provided that writs should issue for a new Parliament within three years after the determination of every Parliament. The necessity of passing the annual Army Bill and the Appropriation Act secures in practice annual sessions.

Provision for Annual Sessions. The British North America Act, 1867[4], expressly provides, that there shall be a session of the Legislature once at least in every year, so that 12 months shall not intervene between the last sitting of the Legislature in each Province in one session and its first sitting in the next session. This rule is also found in Provincial Acts[5].

7. *Enacting Clause.*

Enacting Clause. The enacting clause of a statute varies in the different provinces. In Ontario, Quebec, Manitoba, and British Co-

---

[1] O. R. S. 1887, c. 11, s. 1.   Q. 44 & 45 Vic. c. 7.   N. B. Con. Stat. 1877, c. 4, s. 80.   N. S. Rev. Stat. 1884, c. 3, s. 10.   B. C. Con. Stat. 1877, c. 42, s. 44.   33 Vic. c. 3.   P. E. I. 19 Vic. c. 21, s. 86.

[2] R. S. C. s. 25.

[3] Repealed by the 50 & 51 Vic. (i) c. 59.   [4] s. 86.

[5] O. R. S. 1887, c. 12, s. 86.   33 Vic. c. 3.   B. C. Con. Stat. 1877, c. 42, s. 45.

lumbia a statute professes to be enacted by "Her Majesty by and with the advice of the Legislature."

In Nova Scotia, New Brunswick, and Prince Edward's Island the form is by the "Lieutenant-Governor, the Council and Assembly." In the North West Territories ordinances are enacted by the "Lieutenant-Governor by and with the advice and consent of his Council[1]."

8. *Payment of Members.*

Members of the Legislatures of every province except Nova Scotia receive an allowance or indemnity in addition to a payment for travelling expenses. *Payment of Members.*

In Ontario, if the session does not exceed 30 days, the allowance is $6 for each day on which the member attends : if the session extends beyond 30 days then the member receives such sum as the Assembly may vote. *Sum allowed.*

In Quebec and British Columbia the allowance for a session not exceeding 30 days is $6 a day, and for a session exceeding 30 days a sessional allowance of $600 in Quebec and $400 in British Columbia.

In Manitoba and New Brunswick the plan of a sessional allowance has also been adopted; the former allows $400 and the latter $300 per session. *Sessional allowance.*

A deduction is made from the sessional allowance for each day a member is absent. Such deduction amounts to $4 in Ontario, $6 in Quebec and British Columbia, and $8 in Manitoba. In New Brunswick the deduction is *pro rata*. *Non-allowance.*

No deduction however is made on account of absence due to illness, provided the member is at the place where the Legislature meets in the Provinces of Quebec and New Brunswick or within a certain distance of the place of meeting in the Provinces of Ontario, British Columbia (10 miles) and Manitoba (3 miles). *Illness.*

---

[1] See Todd's *Parl. Gov.* p. 330, where it is suggested that all provincial laws should be enacted in the name of the sovereign.

Allowance
for part
of a
session.

When a member serves for part of a session only and is not entitled to a sessional allowance he is usually paid $4 or $6 a day during the time he is actually a member.

In Prince Edward's Island payment depends on an annual vote. Each member receives $160 and an allowance of $12 for stationery and postage together with his travelling expenses.

Travelling
expenses.

The usual allowance for travelling expenses is 10 cents per mile, but in British Columbia it is 25 cents. The mileage allowed is the distance measured along the nearest mail route as certified by the Speaker between the place of residence of the member and the place where the Legislature meets.

How
payment
is made.

In some provinces a member may draw his allowance up to $4 a day from time to time, but the usual time for payment is at the end of the session, when the members file with the Clerk declarations of the number of days they have attended and the sums to which they are entitled for mileage[1].

[1] O. R. S. 1887, c. 11, ss. 62—70. Q. 49 & 50 Vic. c. 97, ss. 70—74; N. B. 42 Vic. c. 3. Man. Con. Stat. c. 4, ss. 8—22. B. C. Con. Stat. 1877, c. 42, ss. 63—68.

CHAPTER V.

THE PROVINCIAL ASSEMBLIES.

1.   QUALIFICATIONS OF ELECTORS.

THE qualifications required of electors to the Assemblies Electors. vary very considerably in the different provinces.   All agree in requiring electors to be

1.   Males,

2.   Of the age of 21 years,

3.   And not under any special legal disqualification.

British Columbia is the only province that does not exact a property qualification of some kind: Ontario is the only province that accepts an income or wages qualification.

The following is a brief summary of the qualifications in each province.

Ontario.

The qualifications of electors are governed by c. 9 of the Ontario. Revised Statutes of 1887.   The following persons are entitled to be registered as voters.

1.   Persons entered on the assessment roll as owners, Property. tenants, or occupants of real property of the value of (*a*) $200 in cities and towns or (*b*) $100 in villages and townships.

2.   Householders House-holders.

   (*a*)   entered as such on the assessment roll of the municipality, (*b*) and residing at the time of the election in the electoral district for which they vote,

(*c*) and who have resided there continuously since the completion of the previous assessment roll.

Income. 3. Persons assessed at an annual income of $250 and (*a*) residing in the electoral district, and (*b*) who have resided there continuously since the last revision.

Wages. 4. Every person entered on the assessment roll as having earned in any trade or occupation during the previous 12 months not less than $250 and residing in the electoral district.

Land-holders' sons. 5. A landholder's son, stepson, grandson or son-in-law who has resided in his father's house for 12 months prior to the making up of the assessment roll and who is resident within the electoral district. Absence for any period not exceeding six months in the year is not to disqualify, and the time spent at any institution of learning within the Province of Ontario, or as a mariner or as a fisherman in the prosecution of his calling, is reckoned as spent in the father's house.

Indians. 6. (*a*) Where there is a voters' list all Indians or persons with part Indian blood who have been duly enfranchised[1], and all Indians or persons with part Indian blood who do not reside among Indians though participating in the annuities, moneys, or rents of a tribe are entitled to be registered as voters subject to the same provisions as other persons in the electoral district.

(*b*) Where there are no voters' lists, Indians or persons with part Indian blood are entitled to vote only (i) if they have been duly enfranchised, or (ii) if not being duly enfranchised they do not participate in the annuities, interest, moneys or rents of a tribe or body of Indians and do not

---

[1] An enfranchised Indian means an Indian who has by letters patent received a grant in fee simple of a portion of a reserve, see 43 Vic. c. 28, 46 Vic. c. 6.

reside amongst Indians, and if in addition in either case they possess one of the usual qualifications.

In those districts where there is no assessment roll a Where no
assessment
roll. person in order to vote must

(a) be resident and domiciled in the district in which he claims to vote,

(b) own real estate in such district of the value of $200,

(c) be a resident householder in such district at the time of election and,

(d) have been such owner and householder for the six months preceding the election.

Quebec.

The qualifications are governed by the 38 Vic. c. 7, ss. *Quebec.* 7—9. Voters must be,

1. Owners or occupants of real estate of the value of *Property.* $300 in any city municipality entitled to return one or more members, and of the value of $200 in any other municipality, or

2. Tenants of real estate paying an annual rent of $30 *Occupa-* in any city municipality entitled to return one or more *tion.* members, and of $20 in any other municipality, such real estate being of the values of $300 and $200 respectively.

Nova Scotia.

The qualifications of electors depend on the 48 Vic. c. 2 [1]. *Nova* The following persons are entitled to vote. *Scotia.*

1. Persons assessed in respect of real property of *Property.* the value of $150 or of real and personal property of the value of $300.

2. Persons possessed at the previous assessment of real property or of real and personal property of the above

[1] See also N. S. Rev. Stat. 1884, c. 4, s. 14.

amounts and who have been specially exempted from taxation.

Tenancy.   3.   Tenants at the time of the previous assessment of real property of the value of $150 where the assessment was levied on the owner thereof, or persons the assessment value of whose personal property combined with that of the real property occupied by him as tenant is of the value of $300.

Sons.   4.   Sons of persons qualified as above, provided that

(a)   such persons are possessed of sufficient property to qualify more than one voter, and that

(b)   the son has resided in the residence of his father or on the property owned by his father within the district for at least one year prior to the previous assessment.

Sons of widows.   5.   Sons of a widow, provided such widow at the time of the last assessment shall have been in possession of property sufficient to give a vote and such son has fulfilled the conditions of residence just mentioned.

In cases 4 and 5, the elder son is preferred to the younger if the property is not sufficient to qualify both.

Occasional absences from home are not to disqualify sons provided they do not exceed four months in the year.

New Brunswick.

New Brunswick.   The qualifications of electors are regulated by the Consol. Stat. 1877, c. 4, which requires as a qualification to vote

Property.   1.   Assessment for the year, for which the registry is made up, in respect of real estate of the value of $100, or of personal property or of real and personal property together of the value of $400, or

Income.   2.   Assessment for such year at an annual income of $400.

In those districts in which there is no assessment, possession of the qualification is sufficient.

Prince Edward's Island.

The Election Law of 1878 (41 Vic. c. 14) as amended by *Prince Edward's Island.* subsequent Acts was repealed by the 42 Vic. c. 2, reviving the 24 Vic. c. 34. The last mentioned Act has been amended by the 45 Vic. c. 1. The following classes of persons may become voters :

1. Owners of freehold estate in one whole water lot, *Property.* common lot, town lot, or pasture lot, situate in a town, common, or royalty.

2. Owners of freehold estate in land or buildings of the yearly value of 40s.

3. Owners of leasehold estates where the estate with improvements thereon is of a value of £35.

4. Occupants of houses, buildings or land in a town, *Occupation.* common or royalty of the annual value of 40s.

The above qualifications confer a vote for the town, common, or royalty, or electoral district in which the property is situated, provided the property has been owned or possessed for 12 months previous to the *teste* of the writ for holding an election.

5. Persons liable to statute labour who have performed the same and have resided in the polling district *Statute labour.* for 12 months.

6. Persons resident in Charlottetown and Summerside who have paid the provincial or civil poll tax for the *Taxes.* year.

Manitoba.

By the Consol. Stat. 1880, c. 3, the following classes of *Manitoba.* voters are recognised :—

   (*a*) Owners of real estate of the value of $100, *Ownership.*

   (*b*) Yearly tenants of real property of the value of *Tenancy.* $200 and paying an annual rent of $20,

   (*c*) Occupants and bona fide householders on land *Occupancy.* of an annual value of $20.

In each case the person must be resident in the electoral division for three months.

British Columbia.

British Columbia. No property qualification is required[1]. Persons are entitled to be registered as voters provided

Residence. (1) they have resided in the province for 12 months, and

(2) have resided in the electoral district for two months of that period previous to sending in a claim to vote. Indians and Chinese are not entitled to vote.

North West Territory.

N. W. Territories. All *bona fide* residents and householders, not being unenfranchised Indians, within the electoral district, and who have resided in such electoral district for at least 12 months immediately prior to the issue of the writ of election are entitled to vote[2].

Householders.

Persons disqualified. In each Province certain persons are disqualified by law from voting on account of the official positions they hold. The disqualification is usually extended to Judges of Superior, Admiralty and County Courts, Clerks of the Crown and of the Peace, Registrars, Sheriffs, officers in Customs and Excise, agents for the sale of Crown Lands, and Postmasters in cities and towns.

Indians are disqualified in Manitoba and policemen in Quebec[3].

Persons who have been guilty of corrupt practices are subject to temporary disqualifications. They cannot be registered or vote at an election for 8 years in Ontario,

---

[1] B. C. 40 Vic. c. 66.   [2] 43 Vic. c. 25, s. 17.
[3] See O. R. S. 1887, c. 9, ss. 4—6, s. 45. Q. 38 Vic. c. 7, s. 11. B. C. Consol. Stat. 1887, c. 66, ss. 3, 6, and 42 Vic. c. 22, s. 4. Man. Consol. Stat. c. 3, s. 8; 44 Vict. c. 12, s. 6. N. S. Rev. Stat. 1884, c. 4, s. 67.

7 years in Quebec and British Columbia, and 6 years in New Brunswick.

2. QUALIFICATIONS OF ELECTED.

Each province exacts certain qualifications from every Elected. person who sits in the Assembly. Not only must a member fulfil fixed conditions before he takes his seat, but he is liable to lose it under certain circumstances. All the provinces agree in requiring a member of the Assembly to be

    (1)   a British subject by birth or naturalisation,   British
    (2)   a male of the age of 21 years.   subjects, Male.

Some of the provinces impose additional qualifications.

Manitoba and British Columbia require members to be Voter. voters in the province, whilst Nova Scotia requires a member either to be a voter or to possess a freehold or equitable estate of the clear yearly value of $8. British Columbia requires a member to have been a resident within the province for one year preceding his election.

New Brunswick requires a member to be legally seised Property. or possessed for his own use of freehold or leasehold lands in the Province of the value of $1200 over and above all incumbrances.

In Prince Edward's Island the property qualification is fixed at £50, and an oath that he is possessed of such property must be taken by every candidate.

The property qualification in Quebec was abolished by the 45 Vic. c. 7.

In the North West Territories every elector is qualified to be elected to the Council[1].

The following persons are as a rule disqualified in all the provinces from sitting in the Legislative Assembly.

[1] The following statutes may be referred to on the above qualifications: O. R. S. 1887, c. 9; Q. 38 Vic. c. 7, s. 124; N. S. Rev. Stat. 1884, c. 3, s. 3; N. B. 45 Vic. c. 21; Man. Consol. Stat. c. 3, s. 113; B. C. Consol. Stat. 1877, c. 66, s. 5; P. E. I. 19 Vic. c. 21, s. 12; N. W. T., R. S. C., 1886, c. 50, s. 21.

Persons dis-qualified. 1.   Members of the Senate and House of Commons of Canada.

2.   Members of the Legislative Council.

3.   Persons holding provincial offices on the nomination of the Crown to which any salary or emolument is attached.

Members of the Executive Council are exempted from this rule provided they are elected whilst holding office.

4.   Persons holding a federal office of emolument under the Crown, except

> 1.   Officers in the Army, Navy, or Militia, not re-ceiving permanent salary on the staff of the Militia.
>
> 2.   Postmasters whose yearly salary is not over $100 in Quebec.
>
> 3.   Justices of the Peace in Ontario and Manitoba.
>
> 4.   Notaries Public in Ontario.
>
> 5.   Coroners in Manitoba.
>
> 6.   The Chairman of Board of Works in Prince Edward's Island.
>
> 7.   Justices of Lunatic Asylums, except two in Prince Edward's Island.
>
> 8.   Teachers of district Schools in Prince Edward's Island.

5.   Contractors with the Province or contractors with respect to any public service under which the money of the Province is to be paid.

6.   Members of the Legislative Council or Assembly usually vacate their seats on becoming bankrupt or insolvent.

7.   Persons found guilty of corrupt practices are dis-qualified from sitting in the Assembly for 8 years in Ontario, for 7 years in British Columbia and for 6 years in New Brunswick.

In addition to the above persons, each province disqualifies certain other officials too numerous to mention [1].

---

[1] See on disqualifications, O. R. S. 1887, c. 11, ss. 6—14.   Q. 49 & 50 Vic. c. 97.   N. S., R. S. 1884, c. 3, s. 11; 49 Vic. c. 6.   P. E. I. 25 Vic. c. 18,

3. DISTRIBUTION OF SEATS.

Ontario. The British North America Act 1867[1] fixed Ontario. the number of electoral divisions at 82, each returning one member. In 1871 the Ontario legislature re-arranged the constituencies and increased the Assembly from 82 to 89 members[2], and in 1885 the number was increased to 90. One member is returned by each electoral district[3].

Quebec. The Legislative Assembly consists of 65 members[4] Quebec. elected by 65 electoral colleges, each returning one member. An electoral college is formed of an electoral district except in three instances where it is formed of two districts.

At the time of the Union certain districts in Quebec were inhabited by a large Protestant population, and in order to safeguard the representation of these districts it was provided[5], that the limits of such districts should only be altered if the 2nd and 3rd readings of the Bill were passed in the Assembly with the concurrence of the majority of the members representing those districts.

Nova Scotia. The province is divided into 18 electoral Nova Scotia. counties, two returning 3 members each and the remainder 2 members each[6].

New Brunswick. The province is divided into 15 counties New Bruns- and one city. Five counties return 4 members each, one wick. county 3 members, seven counties 2 members each, two counties 1 member each. The city of St John's returns 2 members[7].

Prince Edward's Island. The province is divided into P. E. I. 15 electoral districts each returning 2 members[8].

---

39 Vic. c. 3, 42 Vic. c. 13. N. B. 45 Vic. c. 21. Man. Consol. Stat. c. 5. B. C. 40 Vic. c. 42, ss. 10—24, 40 Vic. c. 66, ss. 5, 6.

[1] s. 70. [2] O. 38 Vict. c. 2, s. 1.

[3] O. 48 Vic. c. 2, s. 7, and see O. R. S. 1887, c. 11, s. 1.

[4] B. N. A. Act, s. 80; Q. 49 & 50 Vic. s. 127.

[5] B. N. A. Act, 1867, s. 80. [6] N. S., R. S. 1884, c. 3, s. 2.

[7] N. B. Consol. Stat. 1877, c. 4, s. 79.

[8] P. E. I., Rev. Stat. 1856, cc. 21, 24.

Manitoba.   *Manitoba.* Here there are 31 electoral districts each
returning one member[1].

British   *British Columbia.* This province is divided into 13
Columbia.   electoral districts, five returning one member each; five
returning 2 members each; two returning 3 members each
and one returning 4 members[2]. By the 48 Vic. c. 3, provision has been made for slightly altering the above arrangement after the next dissolution.

N. W. Ter-   *North West Territories.* Members of the Council are
ritories.   elected by electoral districts not exceeding 1000 square
miles in extent and containing a population of not less than
1000 inhabitants of adult age. Each district returns one
member. The districts are constituted by the Lieutenant-
Governor by proclamation[3].

4. METHOD OF ELECTION.

The methods adopted for returning members to the
Provincial Assemblies, though varying to some extent in
the different provinces, possess some important features in
Notice of   common. The returning officer, on receipt of the writ or
election.   other authority requiring him to hold an election, gives
public notice, that on a certain day he will hold a court, or
attend at a certain place, to receive the nomination of candidates, and that in case a poll be demanded, it will be taken
on a named day.

Nomina-   Candidates are, except in Ontario and Prince Edward's
tion.   Island, nominated in writing. The nomination paper must
be signed by 25 electors in Quebec; by 2 electors in Nova
Scotia; by 12 electors in Manitoba; by 5 electors in British
Columbia; and by one or more in New Brunswick.

---

[1] Man. Consol. Stat. c. 5, s. 2.   M. 44 Vic. c. 12, s. 1.
[2] B. C. Constitution Act, 1871, Sched. A; B. C. 42 Vic. c. 19.
[3] R. S. C. c. 50, s. 18.

In Manitoba and Quebec the nomination paper must be accompanied by the written consent of the person nominated unless at the time he is absent from the province. In Manitoba an affidavit also is required to the effect that the 12 nominators are electors, and that the candidate signed his written consent and the nominators signed the nomination paper, in the presence of the person swearing the affidavit. Special requirements.

In Ontario, Quebec, Nova Scotia, New Brunswick and British Columbia, the vote is taken by ballot. How votes are given.

In Manitoba and Prince Edward's Island votes are recorded by a poll clerk in a poll book.

In Ontario and Quebec the poll remains open from 9 a.m. to 5 p.m.: in Nova Scotia from 8 a.m. to 5 p.m.: in New Brunswick and British Columbia from 8 a.m. to 4 p.m.: in Manitoba it is to open between 8 and 9 a.m. and in Prince Edward's Island between 9 and 10 a.m., and in both these last-mentioned provinces closes at 7 p.m. between the 1st April and 1st October, and at 5 p.m. between the 1st October and 1st April. Hours of polling.

At the close of the poll the returning officer counts the votes and makes a return to the writ. Return.

Corrupt practices, such as bribery, treating, or undue influence on the part of a successful candidate or his agent, render an election void and entail certain disqualifications as regards sitting in the Legislature and voting at an election. As a rule the use of flags, badges, colours, or other party emblems on the day of election is forbidden. Corrupt practices.

Election Petitions are as in England tried before one or two judges of the Superior Court of the province. The result is certified to the Speaker of the Assembly, and the Court is authorized to report on any matter arising during the trial which in the opinion of the Court ought to be reported to the Assembly.

Before taking his seat a member is required to take the oath of allegiance, and in some provinces, e.g. Ontario, he has to file an affidavit that except through his agent he has not made any payment for the purposes of his election beyond his personal expenses and that he has not been guilty of any corrupt practices[1].

5.   QUORUM.

In Quebec and Ontario the same rule prevails as in the Dominion House of Commons, and therefore 20 members are requisite to constitute a quorum : in Manitoba a majority of members is necessary; and in British Columbia the number fixed is 9 including the Speaker[2].

6.   THE SPEAKER.

Appointment of Speaker.

By the British North America Act 1867, s. 87, the election of Speaker in the provinces of Quebec and Ontario originally and on vacancies, the duties of the Speaker, and the procedure in case of absence of the Speaker, are governed by the rules that relate to the Speaker of the House of Commons. These rules[3] have practically been adopted by all the Provincial Assemblies[4].

Power is given to the Speaker to call on any member to take the chair during a temporary absence, and if the Speaker be not present on any day the Assembly elects a member as Speaker for the day.

7.   PRIVILEGES.

The British North America Act 1867, did not expressly confer any privileges on the Provincial Legislatures, nor did it in express terms enable such Legislatures to define their privileges.

[1] O. R. S. 1887, c. 11, s. 15.

[2] B. N. A. A. s. 87.   O. R. S. 1887, c. 11, s. 56.   Man. 44 Vic., c. 12, s. 4. B. C. Con. Stat. 1877, c. 42, s. 39.   [3] See post, c. 12.

[4] See O. R. S. 1887, c. 11, ss. 29—36; Q. 49 & 50 Vic., c. 97, s. 7; N. B. C. S. c. 6.   C. S. Man., c. 5, s. 4.   B. C. Con. Stat. 1877, c. 42, ss. 33, 35.

In the session of 1868—9 the Ontario Legislature passed an Act conferring on the Legislative Assembly the same privileges as were enjoyed by the Dominion House of Commons. The validity of the Act was doubted, and the Dominion Minister of Justice referred the question to the law officers of the Crown in England, who held that it was *ultra vires*[1]. Acts passed defining privileges.

Similar Acts were passed by Quebec in 1870, by British Columbia in 1871, and by Ontario in 1876. All these were allowed to come into force, on the ground that anyone affected by them could test their legality in a court of law.

Amongst the powers conferred by the Quebec Act of 1870 are a number of powers regarding the summoning of witnesses and the punishment of persons disobeying such summons. The validity of these sections was raised in *Ex parte Dansereau*[2], and the appeal side of the Quebec Court of Queen's Bench held that the power of summoning witnesses was necessarily incident to the powers of the Provincial Legislatures, and that a Provincial Legislature had "a right to exercise such powers and privileges as are mere incidents of the powers specifically vested in them and without which they could not properly exercise the duties devolving upon them[3]." *Ex parte Dansereau*.

A somewhat similar point was raised in *Landers* v. *Woodworth*[4] with respect to the right of the Nova Scotia Assembly to remove one of its members for contempt. The Supreme Court of the Dominion held that the Legislative Assembly of Nova Scotia had in the absence of express legislation on the subject, no power to remove one of its members for contempt, unless he was actually engaged in obstructing the business of the House, but that the removal of a member for not making an apology required by the *Landers* v. *Woodworth*.

---

[1] Can. Sess. Papers 1877, No. 89, p. 202.
[2] 19 L. C. Jurist 210: 2 Cart. 165.   [3] per Dorion C. J.
[4] 2 Can. S. C. R. 158; 2 Cart. 220.

House was not within the legal powers of the Assembly in the absence of express legislation. "The House of Assembly of Nova Scotia has no power to punish for any offence not an immediate obstruction to the due course of its proceedings and the proper exercise of its functions, such power not being an essential attribute, not essentially necessary for the exercise of its functions by a local legislature, and not belonging to it as a necessary or legal incident: and that without prescription or statute, local legislatures have not the privileges which belong to the House of Commons of Great Britain by the *lex et consuetudo Parliamenti.*"

It may therefore be taken as established:—

(1) That a Provincial Legislature has, apart from provincial legislation, those implied powers and privileges which are absolutely necessary for the discharge of its functions.

(2) That no privileges or powers in the nature of privileges beyond such essentially implied powers can be exercised in the absence of a statute. The validity of a provincial statute defining legislative privileges might be supported on several grounds. First, that the Act was an amendment of the constitution of the provinces under s. 92 (1) of the British North America Act, a view held by Sanborn, J. in *Ex parte Dansereau.* Secondly, that the powers and privileges in question were corollaries of the other powers conferred on the provinces and were essential to the existence of the Legislatures. Thirdly, that in the case of the provinces existing at the time of the Union the local Legislatures enjoyed such powers and privileges, and that the Union Act cannot be said to have interfered with them.

Acts defining the privileges of the local Legislature have been passed by Ontario[1], Quebec[2], Manitoba[3], British

---

[1] O. R. S., c. 11, ss. 37—55.   [2] 49 & 50 Vic. c. 97, s. 46—56.
[3] Con. Stat. 1880, c. 5, ss. 36—41.

Columbia[1], and Nova Scotia[2]. No Act on the subject, except one relating to the attendance of witnesses[3], has been
passed in New Brunswick.

Freedom of speech. The privilege of freedom of speech Freedom
of speech.
is defined in the Quebec Act as follows—

"No legislative councillor or member of the Legislative
Assembly shall be liable to any action, arrest, or imprisonment, or damages, by reason of any matter or thing brought
by him by petition, bill, resolution, motion or otherwise
before the House or by reason of anything said by him
before such House."

The Ontario Act contains a similar provision ; whilst the
British Columbia Act simply states that "no action at law
or other proceeding shall be brought against any member
of the Assembly for any words spoken by him in the
Assembly."

Freedom from arrest. Freedom from arrest is restricted Freedom
from
as in England to the members personally in civil matters. The arrest.
duration of the privilege varies in the different provinces. In
Ontario and Quebec it begins 20 days before the session opens
and continues until 20 days after the session ends. In British
Columbia the corresponding number of days is 40. In Manitoba
the privilege is restricted to the session. The privilege does
not extend to offences specified in the Acts and committed
by members, as for example taking bribes or disobeying
the order of the House.

Exemption from serving on juries. During the same Service on
Juries.
period that a member is exempt from arrest, all members,
officers in the service of the legislature and all witnesses
summoned to attend, are exempt from serving on juries in
the province. The Quebec Act also exempts them from
attending as witnesses. British Columbia exempts them
only from serving as jurors.

[1] 40 Vic. c. 42, ss. 72—78.   [2] N. S. R. S. 1884, c. 3, ss. 20—40.
[3] N. B. 33 Vic. c. 33.

Witnesses.   *Attendance of witnesses.* Apart from Statute a Provincial Legislature may require the attendance of witnesses [1]. The provincial Acts defining privileges usually regulate this power and confer on the Speaker the power of issuing a warrant to compel attendance.

Publication of papers.   *Publication of papers,* &c. Special provision regarding the publication of papers is made by the British Columbia Act, which enacts, that no action is to be brought on account of the printing or publishing of any documents or papers printed by order of either the Legislative Assembly or the Speaker thereof, and in Ontario the production of an affidavit that the publication was by order of the Legislature empowers the judge to stay all proceedings [2].

Breach of privilege.   *Punishing for breach of privilege.* The Ontario, Manitoba and Nova Scotia Acts enumerate a number of offences which if committed are regarded as a breach of privilege, such as :—

Assaulting, molesting, or libelling any member of the Legislature during the session or 20 days before or after the session.

Obstructing, threatening, or attempting to force or intimidate any member.

Bribing or attempting to bribe any member, as well as the acceptance of any bribe.

Assaulting or interfering with any officer of the House in the performance of his duty.

Suborning or tampering with any witness in regard to evidence to be given by him before the House or any Committee.

Presenting to the House or any Committee any forged or falsified document with intent to deceive the House or Committee.

Forging, falsifying or unlawfully altering any of the records of the House.

---

[1] See *ante*, p. 67.   [2] O. R. S. 1887, c. 11, s. 52.

Persons guilty of infringing any of the privileges of the House are liable to be imprisoned for such time during the session then being held as the Assembly may determine.

8. RESIGNATION OF MEMBERS.

A member may resign his seat in either of the following ways:

1. By giving notice to that effect in his place in any province except Nova Scotia, New Brunswick and Prince Edward's Island.

2. By giving written notice to the Speaker. If there be no Speaker, in Prince Edward's Island the notice must be given to the Lieutenant-Governor: in the other provinces to any two members. In Ontario and British Columbia the notice must be under seal, and in all the provinces except Nova Scotia, New Brunswick, and Prince Edward's Island, the signature must be attested by two witnesses. In the last-mentioned province it must be certified by a notary public.

A member may resign after a general election, and before taking his seat, but such resignation is not to affect his right to contest the election.

A resignation may be either during the session or during the recess.

The Speaker may resign by giving notice from his place in the Assembly, or if the House be not in session by giving notice to any two members[1].

---

[1] O. R. S. 1887, c. 11, s. 25. Q. 49 & 50 Vic., c. 97, ss. 23—27. N. S. R. S. 1884. c. 3. N. B. Con. Stat. 1877, c. 4, s. 76. Man. Con. Stat. c. 5, ss. 23—26. B. C. Con. Stat. 1877, c. 42, ss. 48—50. P. E. I. 19 Vic. c. 21, s. 79, 50 Vic. c. 1.

CHAPTER VI.

PROVINCIAL LEGISLATIVE COUNCILS.

FOUR provinces, viz. Quebec, Nova Scotia, New Brunswick, and Prince Edward's Island, possess Legislative Councils, in addition to Legislative Assemblies. The original constitution of Manitoba made provision for a Legislative Council of 7 members appointed for life by the Lieutenant-Governor[1], but in 1876 the Council was abolished and the Legislature now consists of a Lieutenant-Governor and an Assembly[2].

Legislation in the North-West Territories is effected by a Council partly nominated and partly elected; and the Lieutenant-Governor of Manitoba may have the assistance of a Council in carrying on the government of the district of Keewatin.

Number. The number of Councillors in each province is as follows:—

Quebec, **24**.

Nova Scotia, **15**.

New Brunswick, **18**.

Prince Edward's Island, **13**.

North-West Territories, **20**.

As regards British Columbia not more than 6 can be appointed by the Governor-General; and when a district not

Number.

---

[1] 33 Vic. c. 3.   [2] Man. 39 Vic. c. 28.

exceeding 1000 square miles contains a population of not
less than 1000 inhabitants of adult age it may return one
member to the Council.

Qualifications. In Nova Scotia the Lieutenant-Governor Qualifica-
is no way restricted by statute in the choice of Councillors, tions.
but in the other provinces there are certain statutory
qualifications. These may be classified under the following
heads, (1) citizenship, (2) age, (3) property, (4) residence,
and (5) oath of allegiance.

1. Citizenship. All the provinces agree in requiring 1. Citizen-
a Legislative Councillor to be a British subject by birth or ship.
by naturalization.

2. Age. In Quebec and Prince Edward's Island he 2. Age.
must be 30 years of age. In New Brunswick and the
North-West Territories it is sufficient if he be of full age.

3. Property. A property qualification is required in 3. Pro-
Quebec and New Brunswick. In Quebec such qualification perty.
is the same as for senators, i.e. a councillor must be legally or
equitably seised of freeholds of the value of $4000 over
and above all rents, charges or incumbrances payable out
of the same, and his real and personal property together
must be worth $4000, over and above his debts and
liabilities. If he is not resident in the division for which
elected, his real property qualification must be in such
division.

In New Brunswick a Councillor must be seised of freehold
estate in the province of the value of $2400 over and above
all incumbrances.

In Prince Edward's Island and Manitoba no property
qualification is necessary.

4. Residence. In Quebec, New Brunswick and the 4. Resi-
North-West Territories residence in the province is re- dence.
quired, and in New Brunswick there must be residence for
5 years prior to the issue of the writ of election.

5. Oath.

5. Oath. The Councillor must in every case take the oath of allegiance[1].

Disqualifications.

A member of the Legislative Council becomes disqualified from sitting :—

1. On becoming a member of the Senate or of the House of Commons of Canada.
2. By absence from the Legislature for two consecutive sessions or in Prince Edward's Island for one session.
3. By becoming a subject of a foreign power.
4. By becoming bankrupt or insolvent.
5. By being attainted of treason or of any crime.
6. By ceasing to be duly qualified in respect of property or of residence[2].

In Prince Edward's Island, where the Councillors are elected, the same persons who are disqualified from being candidates for the Assembly are also disqualified from being elected to the Council[3].

How appointed. Quebec, New Brunswick.

How appointed. In Quebec, New Brunswick and Nova Scotia, Councillors are appointed by the Lieutenant-Governor in the Queen's name under the great seal, and in Quebec one Councillor has to be chosen from each district represented by a Senator in the Dominion Parliament[4].

Prince Edward's Island.

In Prince Edward's Island Councillors are elected. The province is divided into seven electoral districts, six of these return two members each, and one district (Charlottetown) returns one member. The voters are the same as for the Provincial Assembly[5].

North-West Territories.

In the North-West Territories the Governor-General by

---

[1] See B. N. A. Act. 1867, ss. 73, 23. N. B. Con. Stat. 1877, c. 4, ss. 4, 11. P. E. I. Rev. Stat. 25 Vic. c. 18, ss. 11, 12, 25 and R. S. C. c. 50, ss. 20, 21.

[2] B. N. A. Act. 1867, s. 74. N. B. Con. Stat. 1877, c. 4, ss. 3—6. P. E. I. 25 Vic. c. 18, s. 11—16. [3] See *ante* p. 61.

[4] B. N. A. Act. 1867, ss. 22, 72. Q. 49 & 50 Vic. c. 97, s. 4. N. S. R. S. 1884, c. 3, s. 1. N. B. Con. Stat. 1877, c. 4, s. 2.

[5] P. E. I. 25 Vic. c. 18, ss. 3—6.

and with the advice of his Privy Council has power to appoint six members by warrant under his privy seal[1]. As regards the other members they are elected by *bona fide* male residents and householders of adult age, within the electoral district, not being aliens or unenfranchised Indians, and who have resided in such electoral district for at least 12 months immediately preceding the issue of the writ for the election[2].

Term of office. In Quebec, New Brunswick, and Nova Scotia, Councillors hold office for life, unless they resign or become disqualified.

In Prince Edward's Island a new election takes place for Charlottetown every eighth year, and for other districts every fourth year, from the date of the last election to the Council[3].

In the North-West Territories elected members of the Council hold office for two years but are eligible for re-election[4].

Quorum. The number required to form a quorum of the Councils is as follows:

in Quebec, 10 including the Speaker[5];

in New Brunswick, 8[6];

in Prince Edward's Island, 6 in addition to the President[7];

and in the North-West Territories a majority of the members[8].

The Speaker or President. In Quebec the Speaker is appointed by the Lieutenant-Governor from amongst the members of the Legislative Council[9].

In New Brunswick and Prince Edward's Island the President of the Council is elected by the Councillors[10].

(marginal notes: Term of office. Quorum. Speaker.)

---

[1] R. S. C. c. 50, s. 7   [2] Ib. s. 20.

[3] P. E. I. Rev. Stat. 25 Vic. c. 18, s. 17.   [4] R. S. C. c. 50, s. 22.

[5] B. N. A. A. 1867, s. 78.   [6] N. B. Con. Stat. 1877, c. 4, s. 8.

[7] P. E. I. Rev. Stat. 25 Vic. c. 18, s. 29.   [8] R. S. C. c. 50, s. 23.

[9] B. N. A. A. 1867, s. 77.

[10] N. B. Con. Stat. 1877, c. 4, s. 7. P. E. I. Rev. Stat. 25 Vic. c. 18, s. 27.

In Quebec the Speaker has a vote and a casting vote [1].

In Prince Edward's Island he has only a casting vote [2].

Privileges.   *Privileges.*   Members of the Legislative Council in Quebec enjoy the same privileges as members of the Assembly [3]. In the other provinces that have Legislative Councils Acts have not as yet been passed to define the privileges of such Councils.

Resignation. A Legislative Councillor may resign his seat by a notice in writing under his hand and seal addressed to the Lieutenant-Governor [4].

---

[1] B. N. A. A. 1867, s. 79.

[2] P. E. I. Rev. Stat. 25 Vic. c. 18, s. 29.   [3] See *ante* p. 69.

[4] B. N. A. Act. 1867, ss. 74, 30.   N. B. Con. Stat. 1877, c. 4, s. 5.   P. E. I. 25 Vic. c. 18, s. 19.

CHAPTER VII.

METHOD OF LEGISLATION.

THE procedure and practice of the Provincial Legislatures are regulated partly by the provisions of the British North America Acts, partly by provincial statutes, partly by orders and resolutions of each Legislature, and partly by usages which though unwritten are recognized and followed.

The hour of meeting varies in the different provinces: in British Columbia it is 11 o'clock, in Nova Scotia 12 o'clock, and in Ontario, Quebec and Manitoba 3 o'clock. If the business of the House is not concluded at 6 o'clock the Speaker leaves the chair until half-past seven. The House at its rising on Friday as a rule stands adjourned until the following Monday. *Hour of Meeting.*

Order of Business. The business in the Provincial Assemblies is generally as follows: *Order of business.*

Every day certain routine business is taken in the following order:—

1. Presenting Petitions.
2. Reading and Receiving Petitions.
3. Presenting Reports by Standing and Select Committees.
4. Motions.

After the above routine business is disposed of, the order of business varies according to the day and the province.

In Ontario, Quebec, and British Columbia the following rules prevail.

Order of business.

On one day the order of business is:—

1. Private Bills.
2. Questions put by Members.
3. Notices of Motions.
4. Public Bills and Orders.

On two other days in the week the order is:—

1. Government Notices of Motions.
2. Government Orders.
3. Public Bills and Orders.
4. Questions put by Members.
5. Other Notices of Motions.
6. Private Bills.

On the remaining two days in the week the order is:—

1. Questions put by Members.
2. Notices of Motions.
3. Public Bills and Orders.
3ᵃ. Government Notices of Motions *in Quebec.*
3ᵇ. Government Orders *in Quebec.*
4. Private Bills.
5. Public Bills and Orders.
6. Private Bills, *in Ontario.*
7. Government Notices of Motions, *in Ontario.*
8. Government Orders, *in Ontario.*

In Nova Scotia the same order of business is followed from day to day.

Public Bills.

Public Bills pass through the same stages as in the Dominion Parliament, except that in some provinces the consent of a second House is not required.

Introduction.

All Bills are introduced upon motion for leave specifying the title of the Bill, or upon motion to appoint a committee to prepare and bring it in: no Bill can be introduced in blank.

Money bills can originate only in the Legislative Assembly and no appropriation can take place unless first
recommended by a message from the Lieutenant-Governor.

Every bill requires except on urgent or extraordinary Readings.
occasions to be read three times on separate days. After the
second reading the House goes into Committee, and all
amendments made are reported to the House. After report
the Bill is open to debate and amendment before it is
ordered for third reading.

Private Bills are initiated by way of petition. No petition Private
Bills.
for a private Bill is received as a rule after the first two
weeks of a session, and no private Bill can be presented after
the first three weeks.

Each Legislature has standing orders, relative to such
petitions, prescribing what notice of the application shall be
given and what particulars must be stated.

The petition comes before the Committee on Standing
Orders, and if such Committee reports favourably, the Bill
is introduced on motion for leave. After being read a second
time it is referred to a Committee, and the subsequent
procedure is similar to that prevailing in the Dominion
Parliament.

CHAPTER VIII.

The Lieutenant-Governor.

In each province an officer called the Lieutenant-Governor, appointed by the Governor-General in Council under the great seal of Canada, presides over the administration and forms a part of the Legislature. As he is not appointed by Her Majesty, and holds no commission from Her, he cannot be regarded as personally representing Her: he is a Dominion officer, and is responsible to the Governor-General and Council[1].

Form of Commission. The Form of Commission appointing a Lieutenant-Governor is as follows:—

L. S.

Canada.

Victoria, by the grace of God of the United Kingdom of Great Britain and Ireland, Queen, Defender of the Faith &c.

To the Honourable A. B. of   in our Dominion of Canada.

Greeting:—

Whereas we did by Letters Patent under the Great Seal of our Dominion of Canada bearing date at the city of Ottawa the   day of   in the   year of our reign appoint A. B. to be Lieutenant-Governor of the Province of   for and during our will and pleasure as upon relation being had to the said recited Letters Patent will more fully and at large appear.

[1] See *Lenoir v. Ritchie*, 3 Can. S. C., p. 575.

And whereas the said A. B. has since died and we have thought fit to appoint you to be such Lieutenant-Governor in his stead. Now know ye, that we reposing special trust and confidence in the prudence, courage, loyalty, and integrity of you the said C. D. of our especial grace, certain knowledge, and mere motion have thought fit to constitute and appoint you, and in accordance with the provisions of the Act of Parliament of the United Kingdom of Great Britain and Ireland passed in the thirtieth year of our reign intituled "the British North America Act, 1867," do hereby constitute and appoint you to be the Lieutenant-Governor in and over the Province of —— during the will and pleasure of our Governor-General of Canada.

And we do hereby authorize and empower and require and command you in due manner to do and execute all things that shall belong to your said command and the trust we have reposed in you, according to the several provisions and directions granted or appointed you by virtue of this our Commission and of the Act above mentioned, according to such instructions as are herewith given to you or which may from time to time be given to you in respect of the said Province of —— under the sign manual of our Governor-General of our said Dominion of Canada, or by order of our Privy Council of Canada, and according to such laws as are or shall be in force within the said Province of ——.

In testimony whereof we have caused these our Letters to be made Patent and the Great Seal of Canada to be hereunto affixed. Witness &c.

By command

_____

Secretary of State.

_____

Attorney-General of Canada.

M. 6

I hereby certify the within to be a true and faithful copy of the record of the original commission as entered in   .

—————————————

Deputy Registrar-General of Canada.

Functions of the Lieutenant Governor. The Lieutenant-Governor discharges important functions as regards the Legislature and the Administration.

As regards the Provincial Legislature his chief duties are :—

To summon, prorogue, or dissolve the Legislature[1].

To appoint Legislative Councillors in Quebec, New Brunswick and Nova Scotia.

To appoint the Speaker of the Legislative Council of Quebec[2].

To recommend the appropriation of the revenues and all money bills[3].

To assent to or veto bills, or reserve them for the consideration of the Governor-General[4].

In British Columbia he is authorized to transmit by message to the Assembly the draft of any laws which it may appear to him desirable to introduce[5], or to return bills for reconsideration with such amendments as he may think fit.

As regards the Executive. As regards the Executive, the Lieutenant-Governor selects his Ministers, but he is bound by constitutional practice to choose them from that party which has the confidence of the majority in the Legislative Assembly. He may dismiss his Ministers or call on them to resign, but for the due and proper exercise of his power he is responsible to the Governor-General in Council[6].

He usually, with the assent of his Executive Council, and

---

[1] See *ante*, pp. 41—52.   [2] B. N. A. Act, 1867, s. 77.
[3] Ib. ss. 90, 54.   [4] Ib. s. 90.
[5] B. C. 34 Vic. c. 42, s. 42.   [6] See *post*, Chap. xv.

subject to the provisions of any Act regulating the Civil Service in the Province, appoints all officers necessary for carrying on the work of administration.

Many other important powers connected with provincial administration have been conferred on the Lieutenant-Governors by the statutes of the respective provinces.

A Lieutenant-Governor holds office as a rule for a period Term of of five years[1], but he may be removed at any time by the office. Governor-General, the fact of such removal being communicated to the Senate and to the House of Commons. In exercising his power of removal the Governor-General is required to act by the advice of his Ministers[2].

[1] B. N. A. Act, 1867, s. 59.   [2] See *post*, chap. xv.

CHAPTER IX.

THE PROVINCIAL ADMINISTRATION.

IN each province the Lieutenant-Governor is assisted in the discharge of his duties by an Executive Council. The members of the Council are appointed by him, and in accordance with constitutional practice, as has been pointed out, he is expected to choose his councillors from that party which has a majority in the Assembly. The Council fulfil in regard to the province functions similar to those discharged by the Dominion Privy Council in regard to the Dominion. The Council in fact is a ministry, and the Lieutenant-Governor in the discharge of his duties is expected to follow its advice.

Number of Ministers. The number of members of the Executive Council varies in the different provinces from four in British Columbia to nine in Prince Edward's Island. The Council of the North-West Territories, which exercises legislative as well as executive functions, consists of 18 members.

Ministers without office. Though as a rule each member of the Council has charge of a department of State, occasionally some members may be without office. For instance, at the present time in New Brunswick two members, in Nova Scotia three members, and in Prince Edward's Island six members, are without office.

The departments of State over which always a minister presides in each of the seven provinces are the following:

The department of the Attorney-General.

The department of Public Works.

The department of Crown Lands.

The office of Secretary of State.

The office of Treasurer.

Besides the above departments, Ontario assigns a minister to the department of Education, Quebec one to Agriculture, and Manitoba one to Railways. Of the ministry in Prince Edward's Island only three preside over departments, one minister undertaking the duties of Secretary, Treasurer, and Commissioner of Crown Lands.

The following table shows the distribution of departments in the different provinces; the provinces being denoted by their initial letters.

	O.	Q.	N.S.	N.B.	M.	B.C.	P.E.I.
Attorney-General	O.	Q.	N.S.	N.B.	M.	B.C.	P.E.I.
Secretary	O.	Q.	N.S.	N.B.	M.	B.C.¹	P.E.I.
Treasurer	O.	Q.		N.B.	M.		P.E.I.
Crown Lands	O.	Q.	N.S.¹	N.B.		B.C.	
Public Works	O.	Q.	N.S.¹	N.B.	M.	B.C.	
Agriculture		Q.			M.		P.E.I.
Railways					M.		
Education	O.						

A brief account may be given of some of the more important departments.

Department of the Law Officer. The Attorney-General of each province holds a most important position in the Ministry. Not unfrequently he is premier. In some cases he is assisted in his department by a Solicitor-General. As law officer he is the official legal adviser of the Lieutenant-Governor. He has the general superintendence of all matters connected with the administration of justice in the province, and it is his duty to see that public affairs are administered in accordance with the law. Not the least important of his

¹ Including mines.

functions is to advise the Lieutenant-Governor on the competence of the Legislature to pass any particular law.

Department of Provincial Secretary. The Provincial Secretary is charged with very varied duties. Besides conducting all correspondence on behalf of his Government, he usually acts as keeper of the Great Seal of the province and as provincial registrar. He is intrusted, except in Ontario, with the control of education, and is charged with the administration of municipal and police laws, the care of the insane, the incorporation of companies, the collection of statistics and Government printing.

Department of Provincial Treasurer. The Provincial Treasurer has the control and superintendence of all financial affairs. He advises on receipts and expenditure and is charged with the preparation of the budget. All provincial revenue as it is collected is paid into banks to the credit of the Treasurer. Moneys are paid only on the warrant of the Lieutenant-Governor and by cheque signed by the Treasurer or his assistant and countersigned by the auditor. On the latter official rests the duty of seeing that no warrant issues for payment of any moneys not appropriated by the Legislature.

Department of Public Works. This provincial department is charged with the construction and maintenance of all public works in the province. The construction of railways, canals, roads, bridges, buildings and other state undertakings is an important part of the work of administration and government.

In Manitoba a separate department has been created for Railways.

Department of Crown Lands. The department of Crown Lands has the control of all lands belonging to the province. The minister grants licences, arranges sales, and enforces forfeitures.

Department of Education. All matters relating to Education are within the jurisdiction of the several provinces, and though the systems adopted differ in details, all are based on the principle of free education, the funds being supplied by the province or by local taxation. In all provinces except Ontario, Quebec, and Manitoba the schools are unsectarian; in the three provinces mentioned there are separate schools for Roman Catholics. Ontario has placed its educational system under a minister; in the other provinces the education is in charge of a superintendent of education.

In the North-West Territories the educational system is under the control of a board of Education, composed of five members, viz. the Lieutenant-Governor and two Protestant and two Catholic members appointed by the Lieutenant-Governor in Council.

The department of Education in Ontario has very ex- Ontario. tensive powers in regard to the Normal, High, Public, and Separate Schools in the province. Power is given to it to make regulations for the organization, discipline, and government of schools, the equipment of school houses, the choice of text books, and the qualifications of inspectors, examiners, teachers and assistants in High Schools: to appoint inspectors and central examiners: to constitute model schools: to set apart schools or colleges for the training of model teachers: to prescribe the conditions under which pupils will be admitted into High Schools: and to make regulations respecting fees and certificates. Power is also given to the department to establish meteorological stations in connection with High Schools [1].

[1] R. S. O. 1887, c. 224.

CHAPTER X.

The Provincial Judicature.

B. N. A.
Act, 1867,
ss. 91, 92. By Sections 91 and 92 of the British North America Act, 1867, "the administration of justice in the Province, including the constitution, maintenance, and organization of Provincial Courts, both of Civil and Criminal jurisdiction, and including procedure in civil matters in these courts," was placed under the jurisdiction of the provinces, whilst criminal law and criminal procedure were placed under the jurisdiction of the Dominion. By a subsequent section the Governor-General was authorized to appoint the judges of the Superior, District, and County Courts in each province, except those of the Courts of Probate in Nova Scotia and New Brunswick. The judges of these last-mentioned courts as well as magistrates and justices of the peace, are appointed by the Lieutenant-Governor of each Province, though the Governor-General also as representing the Crown may appoint justices. In considering the Courts found in the different provinces a distinction must be drawn between (1) Courts of Civil jurisdiction and (2) Courts of Criminal jurisdiction.

I. Courts of Civil Jurisdiction.

Quebec.

*Justices
of the
Peace.* *Justices of the Peace* have jurisdiction in certain civil matters, such as the recovery of school taxes, assessments for

building or repairing churches, parsonages or churchyards, damages caused by animals, disputes between masters and servants in the county, seamen's wages, claims of pawnors against pawnbrokers, and other matters specified in special statutes[1].

The Recorder's Court has jurisdiction for the recovery of certain municipal claims and in disputes between lessors and lessees, and between master and servant[2]. *Recorder's Court.*

Trinity House exercises jurisdiction in matters connected with the shores of the St Lawrence and of the rivers flowing into it, and also with regard to the wages and indemnities due to pilots[3]. *Trinity House.*

Commissioner's Court. This Court is held before one or more unpaid Commissioners in such parishes, townships, or extra-parochial places as may be appointed by the Lieutenant-Governor. *Commissioner's Court.*

The Court has an ultimate jurisdiction,

(a) in all suits purely personal or relating to moveable property, which arise from contract, where the sum or value demanded does not exceed 25 dollars and the debtor resides in the locality of the Court, or if the debtor resides in the same district and within five leagues and the debt has been contracted in the locality, or if the debtor resides in another locality where no court is held; suits for slander, assault and battery, recovery of any fine or penalty, and suits relating to civil status, paternity or seduction, excepted[4];

(b) in suits for the recovery of assessments not exceeding 25 dollars imposed for the building of churches, parsonages, and churchyards.

Circuit Courts. The Circuit Court is held before one judge of the Superior Court in each judicial district and in such of those counties (with certain exceptions) in which the *Circuit Court. Constitution.*

---

[1] Civil Code, Art. 1216.   [2] Ib. Art. 1217.   [3] Ib. 1218.
[4] Ib. Arts. 1188, 1189.

Superior Court does not sit as may be selected by the Governor.

Ultimate Jurisdiction. The Court has an ultimate or final jurisdiction to the exclusion of the Superior Court,

(*a*) in all suits whenever the amount or value of the thing demanded is less than 100 dollars except cases within the exclusive jurisdiction of the Admiralty, and

(*b*) in all suits for school taxes or school fees or concerning assessments for building or repairing churches, parsonages, or churchyards, whatever may be the amount of such suits[1].

Jurisdiction subject to appeal. The Court has an original jurisdiction to the exclusion of the Superior Court but subject to appeal,

(*a*) in all suits in which the sum or the value of the thing demanded amounts to or exceeds 100 dollars but does not exceed 200 dollars[2].

(*b*) in all suits for fees of office, duties, rents, revenue or sums payable to the Crown or which relate to any title to lands or tenements, annual rents or such like matters, whereby rights in future may be bound, even though the amount claimed be under 100 dollars, subject to the right of the defendant to have the suit removed to the Superior Court[3].

Concurrent Jurisdiction. The Court has a concurrent jurisdiction with the Superior Court by means of *certiorari* over judgments rendered by the Commissioner's Court or by Justices of the Peace within the district.

Appellate Jurisdiction. The Court has an appellate jurisdiction over judgments rendered by a Commissioner's Court or by Justices of the Peace for taxes, assessments or penalties, imposed under the Municipal Road Act of Quebec.

Superior Court. *Superior Court.* The Superior Court of Quebec is composed of a Chief Justice and 29 puisne judges[4].

---

[1] Civil Code, Art. 1053.   [2] Civil Code, Art. 1053.
[3] Ib. 1054, 1058.   [4] Q. 50 Vic. c. 11.

The province is divided into 20 judicial districts and sittings of the Court are held at the *chef-lieu* of each district.

The Court has original jurisdiction in all suits or actions which are not exclusively within the jurisdiction of the Circuit Court or of the Admiralty. *Jurisdiction.*

Court of Review. In the following cases a review of a case tried before a Circuit or a Superior Court may be had before three judges of the Superior Court, *Court of Review.*

    (*a*) upon every final judgment on which an appeal lies;

    (*b*) upon every judgment or order given by a judge in summary matters contained in the third part of the Civil Code;

    (*c*) upon any judgment to set aside an attachment before judgment or *capias ad respondendum*[1];

    (*d*) upon judgments given against a defendant by default in cases of attachment[2].

If the judgment reviewed be affirmed the right of appeal to the Queen's Bench is taken away[3].

Court of the Vice-Admiral. This Court, presided over by a judge, exercises jurisdiction in all Admiralty causes. *Court of Vice-Admiral.*

Court of Queen's Bench. The Court of Queen's Bench is composed of a Chief Justice and five puisne judges[4], but the judges of the Superior Court may be called on to sit in the Queen's Bench. Four judges form a quorum and sittings are held in Quebec and Montreal four times a year. *Court of Queen's Bench.*

The Court acts as a Court of Appeal from the Superior and the Circuit Courts[5], *Jurisdiction.*

An appeal lies from the Superior Court,

    (*a*) against any judgment founded upon a general verdict given by a special jury on any question of law;

---

[1] Q. 34 Vic. c. 4.   [2] Civil Code, Art. 483.   [3] Q. 37 Vic. c. 6.
[4] Q. 43 and 44 Vic. c. 4.   [5] Civil Code, Arts. 1114—1116.

(*b*)   against any other final judgment except in cases of *certiorari*, or matters affecting municipal corporations or offices, or where the amount in question does not exceed $200 and the judgment has been confirmed in review before three judges;

(*c*)   against interlocutory judgments in certain cases.

Appeals from Circuit Courts.   An appeal lies from a Circuit Court

(*a*)   where the sum or value of the thing demanded amounts to $100, except in suits for the recovery of assessments for schools or schoolhouses, or for monthly contributions for schools or for the recovery of assessments imposed for the building or repairing of churches, parsonages, and churchyards.   If the evidence has not been taken down in writing the appeal can be only on points of law;

(*b*)   where the demand is less than $100 but relates to fees of office, duties, rents, revenues or sums payable to Her Majesty, or to titles to lands or tenements, annual rents or other matters in which the rights in future of the parties may be affected;

(*c*)   in all actions in recognition of hypothec.

Special measures regulate appeals from judgments given in the Magdalen Islands [1].

ONTARIO.

Division Court.   *The Division Courts.*   In each county there are Courts called Division Courts, not less than three nor more than twelve in number, presided over by the junior County Court Judge.

Each Judicial District is divided into Court Divisions, and once in two months a Court is held in each Division [2].

Causes are heard before the Judge alone, but in actions of tort where the amount sought to be recovered exceeds

---

[1] Civil Code, Art. 1133.   [2] O. R. S. 1887, c. 51.

$10, and in all other actions when such amount exceeds $20, either party may demand a jury.

The jurisdiction extends to, Jurisdiction.

(*a*) all personal actions where the amount claimed does not exceed $60;

(*b*) all claims of debt, breach of contract or money demand where the balance claimed does not exceed $100;

(*c*) all claims of debt or money demand where the balance claimed is under $200 and the original amount is ascertained by signature of the defendant.

The jurisdiction does not however extend to actions for gambling debts, liquor sold in a tavern, ejectment, toll, custom, or franchise, title to land, malicious prosecution, libel, slander, breach of promise, or against Justices of the Peace or relating to the validity of wills and settlements.

An appeal is allowed to the Court of Appeal where the Appeal. amount in dispute exceeds $100.

A County Court is held in every county and is presided County over by a judge who acts as a Local Judge of the High *Court.* Court in all matters assigned to him by Statute or by the Rules of Court.

The jurisdiction of the County Court extends to,

1. all personal actions where the debt or damage claimed does not exceed $200.

2. all causes relating to debt, covenant, and contract up to $400 where the amount is liquidated or ascertained by the act of the parties or by the signature of the defendant.

3. proceedings on bail bonds given to the Sheriff in any County Court whatever be the penalty.

4. recognizances of bail taken in County Courts to any amount.

5. actions of replevin where the value of the goods or property taken does not exceed $200.

6. interpleader matters.

7. actions for the recovery of land where the yearly value of the premises or the rent payable does not exceed $200, (a) where the interest of the tenant has suffered or has been determined by notice to quit, (b) where the rent is 60 days in arrear and the landlord has the right to re-enter.

It is expressly declared that the Court shall not have jurisdiction :

1. where the title to land is in question except in the above-mentioned cases.

2. where the validity of any devise, bequest or limitation under any will or settlement is disputed.

3. in cases of libel, slander, crim. con., or seduction.

4. in actions against a Justice of the Peace for anything done by him in the execution of his office if he objects thereto[1].

Surrogate Court.

Surrogate Court. In each county the senior County Court Judge holds a Surrogate Court, which has jurisdiction in all testamentary matters and causes and in relation to the granting and revoking probates of wills and letters of administration, subject to an appeal to the Chancery Division of the High Court[2].

The Court has a concurrent jurisdiction with the High Court regarding the custody of infants[3].

Maritime Court.

The Maritime Court was constituted by the Dominion Statute 40 Vic. c. 21. It is composed of one Judge for the Province and Surrogate Judges for certain localities appointed by the Governor in Council. It has jurisdiction in all such matters (with certain exceptions) arising out of or connected with navigation, shipping, trade or commerce on any river, lake, canal or inland water of which the whole or part is within the Province of Ontario, as would belong to any existing Vice-Admiralty Court if its process extended to Ontario. By an Ontario Act[4] the Judge of the Court has

[1] O. R. S. 1887, c. 47, ss. 18—22.   [2] O. R. S. 1887, c. 50.
[3] Ib. c. 137, s. 1.   [4] O. R. S. 1887, c. 43.

the same authority as a County Court Judge regarding the use of the Court-house or other buildings for the administration of justice.

Heir and Devisee Commission. This Commission con- *Heir and* sists of the Judges of the Superior Courts and of such other *Devisee Commis-* persons as may be appointed under the Great Seal. The *sion.* duties of the Court, which may be held by three Commissioners, are to ascertain, determine and declare who is the party in whose favour whether as heir, devisee or assign, the patent ought to issue for the lands which form the subject matter of the claim brought before the Commission [1].

Supreme Court of Judicature. In 1881 the separate *Supreme* Courts of Appeal, Queen's Bench, Chancery and Common *Court.* Pleas were consolidated into one Court called the Supreme Court of Judicature for Ontario [2]. This Supreme Court was divided into two divisions, (1) the Court of Appeal, and (2) the High Court of Justice.

The High Court is divided into three Divisions, the 1. *The* Queen's Bench Division, the Common Pleas Division and *High Court.* the Chancery Division, presided over by the Chief Justice of the Queen's Bench, the Chief Justice of the Common Pleas and the Chancellor respectively.

Sittings of the High Court for the trial of causes and Assizes. matters are held twice a year in each county or union of counties.

The High Court possesses all the powers and jurisdiction that were on the 5th Dec. 1859 enjoyed by the Superior Courts of Common Law in England; and on its Equity side it possesses in regard to fraud, accident, trusts, executors and administrators, partnership, account, mortgages, awards, dower, infants, idiots, lunatics, waste, specific performance, discovery, letters patent, and multiplicity of suits, powers similar to those exercised by the Court of Chancery in

[1] O. R. S. 1887, c. 27. [2] O. 44 Vic. c. 5.

England on the 4th March, 1837, as well as the same juris-diction as that possessed by the Court of Chancery on the 10th June, 1857, to administer justice in all cases where there existed no adequate remedy.

Various other powers are possessed by the High Court, as English legislation is followed in so far as the same is appropriate to the wants of the Province[1].

Court of Appeal. *The Court of Appeal* consists of a Chief Justice and three Justices. The jurisdiction of the Court extends to hearing Appeals,

1. from the Queen's Bench, Common Pleas and Chancery Divisions of the High Court.

2. from the Division Court.

3. from County Courts where the case is heard before a judge without a jury[2].

Appeals from the Court of Appeal to the Supreme Court of Canada respecting property and civil rights are not allowed without special leave, unless the title to real estate or the validity of a patent is affected, or unless the matter in controversy exceeds the value of $1000, or unless the question relates to the taking of an annual or quarterly rent, customary or quarterly duty, or a like demand of a general nature affecting future rights[3].

Appeals from the Court of Appeal to Her Majesty in Council are prohibited except when the matter in contro-versy exceeds $4000 in value, or relates to the taking of a rent or any like demand affecting future rights[4]. This how-ever does not affect the right of the Judicial Committee of the Privy Council to sustain any appeal as a matter of grace.

---

[1] O. R. S. 1887, c. 44, ss. 20—42.   [2] O. R. S. 1887, c. 44.
[3] Ib. c. 42, s. 2.   [4] O. R. S. 1887, c. 41.

NOVA SCOTIA.

Justices of the Peace. In all actions of debt where the *Justices.* cause of action does not exceed $20 one Justice has jurisdiction, and where the cause of action exceeds $20 and does not exceed $80 jurisdiction may be exercised by any two Justices of the county in which the defendant resides or in which the debt or cause of action arose. In the latter case either party may have the case tried before a jury[1].

County Courts. Seven County Courts have been es- *County Courts.* tablished, one for each of the seven districts into which the Province has been divided[2].

The Judges of the County Courts are also Masters of the Supreme Court[3].

The County Courts have jurisdiction[4], Jurisdiction.

(*a*) in all actions *ex contractu* where the debt or damage claimed does not exceed $400 and is not less than $20;

(*b*) in all other actions where the damages claimed do not exceed $200;

(*c*) in all actions on bail bonds to the Sheriff in any cause in a County Court;

(*d*) in all actions against the Sheriff or officer of a County Court for nonfeasance or malfeasance in connection with any matter transacted in the County Court.

Except as to actions of debt or assumpsit in which the cause of action is less than $80, the above jurisdiction is concurrent with that of the Supreme Court.

The following matters have been expressly excepted out of the jurisdiction of the Courts, viz. actions where the title to land is in question, or where the validity of any devise, bequest, or limitation is disputed, as well as actions for crim. con., seduction, and breach of promise of marriage.

[1] N. S., R. S. 1884, c. 102, s. 1. [2] N. S., R. S. c. 105, s. 2.
[3] N. S. 49 Vic. c. 50. [4] N. S., R. S. 1884, c. 105, s. 16.

The Courts have jurisdiction in appeals from Justices, Stipendiary Magistrates, City and Municipal Courts.

Admiralty Court.   *The Admiralty Court* exercises jurisdiction in all Admiralty matters.

Probate Court.   *Probate Court.* This Court has jurisdiction in all matters relating to the probates of wills and the administration of estates [1].

Divorce Court.   *Court of Matrimonial Causes and Divorce.* This Court is presided over by the Equity Judge and has jurisdiction over all matters relating to prohibited marriages and divorce; an appeal lying to the Supreme Court in banc [2].

Supreme Court.   *The Supreme Court.* The Supreme Court resembles in organization and jurisdiction the Supreme Court of Judicature in England. It is composed of a Chief Justice and six Puisne Judges. Circuits of the Court are held twice a year in each county and extra sittings are in the summer held in certain towns.

The Court is invested with the powers that were formerly exercised by the Courts of Queen's Bench, Common Pleas, Chancery and Exchequer in England and also with all the powers, except those relating to Probate and Surrogate Courts, that are now exercised in England by the Supreme Court of Judicature [3].

It also exercises an appellate jurisdiction in cases from County Courts.

NEW BRUNSWICK.

Justices.   *Justices' Civil Courts.* Justices of the Peace have in the Counties in which they reside and for which they have been appointed Justices, jurisdiction in the following actions:

---

[1] N. S., R. S. 1884, c. 100.
[2] N. S., R. S. 1873, c. 126, s. 10, N. S. 49 Vic. c. 49.
[3] N. S., R. S. c. 104.

1. Actions of debt where the sum demanded does not exceed $20.

2. Actions of tort to real or personal property where the damages claimed do not exceed $8.

The jurisdiction does not extend to actions where the Queen is a party, or where the title to land is in question, or the action is for a debt exceeding $20 unless the same has been reduced by payment or abandonment to that sum, or where the action is for debt against personal representatives, trustees of absconding debtors, assignees of bankrupts or insolvents, or banking or insurance companies[1].

A rehearing may on affidavit be obtained before a Justice of the Supreme Court.

Local Courts. Stipendiary and Police Magistrates have jurisdiction in the county, town, parish, or district for which they are appointed, *Local Courts.*

1. in all actions where a Justice of the Peace has Civil jurisdiction ;

2. in all actions of debt where the amount claimed does not exceed $40 ;

3. in all actions of tort to real or personal property where the title to land does not come in question and where the damages do not exceed $16.

Civil Courts of St John, Fredericton, Portland. Special Civil Courts have been established in certain towns. *City Courts.*

The Small Debts Court of Fredericton has jurisdiction in actions of debt up to $40, and in tort up to $16.

The City Court of St John and the Civil Court of Portland have jurisdiction in actions of debt up to $80, and in tort up to $20[2].

Parish Courts. In each parish a Court is held before a Commissioner, being a Justice of the Peace appointed by the Lieutenant-Governor in Council[3]. *Parish Courts.*

---

[1] C. S., N. B., c. 60.

[2] C. S., N. B. cc. 53—57.   [3] C. S., N. B. c. 59, 13 Vic. c. 12.

The Court has jurisdiction in

1.   actions of debt where the sum demanded does not exceed $40 ;

2.   actions of tort to real or personal property where the damage claimed does not exceed $16.

The same causes that are excepted out of the jurisdiction of the Justices' Court are also excepted out of this Court substituting $40 for $20.

Divorce Court.

Court of Divorce and Matrimonial Causes. By the 31 Geo. 3, c. 5 (N. B.) the Governor and Council were constituted a Court for hearing and determining causes relating to marriage and divorce.

By the 23 Vic. c. 37 (N. B.) a Court of Divorce and Matrimonial Causes was established, and the jurisdiction formerly vested in the Governor and Council in respect of marriage and divorce is now vested in this Court [1].

An appeal lies to the Supreme Court.

Probate Court.

Probate Court. Probates of Wills and Letters of Administration were at first granted by the Governor under the Royal Instructions; Surrogates being appointed for that purpose in the different counties [2]. The Court of Probate has now full jurisdiction in all matters relating to wills or administrations, an appeal lying to the Supreme Court [3].

County Courts.

County Courts. When the province was first established County Charters or Letters Patent were issued creating the several districts, into which the province was for that purpose divided, separate counties, and constituting a separate judicial system for each district. Amongst the Courts established were the Inferior Courts of Common Pleas with jurisdiction in all causes arising within the county and in which the amount claimed exceeded 40s. and did not exceed £50 in value and in which the title to lands did not come

[1] C. S., N. B. c. 50.

[2] Report on Judicial Institutions of N. B. p. 35.

[3] C. S., N. B. c. 52, 41 Vic. c. 30.

in question. In 1795 the jurisdiction was extended by giving to these Inferior Courts a concurrent jurisdiction with the Supreme Court[1]. These Inferior Courts of Common Pleas were abolished in 1867 and County Courts substituted for them[2].

A County Court sits in each county from time to time *Jurisdiction.* and has jurisdiction in all personal actions of debt, covenant and assumpsit where the debt or damages claimed do not exceed $200, and in actions on bonds given to the sheriff or otherwise in any case in a County Court and in actions on other bonds where the real debt does not exceed $400[3]; except (1) where the title to land is in question, (2) where the validity of any devise, bequest or limitation is disputed, (3) crim. con. and seduction, (4) breach of promise of marriage, (5) actions against justices of the peace for anything done in the execution of their office[4].

An appeal lies to the Supreme Court by any party feeling himself aggrieved by the decision of a judge upon any point of law, or with the charge to a jury, or with the decision upon motion for a non-suit or for a new trial or in arrest of judgment[5].

County Courts have concurrent jurisdiction with the Circuit Courts in all criminal cases except capital offences[6].

Supreme Court. The Supreme Court of New Bruns- *Supreme Court.* wick was established by General Thomas Carleton, the first Governor, under the authority of the King's Commission. It was invested with the powers and authorities of the three Superior Courts of Law at Westminster Hall. Its constitution and practice have from time to time been modified by local statutes[7].

---

[1] N. B. 35 Geo. 3, c. 2: see Report of Commissioners on Judicial Institutions of the Province, 1833.

[2] N. B. 30 Vic. c. 10.   [3] N. B. 49 Vic. c. 18.

[4] C. S., N. B. c. 51.   [5] Ib. s. 50.   [6] Ib. s. 62.

[7] C. S., N. B. 37. N. B. 36 Vic. c. 31; 42 Vic. c. 7; Ib. c. 8; 44 Vic. c. 12.

In 1879 a separate Judge in Equity was appointed to hold separate Equity sittings and to exercise all the powers of the Supreme Court in Equity. The original jurisdiction of the Supreme Court was preserved and an appeal was allowed to the Court from the Judge in Equity[1].

The Court is now composed of a Chief Justice, a Judge in Equity and four Puisne Judges[2]. Sittings of the Court are held at Fredericton and St John, and the Court goes on circuit in the different counties. The Judge in Equity holds sittings in counties at such times and places as he may appoint[3].

By a recent Act[4] the Lieutenant-Governor is authorized to appoint three referees to assist in discharging the business of the Supreme Court in Equity.

MANITOBA.

County Courts.

County Courts are held in counties from time to time[5].

The Courts have jurisdiction,

    (*a*) in all personal actions of *tort* where the damages claimed do not exceed $100;

    (*b*) in all actions of replevin where the value of the goods does not exceed $100;

    (*c*) in all actions *ex contractu* where the amount payable does not exceed $250.

The following actions are excepted:

    (*a*) for a gambling debt;

    (*b*) for spirituous liquor drunk in a tavern;

    (*c*) on notes of hand given for a gambling debt or for liquor drunk in a tavern;

    (*d*) of ejectment;

[1] N. B. 42 Vic. c. 7. Ib. c. 8.   [2] N. B. 44 Vic. c. 12.
[3] N. B. 43 Vic. c. 10.   [4] N. B. 49 Vic. c. 9.
[5] C. S. Man. 1880, c. 34. M. 48 Vic. c. 22.

(e) relating to validity of devises or limitations under a will or settlement;

(f) for malicious prosecution, libel, slander, crim. con., seduction or breach of promise of marriage;

(g) against justices of the peace or peace officers for anything done in the execution of their office.

A *Surrogate Court* has been established for each judicial district. The Senior County Court Judge for the district presides. *Surrogate Court.*

The Court has jurisdiction in all matters relating to probates of wills and letters of administration in the Province [1].

Court of Queen's Bench. The Court of Queen's Bench consists of a Chief Justice and three Puisne Judges and sits at Winnipeg [2]. *Court of Queen's Bench.*

The Court as a Court of original and appellate jurisdiction possesses "all such powers and authorities as by the laws of England are incident to a Superior Court of record of civil and criminal jurisdiction in all matters civil and criminal whatsoever and shall have use enjoy and exercise all the rights incidents and privileges as fully as the same were on the 15th July 1870, possessed used exercised and enjoyed by any of Her Majesty's Superior Courts of common law at Westminster or by the Court of Chancery at Lincoln's Inn or by the Court of Probate or any Court in England having cognizance of property and civil rights and of crimes and offences [3]."

The Court has therefore both civil and criminal as well as legal and equitable jurisdiction [4].

Courts of Assize for civil causes are held by one of the judges of the Queen's Bench twice a year at Winnipeg for the Eastern Judicial District, and at Portage la Prairie for *Assizes.*

---

[1] M. 44 Vic. c. 28, s. 93.   [2] M. 48 Vic. c. 15, ss. 11, 13.
[3] Ib. s. 6.   [4] Ib. s. 7.

the Central Judicial District, and at Brandon for the Western Judicial District[1].

As a Court of Appeal the Queen's Bench hears appeals on points of law from County Courts[2]; appeals from the decision of an election judge on any question of law or facts[3]; appeals from a judge in chambers[4] and from the Surrogate Courts[5].

BRITISH COLUMBIA.

Small Debts Court. *Small Debts Court.* Actions in which the sum demanded does not exceed $100 may be tried before a stipendiary or a police magistrate[6].

County Court. *County Courts.* Six County Courts have been established under the 46 Vic. c. 5. They exercise jurisdiction in all civil causes up to $1000 and in equity up to $2500, and are invested with the powers of a Court of Probate. An appeal on points of law lies to the Supreme Court.

Supreme Court. *Supreme Court.* By a commission dated the 2nd Sept. 1858, Her Majesty appointed Matthew Baillie Begbie to be a judge of the Colony of British Columbia with full power to hold Courts of Judicature and to administer justice. Governor Carleton on his arrival issued a proclamation which had the force of law declaring that the Court held before Judge Begbie should be known as the Supreme Court of Civil Justice of British Columbia and ordained that the Court should be invested with "complete cognizance of all pleas whatsoever" and "with jurisdiction in all cases civil as well as criminal arising within the Colony."

Previous to this an order in Council dated the 4th April 1856, had constituted a Supreme Court for Vancouver's

---

[1] M. 48 Vic. c. 16.   [2] C. S. Man. c. 34, s. 206.
[3] Ib. c. 4, s. 93.   [4] Ib. c. 31, s. 24.
[5] M. 44 Vic. c. 28, s. 123.   [6] B. C. 49 Vic. c. 6.

Island. After the union of the Island with British Columbia the two Courts were merged in one Court called the Supreme Court of British Columbia[1], such Court to possess all the powers of the two previously existing Courts.

Subsequently the Legislature passed an Act[2] constituting a Provincial Supreme Court under the name of the Court of Queen's Bench to be composed of the same Judges as the Supreme Court, and to have all the powers and jurisdiction of that Court.

The Supreme Court now consists of a Chief Justice and four Puisne Judges. Courts of Assize are held in different towns throughout the Province on fixed days[3].

PRINCE EDWARD'S ISLAND.

Civil Jurisdiction of Justices. Where a debt does not *Justices.* exceed $32 a debtor may be arrested and brought before a Justice of the Peace, and unless he gives security for appearing at the County Court to answer the plaintiff's suit, two Justices may try the cause, an appeal lying to the County Court[4].

Courts for trial of Small Debts to be held before Com- *Small Debts Court.* missioners were in 1860 established throughout the province. Jurisdiction was conferred in matters of debt and trover for the recovery of sums not exceeding £20, except where a question of title was involved, or the action was for a gambling debt. Actions for rent were also excluded unless no distress could be found on the premises[5].

County Courts. The County Courts have jurisdiction, *County Court.*

(*a*) in all actions *ex contractu* and *ex delicto* where the debt or damages claimed do not exceed $150;

[1] B. C. Ordinances, 1st March, 1869, 22nd April, 1870.
[2] B. C. 45 Vic. c. 3. [3] B. C. 48 Vic. c. 6; 49 Vic. c. 3; 50 Vic. c. 8.
[4] P. E. I. 37 Vic. c. 1. [5] P. E. I. 23 Vic. c. 16.

(*b*) in actions on bail bonds given to a sheriff in a County Court or where the penalty is recoverable before the Court of Commissioners for the recovery of small debts;

(*c*) in all actions for any amount recoverable under any statute before the Court of Commissioners for the recovery of small debts.

The following actions are excepted,

(*a*) of detinue, replevin or ejectment where the title to land is brought in question;

(*b*) in which the validity of any devise, bequest or limitation is disputed;

(*c*) crim. con. and seduction;

(*d*) for breach of promise of marriage;

(*e*) against executors or administrators;

(*f*) against Justices of the Peace for anything done in the execution of their office;

(*g*) upon judgments in the Supreme Court[1].

An appeal is allowed to the Supreme Court[2].

Marine Court. A *Marine Court of Enquiry* established by the 27 Vic. c. 23 has jurisdiction in collisions, casualties resulting in loss of life and charges of misconduct against masters of vessels.

Surrogate Court. *Surrogate Courts.* Jurisdiction in matters relating to wills belongs to the Surrogate Courts[3].

Insolvents' Court. *Insolvents' Courts* were established by 31 Vic. c. 15.

Divorce Court. *Court of Divorce.* In 1835 the Lieutenant-Governor and Council were authorized to hear and determine all matters relating to divorce, and power was given to the Lieutenant-Governor to appoint the Chief Justice to preside in his stead[4].

Supreme Court. *Supreme Court.* The Supreme Court was established by Governor Patterson under the powers conferred by his Com-

---

[1] P. E. I. 41 Vic. c. 12, ss. 16—17.   [2] Ib. s. 93.
[3] P. E. I. 36 Vic. c. 21.   [4] P. E. I. 5 Will. 4, c. 10.

mission [1]. As a Court of Common Law it is composed of a Chief Justice and two Puisne Justices, who exercise a jurisdiction similar to that enjoyed by the old Courts of Queen's Bench and Common Pleas.

Jurisdiction in Equity belongs to the Master of the Rolls [2] and to the Vice-Chancellor [3], who act also as Puisne Judges on the Common law side of the Supreme Court. An appeal in Equity lies to the Chief Justice, the Master of the Rolls and the Vice-Chancellor [4]. Except when sitting in the Court of Appeal the Chief Justice has no equity jurisdiction.

The Master of the Rolls as such has similar powers to those formerly enjoyed by the Master of the Rolls in England [5], and the Vice-Chancellor as such has co-ordinate jurisdiction [6].

The Chief Justice, the Master of the Rolls and the Vice-Chancellor act as a Court of Appeal in Chancery [7], and all right of appeal to the Lieutenant-Governor as Chancellor has been taken away [8].

NORTH-WEST TERRITORIES.

The Supreme Court consists of five Puisne Judges, each of whom is required to reside at such place in the territories as the Governor in Council directs [9]. A judge usually exercises jurisdiction within the district in which he resides, and is invested with all the powers of the Court other than those usually exercised by a Court sitting in banc. *Supreme Court.*

The Court possesses the same powers as the Court of Queen's Bench of Manitoba [10], and has all the powers vested in the Stipendiary Magistrates on the 2nd June 1886. *Jurisdiction.*

[1] See *ante*, p. 32.
[2] P. E. I. 11 Vic. c. 6.
[3] P. E. I. 32 Vic. c. 4.
[4] Ib. 46 Vic. c. 6.
[5] P. E. I. 11 Vic. c. 6.
[6] P. E. I. 32 Vic. c. 4.
[7] Ib. P. E. I. 46 Vic. c. 6.
[8] P. E. I. 44 Vic. c. 16, s. 3.
[9] R. S. C. c. 50, ss. 41—45.
[10] Ib. s. 48.

Every Judge is authorized to hold a Court at such times and places as he thinks proper and to decide any claim or dispute in a summary manner, except in actions of debt or contract where the claim exceeds $1000, and in actions of tort where the amount claimed exceeds $500, in which cases either party may demand a jury[1].

COURTS OF CRIMINAL JURISDICTION.

By section 91 of the British North America Act 1867, the Criminal law including Criminal procedure was placed within the legislative jurisdiction of the Dominion whilst the Constitution of Courts of Criminal jurisdiction was handed over to the province.

A uniform code of Criminal law and procedure has been for some years in force in the Dominion.

Justices. *Justices of the Peace.* Justices of the Peace and Stipendiary magistrates have by various statutes jurisdiction to try in a summary manner minor offences. They are also authorized to try summarily certain indictable offences such as larceny, embezzlement, obtaining money under false pretences, aggravated assaults, assaults on children or magistrates, using premises for betting, provided the accused consent to be so tried. Persons under 16 years of age charged with larceny may be tried before one stipendiary magistrate or two justices[2]. An appeal from any conviction of justices lies in Ontario to the Sessions, in Quebec to the Queen's Bench, in Prince Edward's Island and North-West Territories to the Supreme Court, and in the other provinces to the County Court[3].

Sessions. *General or Quarter Sessions, Recorder's Court.* These courts sit at least four times a year and have as a rule power

---

[1] R. S. C. c. 50, s. 88.   [2] Ib. cc. 174, 176.   [3] Ib. c. 178, s. 76.

to try all indictable offences except treason, felony punishable with death, libel, and fraudulent acts of agents, bankers, factors, trustees, directors, keepers of warehouses or partners[1].

County Courts. In some provinces such as Manitoba, *County Courts.* Nova Scotia and New Brunswick, the County Court exercises a criminal jurisdiction, as appeals from decisions of Justices are in these provinces taken to the County Court.

Courts of Oyer and Terminer. Courts of Oyer and *Courts of Oyer and Terminer.* Terminer and general gaol delivery are held periodically in the different provinces. Such Courts have general jurisdiction in treason, felonies, and other indictable offences[2].

The Supreme Court of each province has on its Common *Provincial Supreme Court.* law side jurisdiction in all indictable offences.

Court for consideration of Crown Cases reserved. Any *Court for consideration of reserved cases.* question of law arising on a trial where a person is convicted on indictment of any treason, felony or misdemeanour may be reserved by the Judge for the consideration of this Court[3].

The Court for the consideration of Crown cases reserved is

in Ontario, any division of the High Court of the province;

in Quebec, the Court of Queen's Bench on its appeal side;

in Nova Scotia, New Brunswick, British Columbia, and Prince Edward's Island, the Supreme Court of the province;

in Manitoba, the Court of Queen's Bench of the province;

in the North-West Territories, the Supreme Court of the Territories[4].

---

[1] R. S. C. c. 174, ss. 4, 6.   [2] Ib. c. 174, s. 3.
[3] Ib. c. 174, s. 259.   [4] Ib. c. 174, s. 2.

CHAPTER XI.

THE DOMINION PARLIAMENT.

1. *Parties to Legislation.*

THE legislative power of the Dominion is generally re-presented as being vested in (1) the Parliament of Canada, consisting of two Houses, viz. a Senate and a House of Commons, and (2) the Governor-General. Inasmuch, how-ever, as the Crown may veto any Canadian Act, it is more correct to say that the Legislature of the Dominion consists of (1) the Crown, (2) the Governor-General and (3) the Parliament of Canada[1]. Reserving for later consideration the relations of the Crown and the Governor-General to legislation, an account will now be given of certain matters relating to Parliament generally and then the constitution and functions of each House will be considered in detail.

2. *How summoned.*

Though the British North America Act, 1867, makes provision for the appointment of senators, the election of members of the House of Commons, and the meeting of Parliament once a year, it is silent as to the manner in which Parliament is summoned, except in so far as it provides by section 38 that the Governor-General may summon the

[1] B. N. A. Act, ss. 17, 55, 57.

House of Commons in the Queen's name under the great seal.

By the Letters Patent[1] constituting the office of Governor-General the Crown authorizes and empowers the Governor-General to exercise all powers belonging to the Crown in respect of the summoning, proroguing or dissolving of the Canadian Parliament. The Governor-General has therefore full legal power to exercise the prerogative rights of summoning or dissolving Parliament. In exercising these powers he follows closely the practice adopted by the Crown in England.

The Dominion like the English Parliament is summoned for the despatch of business by proclamation issued by and with the advice of the Ministry. Various months have been selected for the time of meeting but it is now understood that Parliament will be summoned as early in the year as possible. *Summons.*

The form of proclamation is as follows. *Form of proclamation.*

Lansdowne,

CANADA.

VICTORIA by the Grace of God of the United Kingdom of Great Britain and Ireland QUEEN Defender of the Faith &c., &c.

To our beloved and faithful the Senators of the Dominion of Canada and the Members elected to serve in the House of Commons of our said Dominion and to each and every of you:—GREETING:—

A PROCLAMATION.

Whereas the meeting of our Parliament of Canada stands Prorogued to the 17th day of the month of December next, Nevertheless, for certain causes and considerations, We have thought fit further to prorogue the same to Thursday the

---

[1] See Appendix.

seventeenth day of the month of January next, so that neither
you nor any of you on the said seventeenth day of December
next at Our city of Ottowa to appear are to be held or
constrained : for we do will that you and each of you, be as
to Us, in this matter, entirely exonerated ; commanding and
by the tenour of these presents, enjoining you and each of
you and all others in this behalf interested that on Thursday, the seventeenth day of the month of January next at
Our city of Ottawa aforesaid, personally be and appear for
the despatch of business to treat, do, act, and conclude upon
those things which in our said Parliament of Canada by the
Common Council of our said Dominion, may by the favour
of God be maintained.

In testimony whereof We have caused these our Letters
to be made Patent and the Great Seal of Canada to be
hereunto affixed. Witness &c.

Proceed-
ings in the
House of
Commons.

3.   *The opening of Parliament.*

When a new House of Commons is elected, the members
assemble in their Chamber on the morning of the day mentioned in the proclamation and at an hour fixed by the
clerk, for the purpose of taking the oath and signing the
roll.   The Clerk of the Crown in Chancery attends at the
table and delivers to the clerk of the House a roll containing the names of duly elected members.   The oath of
allegiance in the form set out in the British North America
Act 1867,

> I ———— do swear that I will be faithful and bear
> true allegiance to her Majesty Queen Victoria ;

is administered by one of the clerks or the Sergeant-at-
arms authorized for that purpose by the Governor-General[1].

Election of
Speaker.   By the British North America Act 1867, section 44, the
House of Commons on its first assembling after a general

---

[1] B. N. A. Act, 1867, s. 128.

election is to "proceed with all practicable speed to elect one of its members to be Speaker." The House might evidently under this provision at once elect its Speaker, and such election would be complete without any confirmation by the Governor-General.

The customary method of proceeding to the election is Election of Speaker. as follows:—

Shortly before the hour fixed for the opening of Parliament, the members re-assemble. On the Usher of the Black Rod presenting himself at the door, which he strikes three times with his rod, he is admitted. Advancing up the floor of the House he makes three obeisances and says in French and in English—

"Gentlemen [or Mr Speaker *in subsequent sessions*], his Excellency the Governor-General desires the immediate attendance of this honourable House in the Senate chamber."

The Usher then retires and the members proceed to the Senate chamber in order to hear the message relating to the election of Speaker. The Speaker of the Senate thereupon addresses the members as follows:

"His Excellency the Governor-General does not see fit to declare the causes of his summoning the present Parliament of the Dominion of Canada until a Speaker of the House of Commons shall have been chosen according to law, but to-morrow, at the hour of — his Excellency will declare the causes of his calling this Parliament."

The Commons then return to their chamber. The clerk presides and the election of Speaker is proceeded with, any question relating thereto being put to the House by the clerk. The member duly elected is conducted to the Chair by his proposer and seconder, where he returns his thanks to the House for the honour conferred on him. The mace is

M.   8

then placed on the table and the House adjourns to the following day. Upon its re-assembling the Usher of the Black Rod again desires its attendance in the Senate chamber. The Speaker-elect then informs the Governor-General of his election and claims for the House "all their undoubted rights and privileges." The Speaker of the Senate on behalf of his Excellency replies that "he fully confides in the duty and attachment of the House of Commons to Her Majesty's person and government and upon all occasions will recognize and allow their constitutional privileges."

Approval of Speaker.

In the English House of Commons the choice of a Speaker is "confirmed and approved" by the Crown. This course was followed in some of the Legislatures of the old provinces; but when in 1827 Lord Dalhousie, then Governor-General, refused to approve the election of Mr Papineau as Speaker of the Legislative Assembly of Lower Canada, the Assembly passed a resolution declaring the action of the Governor-General to be unconstitutional, as the Act constituting the Legislature did not require the choice of Speaker to be approved by the Governor-General. The form of approval remained in force in Upper and Lower Canada until the union of the two provinces in 1841, but the Act of Union is silent on the point.

After the delivery of the usual speech by the Governor-General the members return to their own House, the Speaker after taking the chair informs the House that the usual privileges had been granted to the House by the Governor-General. The reports of Judges and returns of the Clerk of the Crown in Chancery respecting elections are then presented, and in accordance with the custom prevailing in the English House of Commons a bill is read a first time *pro forma* in order to assert the right of the House to deal with any business it may think right to discuss before proceeding to the consideration of the matters contained in the speech.

Reading bill *pro forma*.

The Speaker then reports to the House that his Excel- Considera-
tion of
Speech.
lency the Governor-General has that day made a speech to
both Houses of Parliament of which he has obtained a copy.
The speech is entered on the journals as read, and a member
of the Government then moves that the speech be taken
into consideration on a future day. When this is agreed to,
formal resolutions are passed appointing standing committees,
and the librarian's report and other papers are presented.

In England the Queen's Speech is invariably taken into
consideration on the same day on which it is delivered; but
in Canada, though the custom is to debate the Speech on the
following day, yet when important matters are likely to come
up for debate its consideration may be postponed for a time.
An instance of this occurred in 1873, when the House thought
it advisable to consider at once matters relative to the Canadian Pacific Railway[1].

A resolution for an address in reply to the Speech is
moved and seconded. Each paragraph of the resolution is
put as a separate resolution, and a general debate may take
place on such paragraph and amendments may be moved.
When the resolution has been agreed to, it is referred *pro
forma* to a Committee to prepare and report the draft of
an address. The Chairman of this Committee reports the
address, which is read a second time and usually agreed to
without any discussion. The address is then ordered to be
engrossed and presented to the Governor-General by such
members of the House as are Privy Councillors.

On the opening of a New Parliament the Senators meet Proceed-
ings in
Senate.
in their chamber, and the Speaker informs the House when
the Governor-General will proceed to open the session. If
a new Speaker has been appointed by the Governor-
General[2] the Clerk of the House, as soon as the Senate has
met, reads the Commission making the appointment, and the
Speaker-elect is conducted to the Chair by two prominent

[1] Can. Com. J., 1873, Oct. sess. p. 119.   [2] B. N. A. A., 1867, s. 34.

Senators. The mace is placed on the table and prayers are read. New members present their certificates of appointment and take the oath of allegiance[1]. The House then adjourns until the hour when the Governor-General is to be present.

At the appointed time the Governor-General takes his seat and the Speaker directs the Usher of the Black Rod to summon the Commons. The Commons attend with their Speaker and the Governor-General reads the Speech.

Considera-
tion of
Speech. After the Commons have returned to their chamber and the Governor-General has retired, a bill is introduced *pro forma*[2] and the Speaker reports the speech, which is then usually ordered to be taken into account on the following day. All the members present are then appointed a committee to consider the orders and customs of the House and privileges of Parliament. To this committee is referred every matter affecting the privileges of the House or of its members. The procedure followed on the consideration of the address was up to 1870 similar to that adopted in the Commons, but in that year the custom of moving the address directly without any previous resolution was introduced and has since been followed. The address being agreed to is ordered to be presented by those Senators who are Privy Councillors.

4. QUORUM.

By Sections 35 and 48 of the British North America Act, 1867, it is provided that at least 15 Senators and 20 Members of the House of Commons, including the Speaker, are necessary to constitute a meeting of the Senate and of the House of Commons respectively. In the Senate if, 30 minutes after the Speaker takes the chair, there is not a quorum, he adjourns the House until the

---

[1] B. N. A. A. 1867, s. 128.　　　[2] See *ante*, p. 115.

next day. In the House of Commons the Speaker may, if the necessary number of members be not present, adjourn the House as soon as he takes the chair, and is bound to do so if his attention is called to the fact that there is no quorum present and such proves to be the case after counting the House[1]. A count out is very rare in the Canadian House of Commons[2].

5. PRIVILEGES.

By the British North America Act, s. 18, power was given to the Parliament of Canada to define the privileges, immunities and powers to be enjoyed by the Senate and House of Commons, but a proviso was added, that the same should never exceed those "at the passing of *this* Act" enjoyed by the English House of Commons. As it was doubtful whether the words "this Act" applied to the British North America Act, 1867, or to any Dominion Act passed to define the privileges of the Houses of Parliament, it was enacted by the Imperial Act, 38 and 39 Vic. c. 38, that the privileges to be enjoyed should not exceed those enjoyed by the English House of Commons at the time of the passing of the Dominion Act. *Power to define Privileges.*

By c. 11 of the Revised Statutes of Canada the Senate and the House of Commons respectively and the members thereof are to hold and enjoy "the like privileges, immunities and powers as at the time of the passing of the British North America Act, 1867, were held, enjoyed and exercised by the Commons House of Parliament of the United Kingdom and by the members thereof so far as the same are consistent with, and not repugnant to, the said Act." Such privileges are to be noticed judicially in all courts in Canada. *Privileges defined.*

The Canadian Act does not attempt to enumerate the

---

[1] Senate S. O., 5, 6. Com. S. O., 1, 4.   [2] Burinot, p. 218.

privileges specifically, nor is this necessary[1], but express provision is made for the stay of proceedings, civil or criminal,

Publications by order of House. for publishing any report, paper, vote or proceeding under the authority of the Senate or House of Commons on production of a certificate of the Speaker or Clerk of the Senate or House of Commons stating that the report, paper, vote, or proceeding was published under the authority of the Senate or House of Commons, together with an affidavit verifying such certificate[2].

Publication of Copies. Civil or criminal proceedings for publishing a copy of any report, paper, vote, or proceeding are also to be stayed on the production of the report, paper, vote or proceeding and an affidavit as to correctness.

In any proceedings for printing an extract from, or abstract of, any such report, paper, vote or proceeding, such report, paper, vote or proceeding may be given in evidence, and if shewn to the jury that the extract or abstract was published without malice, a verdict of not guilty is to be entered.

6. PAYMENT OF MEMBERS.

Payment of Members. Members of the Senate and House of Commons are paid for their attendance and receive an allowance for travelling expenses[3]. The sum allowed is **10** dollars a day if the session does not exceed 30 days, but if the session is longer a member receives a sessional allowance of **1000** dollars.

From this allowance a deduction of 8 dollars a day is made for every day on which the member does not attend a sitting of the House or of some Committee, provided the House sits on such day. Days on which the House does not sit, or on which the member is prevented attending by

---

[1] *Dell* v. *Murphy*, 1 Moore's P. C. N. S. 487.

[2] R. S. C. c. 11, s. 6.   [3] R. S. C. c. 11, ss. 25—33.

illness, provided he be within 10 miles of the place of meeting, are reckoned days of attendance. In some very exceptional cases the House has resolved that an absent member should receive the sum he would have been entitled to had he not been so absent. The legality of such a proceeding is very doubtful[1].

When a person is member for at least 30 days of a session, 8 dollars a day is deducted from the sessional allowance for each day before he was elected or after he ceased to be a member.

Member for part of session.

An allowance of 10 cents per mile is given for travelling expenses, both on going and on returning, between the place of residence of the member and the place where the session is held, according to the nearest mail route, the distance being determined and certified by the Speaker of the Senate or of the House of Commons as the case may be.

Travelling expenses.

A member may draw his sessional allowance from time to time to the extent of 7 dollars a day, the balance being payable at the end of the session on the member making a declaration as to the number of days he has attended and the number of miles travelled.

How paid.

The Speakers of the Senate and of the House of Commons receive each a salary of 4000 dollars per annum[2].

Salary of Speaker.

7. ADJOURNMENT.

A motion to adjourn is always in order and always takes precedence of the question before the House. In the Commons no amendment can be moved to such motion, and if the motion be lost no second motion to the same effect can be made until after some intermediate proceeding shall have been had[3]. A wide latitude of debate is allowed on a motion for

---

[1] See Burinot, p. 148. [2] R. C. S. c. 11, s. 24.
[3] Com. S. O. 30.

adjournment, as the Canadian Parliament has not adopted the rule that the speeches should be relevant to the question of adjournment.

8. PROROGATION.

Proroga-
tion.

In Canada Parliament is usually prorogued by the Governor-General in person. As soon as the business of the two Houses is completed, the Governor-General, through his secretary, and with the advice of his ministers, informs the Speaker of each House that at a certain hour on a given day he will prorogue Parliament. The Commons are summoned in the usual manner to attend in the Senate chamber, and after assent is given to bills that have been passed, the Governor-General delivers the customary speech in English and French. At the conclusion of the speech the Speaker declares that:—

> "It is his Excellency the Governor-General's will and pleasure that this Parliament be prorogued until —— and to be then here holden; and this Parliament is accordingly prorogued until —— ".

The fact of the prorogation is also notified in the "Canada Gazette[1]."

Its effect.

The effect of the prorogation is to put an end to the session. Proceedings on all bills pending in either House cease to have any effect, and such bills will require to be introduced again and go through all the necessary stages in the following session. Where a session ends unexpectedly it is customary as in England to protect parties promoting private bills, and by a series of resolutions to permit such bills to be advanced in the following session by unopposed motions to the stages at which they stood when the prorogation took place[2]. All committees, standing or select, are dissolved by the prorogation.

---

[1] Burinot, p. 236.   [2] Burinot, p. 239.

9. DISSOLUTION.

The Parliament may be dissolved by the Governor-General at any time[1], and though the Governor-General is expected to pay the greatest attention to the advice of his ministers, yet he is not bound to grant a dissolution whenever and as often as they demand it. The dissolution of Parliament is a prerogative right and the Governor-General, as representing the Crown, is required to act on his own responsibility[2].

Dissolution a prerogative right.

The following examples illustrate the above principle. Sir Edmund Stead, Governor-General of Canada, refused to dissolve Parliament in 1858, on the grounds that a general election had been held the previous winter, that important business remained to be finished, and that there was no reasonable probability that the verdict of the previous election would be reversed[3].

Lord Mulgrave, Governor of Nova Scotia, refused a dissolution in 1860, on the ground that it was neither expedient, nor for the public interest, that a dissolution should take place a short time after a general election[4].

When in May, 1872, the Legislative Assembly of Victoria passed a vote of want of confidence in the administration, the ministry informed the Governor that they were bound either to resign or to recommend a dissolution, and they accordingly advised a dissolution. The Governor declined to dissolve, as he believed a ministry could be formed without having recourse to a dissolution[5].

In the last-mentioned case the ministers maintained that the alternative of resignation or dissolution is left absolutely to their discretion and responsibility. The Governor dissented from this proposition, maintaining that as a colonial Governor, it was his duty to exercise a due discretion. Lord Mulgrave in explaining his conduct in the case referred to

Position of Ministers.

---

[1] B. N. A. Act, s. 50.   [2] See *post*, chap. xv.
[3] See Todd, p. 529.   [4] Ib. p. 537.   [5] Ib. p. 539.

above summed up the position as follows:—"I quite admit that when a Council is backed by a majority of the House a Governor is bound in ordinary cases to follow their advice and that it is chiefly by his influence and persuasion that he must endeavour to direct their conduct, but the premier would place a Governor in the same position as the Queen, and the Council in the position of the Cabinet at home, forgetting entirely that the Governor is himself responsible to the home government and that it is no excuse for him to say in answer to any charge against his administration of affairs, I did so by the advice of my Council[1]."

Lapse of time.

The Parliament is also dissolved by lapse of time, as the British North America Act, s. 50, provides that, subject to the above-mentioned power of dissolution by the Governor-General, every House of Commons shall continue for five years from the day of the return of the writs for choosing the House.

Demise of the Crown.

The Canadian Parliament is not affected by the demise of the Crown, an Act to that effect[2] having been passed in the first session of the Parliament of the Dominion.

---

[1] Todd, p. 537.   [2] R. S. C. c. 11, s. 1.

CHAPTER XII.

THE HOUSE OF COMMONS.

1. NUMBER.

THE House of Commons now consists of 215 members, Number.
distributed as follows [1] :

Ontario	92
Quebec	65
Nova Scotia	21
New Brunswick	16
Manitoba	5
British Columbia	6
Prince Edward's Island	6
North-West Territories	4
	215

Originally the House consisted of 182 members, but
provision was made by the British North America Act,
s. 57, for a decennial adjustment of representation. To
Quebec was assigned a fixed number, viz. 65 members:
to the other provinces was assigned such a number of
members as would bear the same proportion to the number
of its population (ascertained every ten years) as the number
65 would bear to the number of the population of Quebec

[1] 50 and 51 Vic. c. 4.

so ascertained. Any adjustment only comes into effect on the termination of the then existing Parliament. After the census of 1871 the number of members was increased to 200, and in 1881 eleven additional members were added. Representation was conceded to the North-West Territories in 1886. After the then next general election four electoral districts in these Territories were to return one member each[1]. The first members for these Territories were elected in 1886[2].

Electoral Districts.

In Ontario, Quebec and Manitoba and the North-West Territories one member is returned by each electoral district: in Nova Scotia, three electoral districts, in New Brunswick and British Columbia one electoral district, return two members each, otherwise in these three provinces the rule of single member constituencies is followed. In Prince Edward's Island each district returns two members[2].

2. QUALIFICATIONS OF ELECTORS.

By the British North America Act, 1867, it was provided, [s. 41] that until the Parliament of Canada should otherwise provide the voters in each province for members of the Dominion House of Commons should be the voters qualified to vote for members of the provincial Assembly. For several years no attempt was made to introduce a uniform franchise, but with the increased development of the provinces it began to be seen that so long as the Provincial Parliaments retained power to alter the franchise, the Federal Parliament was exposed to serious disturbance. Bills providing for a uniform franchise were brought before the Canadian Parliament in 1883 and 1884, but were strongly opposed by the advocates of provincial rights[3], and it was not until 1885

---

[1] R. S. C. c. 7.   [2] Ib. c. 6.
[3] Dominion Annual Register 1885, p. 54.

that a general law was passed. This Act was subsequently amended, and the franchise is now governed by c. 5 of the Revised Statutes of Canada, 1886.

In both cities and towns a voter must be registered as such, and

(1) be a British subject by birth or naturalization; British subjects.

(2) be 21 years of age; Full age.

(3) fall within one of the following classes:—

(*a*) Owners of real property of the actual value of Owner-ship. (1) $300 in a city, or (2) $200 in a town, or (3) $150 in any place not in a city or town.

(*b*) Tenants holding under a lease at a rent of $2 Tenancy. monthly, or $6 quarterly, or $12 half-yearly, or $20 yearly who (1) have been in possession for one year, and (2) have *bona fide* paid one year's rent or $20 of such rent if the rent be over $20 and payable yearly.

(*c*) Occupants occupying real property of a value Occu-pancy. of $300 in a city, or $200 in a town, or $150 elsewhere, who have been in occupation for one year.

(*d*) Persons residing within the electoral district Income. who have been residents in Canada for one year and who enjoy an income of $300 annually.

(*e*) Persons residing for one year in the electoral Annuity. district who are in receipt of a life annuity secured on real estate in Canada of at least $100.

(*f*) Son of the owner or the occupant under a lease Farmer's sons. for 5 years of a farm of not less than 20 acres where (1) the value of the farm or real property is sufficient to qualify both, and (2) the son has resided with father for 12 months. All sons may qualify, but if the value of the farm or real property will not qualify all, preference is given to the elder sons.

(*g*) Son of an owner of real property where similar conditions are fulfilled.

In the two last-mentioned cases 'son' includes grandson, step-son and son-in-law. Occasional absences not exceeding six months in the year will not disqualify, and the time spent at an institution of learning or as a mariner or a fisherman is considered to be spent at home.

Fishermen.

(*h*) Fishermen, if resident and owning real or personal property of the value of $150.

Indians.

(*i*) Indians on a reserve not in Manitoba, British Columbia, Keewatin or the North-West Territories, and in occupation of a plot of land on such reserve, and whose improvements are of the value of $150, and who are otherwise qualified [1].

The Act contains some special provisions relating to the North-West Territories and to Prince Edward's Island and British Columbia.

North-West Territories.

In those districts in the North-West Territories that are entitled to send representatives to the House of Commons, an elector is described as :—

"A *bona fide* male resident and householder of adult age who is not an alien or an Indian within the electoral district, and who has resided in such district for at least 12 months immediately preceding the issue of the writ of election [2]."

P. E. I.

In the provinces of Prince Edward's Island and of British Columbia all voters who were qualified by the laws of these two provinces to vote at the passing of the Electoral Franchise Act, 1885, are to have a right to be registered as voters and to vote so long as they shall continue to be qualified to vote under such laws [3].

Persons disqualified.

Persons disqualified from voting. The following persons are disqualified from voting [4]:

1. Judges.

1. Judges of every Court whose appointments rest

---

[1] See s. 11 of 48 and 49 Vic. c. 40.   [2] R. S. C. c. 7, s. 4.
[3] R. S. C. c. 5, s. 10.   [4] R. S. C. c. 8, s. 42, 49 and 50 Vic. c. 6.

with the Governor-General. The Judges therefore of the Supreme Court of Canada, of the Superior, District and County Courts of the provinces cannot vote.

2. Revising officers, returning officers and election clerks for the electoral district for which they hold their office, but deputy returning officers, poll clerks and constables may vote [1]. *2. Election officers.*

3. Any person employed for money at time of election except the returning officer in case of an equality of votes, when he may give a casting vote. *3. Paid election agents.*

4. Indians (a) in Manitoba, British Columbia, Keewatin and North-West Territories, (b) in the other provinces who do not fulfil the conditions above referred to. *4. Indians.*

5. Persons of Mongolian or Chinese race [2]. *5. Chinese.*

6. Persons found guilty of corrupt practices at elections. Their disqualification lasts for eight years [3]. *6. Persons guilty of corrupt practices.*

The Governor-General appoints revising officers to revise the list of voters every year. A preliminary revision is held in June, and the corrected lists are required to be printed and published before the 1st September. Within five weeks the final revision takes place, when objections are heard and examined, and the list as finally revised is certified and a duplicate sent to the Clerk of the Crown in Chancery at Ottawa before the 1st of November [4]. *Revision of Voters' lists.*

If the revising officer be not a Judge an appeal lies from his decision. In Quebec the appeal is to the Judge of the Superior Court resident in or having charge of the judicial district in which the polling district in respect of which the appeal arises is situate.

[1] 49 and 50 Vic. c. 6, s. 1.
[2] Ib. c. 5, s. 2.   [3] Ib. c. 8, s. 98.
[4] R. S. C. c. 5, ss. 11—32.

In the other provinces the appeal is to the Judge of the County Court, but in British Columbia, if the electoral district is not within the jurisdiction of a County Court, the appeal is to a Judge of the Superior Court [1].

Voters qualified to vote in respect of income can only be registered and vote in the polling district in which they reside: other voters are registered and vote where their real property is situated, but if the property is partly in one polling district and partly in another, they may be registered and may vote in either district [2].

3. QUALIFICATIONS OF ELECTED.

No property qualification is required of any member of the House of Commons. He must be a subject of the Crown by birth or naturalization [3], and must not be disqualified by law from sitting.

The following persons are so disqualified:

Members of Provincial Parliaments.

1. Members of any provincial Legislative Council or Legislative Assembly [4]. This disqualification is not found in the British North America Act, 1867, but has been adopted not only by the Dominion Parliament but by the Provincial Assemblies.

A member of the House on being appointed a member of a Provincial Assembly or elected to a Provincial Assembly vacates his seat in the House, unless the appointment or election was without his consent, and provided (1) he does not take his seat in the Provincial Council or Assembly, and (2) he resigns such seat within ten days after being notified of his election, or if not within the province, then within ten days after his arrival there, and (3) gives notice to the Speaker of the House of Commons that he has so resigned [5].

---

[1] R. S. C. c. 5, ss. 33, 34.　　　　[2] 48 and 49 Vic. c. 40, s. 7.
[3] R. S. C. c. 8, s. 20.　　　　[4] Ib. c. 13, s. 1.　　　　[5] Ib. s. 3.

A member of a Provincial Council or Assembly who sits in the House of Commons incurs a penalty of $2000 for every day he sits or votes, which penalty may be recovered by any person who sues for the same [1].

2. Persons holding any office of emolument under the government of Canada on the nomination of the Crown to which any salary is attached [2], except

Persons holding Offices of Emolument.

(*a*) a Minister of the Crown, provided he has been elected while holding office;

(*b*) a Minister of the Crown resigning one office and accepting another within one month, unless a new administration be formed;

(*c*) officers of militia, or militia men receiving only their daily pay when called out [3], or pay for care of arms or for giving drill instruction [4];

(*d*) a person holding any office, commission or employment, if by his commission or instrument of appointment it is declared that he shall hold such office without any salary [5].

3. Contractors.

Contractors.

(1) Persons undertaking any contract for which money is to be paid by the government of Canada [6].

(2) Shareholders in companies undertaking contracts for building public works [7].

The Act excepts

(*a*) persons on whom a contract devolves by descent, limitation or agreement until 12 months has elapsed [8];

(*b*) lenders of money to the government [9].

It is also provided that government contracts shall contain a clause that no member shall become interested in them [10].

---

[1] R. S. C. c. 13, s. 4.   [2] Ib. c. 11, s. 9.
[3] Ib. s. 17.   [4] Ib.
[5] Ib. s. 9.   [6] Ib. s. 10.
[7] Ib. s. 15.   [8] Ib. s. 17.   [9] Ib.   [10] Ib. s. 16.

A person disqualified, if a member, vacates his seat and incurs a penalty of $200 a day[1].

Corrupt Practices.

4. Persons guilty of corrupt practices at elections.

(*a*) If it be proved on the trial of an election petition that any corrupt practice has been committed by any candidate, or with his actual knowledge, or if any candidate be convicted of bribery or undue influence, the election is void, and such candidate is to be incapable of being elected to the House for seven years[2].

(*b*) Persons other than candidates found guilty of corrupt practices are to be incapable of being elected to the House for a period of eight years[3].

Revising officers.

5. A revising officer cannot be a candidate for the electoral district for which he is revising officer, nor for two years after he resigns his office[4].

Other officers.

6. Sheriffs, Registrars of Deeds, Clerks of the Peace and County Crown Attornies are also disqualified[5].

4. METHOD OF ELECTION.

Every writ for the election of a member is dated and is returnable at such time as the Governor-General determines. The day on which the nomination of candidates is to take place is mentioned in the writ, and such day must, in the case of a General Election, be the same for the whole Dominion, except in the electoral districts in British Columbia and the districts of Algoma in Ontario, and of Gaspé, Chicoutimi and Saguenay in Quebec, where the day is fixed by the returning officer[6].

Form of Writ.

The usual form of writ is as follows:—

Victoria, by the grace of God of the United Kingdom of Great Britain and Ireland, Queen, Defender of the faith. To the [*Returning Officer*]

[1] R. S. C. c. 8, s. 13.   [2] Ib. s. 96.
[3] Ib. s. 98.   [4] Ib. s. 20.
[5] Ib. c. 11, s. 9.   [6] Ib. c. 8, ss. 4—5.

GREETING.

Whereas by the advice of our Privy Council for Canada We have ordered a Parliament to be holden at Ottawa on the   day of   [*Omit this preamble except in case of a General Election*], We command you that notice of the time and place of election being duly given You do cause Election to be made according to law of a Member to serve in the House of Commons of Canada for the Electoral District of   [*Except in the case of a General Election insert here* in the place of   deceased *or otherwise stating the cause of vacancy*] and [*except in the Electoral Districts mentioned in s.* 2 *of* 37 *Vic. c.* 9] that you do cause the nomination of Candidates at such Election to be held on the   day of   next and that you do cause the name [*or* names] of such member [*or* members] when so elected whether he [*or* they] be present or absent to be certified to our Clerk of the Crown in Chancery on or before the   day of   next.

WITNESS Our Right Trusty and Well-beloved &c., Governor-General of our Dominion of Canada at our City of Ottawa, the   day of   in the   year of Our Reign and in the year of Our Lord 18

Where a vacancy occurs in any Electoral District owing to death, resignation or other cause, the fact of the vacancy is brought to the Speaker's notice in either of two ways, (1) by a member giving notice from his place, or (2) by a notice in writing under the hands and seals of any two members.

Vacancies.

The usual form of notice is as follows:

Notice of Vacancy.

Dominion of Canada }
   To wit   }   House of Commons.

To the Hon. the Speaker of the House of Commons.

We the undersigned hereby give notice that a vacancy hath occurred in the representation in the House of Commons for the Electoral District of [*here state Electoral District, cause of vacancy and name of Member vacating seat*].

Given under our Hands and Seals at   this day of   18

——— *Member for the Electoral District of*

———   „   „   „   *of*

Warrant for Election.   The Speaker then issues his warrant to the Clerk of the Crown in Chancery for the issue of a new writ for the election of a Member to fill the vacancy[1]. The warrant is as follows :

Dominion of Canada }   House of Commons.
     To wit   }

To the Clerk of the Crown in Chancery.

These are to require you to make out a new writ for the election of a Member to serve in this present Parliament for the Electoral District of   in the room of   who since his election for the said Electoral District hath [*here state reason for issue of warrant*]

Given under my hand and seal this   day of   in the year of Our Lord

——— *Speaker.*

If there be no Speaker, or if the Speaker be absent from Canada, then any two members can issue such warrant[2].

If a vacancy occur after a General Election, but before the meeting of Parliament, a new writ is to issue, but this is not to affect the rights of any person entitled to contest the previous election.

Proclamation.   Within a certain time, varying in the Provinces from 8 to 20 days after the receipt of the writ, the returning officer

---

[1] R. S. C. c. 13, s. 9.   [2] Ib. s. 13.

issues a Proclamation stating the place and time for the nomination of candidates, the day on which a poll will be taken if necessary, the polling stations fixed by him and the place and time where he will count the votes.

Before issuing the proclamation it is the duty of the Returning Officer, after ascertaining the number of persons qualified to vote, to see that there are a sufficient number of polling districts, and power is given him to subdivide the districts appointed by the Legislature or by the local authorities so that there may be one polling district for every 200 voters.

Duties of Returning Officer.

Proclamation.

Form of Proclamation.

Electoral District of   to wit.

Public notice is hereby given to the Electors of the Electoral District aforesaid, that, in obedience to Her Majesty's writ to me directed and bearing date the   day of   , I require the presence of the said Electors at   in the County [*or* City *or* Town] of   on the   day of   month of   from noon until two of the clock in the afternoon, for the purpose of nominating a person [*or* persons] to represent them in the House of Commons of Canada: and that in case a Poll be demanded and allowed in the manner by law prescribed, such Poll will be opened on the   day of the month of   in the year   from the hour of 9 in the morning till 5 of the clock in the afternoon, in each of the Polling Districts, that is to say:

For the Polling District No. 1, consisting of at

And further that on the   day of   at I shall open the ballot boxes, sum up the votes given for the several candidates and return as elected the one having the majority of votes.

Of which all persons are hereby requested to take notice and govern themselves accordingly.

Given under my hand at   this   day of in the year

A. B.

Returning Officer.

Nomination of Candidates. Candidates are nominated in writing signed by 25 electors. The nomination paper is not valid unless accompanied by the written consent of the candidate, except when he is absent from the Province, in which case such absence is to be stated in the nomination paper.

One of the persons filing the nomination is required to make oath before the Returning Officer that he knows the several persons who have signed the nomination paper to be electors duly qualified to vote; that they signed the paper in his presence; and that the consent of the candidate was signed in his presence, or that the candidate was absent from the Province.

Deposit. A sum of 200 dollars also has to be deposited with the Returning Officer. This sum is returned to the candidate if he is elected, or if he polls half as many votes as those given the successful candidate: otherwise the sum is to belong to the Dominion and to be applied by the Returning Officer in defraying the expenses of the election[1].

Poll. If a poll is necessary, it takes place on the day fixed. The voting takes place by ballot, and the poll remains open from nine in the morning till five in the afternoon. On the close of the poll the Returning Officer counts the votes and declares that candidate who is found to have a majority of votes elected. If an equality of votes exists between two or more candidates, the Returning Officer may give a casting vote.

---

[1] R. S. C. c. 13, s. 8, ss. 19—23.

Within four days after the declaration of the poll any Recount. "credible witness" may apply to the County Court Judge or to the District Judge, or in the Province of Quebec to the Judge of the Superior Court discharging his duties in the district, for a recount of the votes on any of the following grounds, viz. that the Returning Officer (1) improperly counted, or (2) improperly rejected ballot papers, or (3) that a person, whose name was included in or excluded from the list of voters, was by the judgment of a Court not entitled or was entitled to have his name on such list, or (4) that the Returning Officer improperly summed up the votes. The application must be supported by affidavit, and if security is given to the amount of 100 dollars, the Judge is to hold a recount and certify the result to the Returning Officer.

In order to allow time for an application for a recount Return. the Returning Officer is not required to make his return to the writ of election until after the sixth day from the declaration of the poll.

The return is in the following form :—

I hereby certify that the Member [*or* Members] elected for the Electoral District of in pursuance of the within given writ as having received the majority of votes lawfully given is [*or* are] A, B and C [*names as in nomination papers*]

Signed R. O.
Returning Officer.

The return, together with a report, and other documents are transmitted by post to the Clerk of the Crown in Chancery. A duplicate of the return is sent to each candidate, and a notice of the return is published in the Canada Gazette.

The expenses of the Returning Officer are borne by the Expenses. Dominion. The Governor-General by warrant directs the Minister of Finance to pay the necessary fees, allowances and disbursements out of the Consolidated Revenue[1]. If a candidate, as already pointed out, does not poll half as many votes as the candidate elected, he forfeits the 200 dollars deposit, which will then be applied by the Dominion towards the expenses of the election.

Acts forbidden. The use of flags or ribbons or favours on the day of election, and within eight days before such day is forbidden[2]. Taverns are to be closed on the polling day[3]. Corrupt practices, such as bribery or treating, or personation, or paying for the conveyance of voters are forbidden under heavy penalties[4].

Return to the Writ. At the beginning of each Parliament a return book is furnished by the Clerk of the Crown to the Clerk of the Commons and is sufficient evidence of the return. In addition to the return book the Clerk of the Crown sends to the Clerk of the Commons a certificate of the return to each writ "deposited as of record" in the Crown Office, and this certificate is usually required before a member takes his seat. Not unfrequently members are sworn before such certificate is made out, but in such cases a resolution is passed admitting the member to take his seat, and recommending an adherence to the practice of requiring the certificate of the Clerk of the Crown to the return of the writ.

The Oath. By the British North America Act, s. 128, every member before taking his seat must take and subscribe before the Governor-General, or some person authorized by him, the following oath of allegiance:—

I   do swear that I will be faithful and bear true allegiance to Her Majesty Queen Victoria.

The Clerk is the person usually authorized by the Governor-General to administer the oath.

---

[1] R. S. C. c. 13, ss. 121—123. [2] Ib. s. 81.
[3] Ib. s. 83. [4] Ib. ss. 84—99.

No penalty is incurred by a member who sits or votes without taking the oath. In 1875 attention was called to the fact that Mr Orton, Member for the Electoral District of Centre Wellington, had sat and voted without taking the oath. The Committee of Privileges, to whom the matter was referred, held that, as there was no law on the subject, he had neither incurred any penalty nor vacated his seat, but that his votes recorded before taking the oath should be struck out of the division list and the journals [1].

Since the year 1879 all new members elected after or at a General Election, including Ministers after re-election, have been introduced on taking their seat. Previous to that year the practice was not uniform. The practical advantage of a formal introduction is that it secures the administration of the oath not being overlooked.

Introduction of Members.

The form of introduction is as follows: the new member standing between two other members is presented to the Speaker in these words,

"Mr Speaker, I have the honour to present to you A. B., Member for the Electoral District of who has taken the oath and signed the roll and now claims the right to take his seat."

The Speaker thereupon replies: "Let the Honourable Member take his seat."

The member then advances to the Chair and pays his respects to the Speaker.

5. ELECTION PETITIONS.

The trial of Election Petitions is regulated by the Dominion Controverted Elections Act [2].

Any corrupt practice committed by a candidate or by his agent, with or without the candidate's knowledge, voids

---

[1] See Burinot, p. 143.   [2] R. S. C. c. 9.

an election. Corrupt practices include bribery, treating, undue influence, or personation.

Trial of
Petitions.

The Act confers jurisdiction to try Election Petitions on the following Courts:

in Quebec: the Superior Court of the Province;

in Ontario: the Court of Appeal, and the High Court of Justice of the Province;

in Nova Scotia, New Brunswick, Prince Edward's Island and the North West Territories: the Supreme Court; and

in Manitoba: the Court of Queen's Bench of the Province.

A Petition may be presented either by a candidate or by any one who had a right to vote at the election to which the Petition relates.

The Petition is heard before one Judge without a jury and takes place in the Electoral District, to which the return in question relates, unless the Court is of opinion that the trial could be held more conveniently elsewhere.

Appeal.

An Appeal is allowed in Quebec to any three judges of the Superior Court of Quebec or of Montreal, and in the other provinces to the Court of which the Judge trying the Petition is a member.

Such Appeal must be limited to a preliminary objection, which, if allowed, would have put an end to the Petition, or to an Appeal from the decision of the Judge who tried the Petition on a point of law [1].

At the conclusion of the trial the Judge makes his report to the Speaker who communicates it to the House.

6. OFFICERS OF THE HOUSE.

The
Speaker.

The Speaker is elected by the House [2], though after his election he proceeds, accompanied by the members, to the Senate Chamber to inform his Excellency the Governor-

[1] R. S. C. c. 9, s. 50.   [2] B. N. A. Act, 1867, ss. 44, 45.

General that the House has "elected him to be their Speaker." The choice of the Speaker is not "confirmed" and "approved" by the Governor-General, as it is by the Crown in England. Up to 1840 the election of the Speaker of the Legislative Assembly in both Upper and Lower Canada was always "approved" by the Governor, but such approval is not essential[1].

When a Speaker dies or resigns during a prorogation, the House of Commons at the opening of the next Session adopts the English practice of proceeding to the Senate Chamber and asking the authority of the Governor-General to proceed to the election of a Speaker according to law[2].

The duties of the Speaker are prescribed by Standing Orders, by the customs of the House, and by English precedents. *Duties of Speaker.*

He presides over all meetings of the House[3], and receives and puts all motions. He communicates to the House all messages received from the Governor-General or from the Senate. If necessary he reprimands members and under the instructions of the House commits persons to the custody of the Sergeant at Arms. He decides points of order, subject to an appeal to the House, and enforces all rules, and is the official mouthpiece of the House when an address is presented to the Crown or to the Governor-General.

If the Speaker from any cause finds it necessary to leave the Chair, he may call upon the Chairman of Committees, or in his absence, upon any member, to take the Chair during the remainder of the day[4]. *Absence of Speaker.*

If the Speaker is unavoidably absent the Chairman of Committees acts as Deputy Speaker[5].

The Clerk of the House is appointed by Commission under the Great Seal to hold office during pleasure. He *The Clerks.*

---

[1] See *ante* p. 114. [2] Burinot, p. 163. [3] B. N. A. Act, 1867, s. 46.
[4] R. S. C. c. 14, s. 1. [5] Ib. s. 2.

acts as recorder and keeps the journals of the House. The Clerk Assistant is appointed by the Speaker to assist the Clerk.

The drafting of all public bills, and their revision after passing the various stages are entrusted to the "law clerk".

Sergeant at Arms. The Sergeant at Arms is appointed by the Crown and acts as the chief executive officer of the House, fulfilling similar functions to those performed by the same officer in the English House of Commons.

7. INTERNAL ARRANGEMENTS.

Each member is provided with a seat and a desk to which is affixed a card with his name. It is the duty of the Sergeant at Arms to see to the allotment of seats.

Strangers are admitted to the galleries by tickets distributed to members by the Sergeant at Arms, and to the Speaker's gallery by order of the Speaker. Strangers are not obliged to withdraw when a division takes place, but either the Speaker or the House may order the withdrawal of strangers.

8. RESIGNATION.

A member resigns or vacates his seat:

(1) By giving notice of resignation from his place in the House.

(2) By giving written notice under seal attested by two witnesses to the Speaker, or if there be no Speaker or if the member be Speaker, to two members. No member can resign while his election is contested, nor until the time during which it may be contested has elapsed [1].

---

[1] R. S. C. c. 14, s. 12.

(3) By death.

(4) By accepting certain offices [1].

The House of Commons on at least one occasion since the Confederation has expelled a member. Previous to the Union the Legislative Assemblies of Lower and Upper Canada had several times exercised the power of expulsion [2]. In 1874 Louis Riel accused of the murder of Thomas Scott, was expelled as a fugitive from justice, and when he was returned again in 1875, a new writ was ordered to be issued for the election of a new member "in the room of Louis Riel adjudged an outlaw."

Expulsion of Members.

[1] R. S. C. c. 14, ss. 5—7. See *ante*, p. 129.

[2] See cases in Burinot, p. 150.

CHAPTER XIII.

THE SENATE.

1. NUMBER.

THE number of senators by the B. N. A. Act, 1867, s. 22, was limited to 72, 24 being assigned to Ontario, 24 to Quebec, 12 to Nova Scotia and 12 to New Brunswick. On the admission of British Columbia the Order in Council of the 16th May, 1871, assigned three senators to the province and thus increased the number to 75. When Prince Edward's Island was admitted in 1873, no addition was made to the Senate, but in accordance with section 147 of the B. N. A. Act, 1867, Nova Scotia and New Brunswick were each deprived of two senators, and the four places thus obtained were given to the newly admitted province. Manitoba by the 33 Vic. c. 3, s. 3, had three senators assigned to it under the powers conferred on the Dominion Parliament by the Imperial Act 34 and 35 Vic. c. 28, thus bringing the number up to 78. Any doubt as to the validity of the addition of senators by the last mentioned act was set at rest by the Imperial Act 49 and 50 Vic. c. 35, which confers on the Dominion Parliament full power to make provision for the representation in the Senate of any new province or of any territory.

N. W. T.　In 1887 a Dominion Act[1] provided that the North-West Territories were to be represented by two senators possessing the same qualification as other senators.

[1] 50 and 51 Vic. c. 3.

The 26th section of the B. N. A. Act of 1867 empowered the Crown on the recommendation of the Governor-General, to direct at any time, that three or six members be added to the Senate.

In Dec. 1873 the Canadian Privy Council, nominally "in the public interests," but in reality to increase the supporters of the Ministry in the House, advised that an application be made to Her Majesty to add six members. The recommendation was forwarded by the Governor-General to the Colonial Secretary who, under the circumstances, declined to advise Her Majesty to comply with the request.

"After a careful examination of the question," said the Colonial Secretary, "which is one of considerable importance, I am satisfied that the intention of the framers of the 26th section of the B. N. A. Act, 1867, was that this power should be vested in Her Majesty, in order to provide a means of bringing the Senate into accord with the House of Commons in the event of an actual collision of opinion between the two Houses. You will readily understand that Her Majesty could not be advised to take the responsibility of interfering with the constitution of the Senate, except upon an occasion when it had been made apparent that a difference had arisen between the two Houses of so serious and permanent a character that the Government could not be carried on without Her intervention, and where it could be shown that the limited creation of senators allowed by the Act would apply an adequate remedy. This view is, I may observe, strongly confirmed by the provisions of the 27th section, which shew that the addition to the Senate is only to be temporary and that the Senate is to be reduced to its usual number as soon as possible after the necessity for the exercise of the special power has passed away[1]."

[1] Can. Sess. Papers, 1877, No. 68.

2. QUALIFICATIONS OF SENATORS.

By section 23 of the B. N. A. Act, 1867, the qualifications required of a Senator are as follows :—

Age.   1. He must be 30 years of age.

Subject.   2. He must be either

    (*a*)   a natural born subject of the Queen, or

    (*b*)   a naturalised subject.

Naturalisation is one of the subjects specifically reserved to the Dominion Parliament, and therefore an alien can only be naturalised by force of a Dominion or of an Imperial Act of Parliament. The status of aliens naturalised before the Union by a Provincial Legislature is recognised, and such subjects may be Senators.

Property.   3. His real and personal property must be of the value of 4000 dollars over and above his debts and liabilities.

    (*a*)   Of this property a certain minimum amount must consist of freeholds of which he is seised for his own benefit. The lands referred to in the Act[1] are "lands or tenements held in free and common socage...or held in franc-alleu or in roture."

    (*b*)   The minimum amount of freehold property is 4000 dollars, and such amount is calculated "over and above all rents, dues, debts, charges, mortgages, and incumbrances due or payable out of, or charged in or affecting the same."

    (*c*)   It is not necessary that the freeholds should be in the particular Electoral District of the Province for which the Senator sits, except in the case of Quebec Senators who are non-resident in the Province of Quebec[2].

     4. He must be resident in the Province for which he is appointed[3]. The Senators from Quebec are an exception to

---

[1] B. N. A. A. s. 23, (31).   [2] See below.   [3] B. N. A. A. s. 23 (5).

this rule, as it is sufficient if non-residents have the real
property qualification in the electoral division for which
they are appointed[1].

5. Before taking his seat a Senator must subscribe the Oath.
Oath of Allegiance, and make a declaration that he is duly
qualified in respect of property for sitting in the Senate[2].

In 1880 a resolution was adopted by the Senate by
which every member is required, within the first twenty
days of the first session of each parliament, to take before
the Clerk in the form prescribed by the B. N. A. Act
1867, a renewed declaration as to his property qualification.

A Senator is forbidden, under a penalty of 200 dollars Senators
a day, to be directly or indirectly a party to or concerned not to be
parties to
in a contract with the government, but this is not to affect government
a Senator who is a shareholder in a public company that contracts.
has with the government a contract not relating to the
building of any public work[3].

All questions relating to the qualification of a Senator Questions
as to
or to a vacancy in the Senate are heard and determined by Qualification.
the Senate[4].

3. HOW APPOINTED.

Senators in Canada are not, as in the United States,
elected by the legislative bodies in the different states. They
are appointed by the Governor-General, but the Governor-
General in making the appointments is required to nominate
a certain fixed number from the residents in each province
except Quebec.

A Senator is appointed by instrument under the Great
Seal. The form in use is as follows:—

---

[1] Ib. sec. 23 (6).   [2] B. N. A. Act, 1867, s. 128.
[3] R. S. C. c. 11, s. 18.   [4] B. N. A. Act, s. 33.

CANADA.

Dufferin.

(L. S.)

VICTORIA by the grace of God of the United Kingdom of Great Britain and Ireland Queen, Defender of the Faith &c.

To our trusty and well-beloved   of our Province of in our Dominion of Canada.

GREETING :—

Know ye that as well for our especial trust and confidence we have manifested in you as for the purpose of obtaining your advice and assistance in all weighty and arduous affairs, which may the state and defence of Our Dominion of Canada concern, We have thought fit to summon you to the Senate of our said Dominion [and we do appoint you for the   electoral division of Quebec] and we do command you the said   that all difficulties and excuses whatsoever laying aside, you be and appear for the purpose aforesaid in the Senate of our said Dominion at all times whenever and wheresoever Our Parliament may be in Our said Dominion convoked and holden : and this you are in no wise to omit.

In testimony whereof we have caused our letters to be made Patent and the Great Seal of Canada to be hereunto affixed.   Witness &c.

By command

————

Clerk of the Crown in Chancery,
Canada.

The form of Introduction may be illustrated by an extract from the Senate Journals of Canada.

"The Honourable the Speaker informed the House that there was a Member without, ready to be introduced.

"When the Honourable A. B. was introduced between the Introduc-
tion. Members X and Y,

"The Honourable A. B. presented Her Majesty's writ summoning him to the Senate.

"The same was then read by the Clerk and *ordered* to be put upon the Journal.

"Then the Honourable A. B. took and subscribed the oath prescribed by law which was administered by C. D. a Commissioner appointed for that purpose and took his seat accordingly.

"The Honourable the Speaker acquainted the House that the Clerk of the Senate had laid upon the table the certificate of one of the Commissioners setting forth that the Honourable A. B., a member of the Senate, had made and subscribed the Declaration of Qualification required by the British North America Act 1867."

4. MEETING OF THE SENATE.

Fifteen Members, including the Speaker, are necessary Quorum. to form a quorum[1].

The Speaker is appointed by the Governor-General and is removable by him[2].

All questions are decided by a majority of votes. The Speaker in all cases has a vote as well as a casting vote[3].

Senators enjoy the same privileges as members of the Privileges. House of Commons, and are entitled to payment for their services.

5. TENURE OF OFFICES.

A Senator holds his office for life[4], but he may resign by a writing under his hand addressed to the Governor-General[5].

His place is liable to become vacant in the following cases :—

[1] B. N. A. Act, s. 35.   [2] Ib. s. 36.   [3] Ib.
[4] B. N. A. Act, s. 29.   [5] Ib. s. 30.

1.   If for two consecutive sessions of the Parliament he fails to give his attendance.

2.   If he takes an oath or makes a declaration or acknowledgment of allegiance, obedience, or adherence to a foreign power, or does an act whereby he becomes a subject or citizen, or entitled to the rights or privileges of a subject or citizen, of a foreign power.

3.   If he is adjudged bankrupt or insolvent, or applies for the benefit of any law relating to insolvent debtors, or becomes a public defaulter.

4.   If he is attainted of treason, or convicted of felony or of any infamous crime.

5.   If he ceases to be qualified by property or residence ; but a Senator holding an office under the Government requiring his presence at the seat of Government is not to be disqualified by reason of his residence there.

CHAPTER XIV.

THE METHOD OF LEGISLATION.

THE method of legislation is regulated by (1) statutes, How regulated. (2) standing orders and rules adopted by Parliament, and (3) customs.

Some provisions affecting the procedure of Parliament Statute. are to be found in the British North America Act 1867. The 54th section, for instance, enacts, that it is not lawful for the House of Commons to pass any vote, resolution, address, or bill for the appropriation of any part of the public revenue or any tax, to any purpose that has not been recommended to that House by message of the Governor-General, and the 133rd section requires all acts of the Parliament of Canada to be printed in both French and English.

With the above exceptions the procedure in either House Standing orders, is mainly governed by rules based on the practice of the rules, and English Parliament. In the early legislative councils of resolutions. Upper and of Lower Canada the practice of the House of Lords was adopted[1]; but when legislative assemblies were summoned they resolved to follow as far as circumstances would permit the rules, orders and usages of the English House of Commons[2]. When the Dominion Parliament met in 1867, the House of Commons appointed a Committee to frame rules for governing the procedure in that House, and

---

[1] Burinot, p. 212.   [2] Ib. p. 212. Christie's *Low. Can.* 130–139.

the Committee practically adopted the rules previously in force in the former legislative assembly of Canada.

Sessional orders. Sessional orders are rules of a temporary nature intended to govern the business of the session, such as the time of adjournment or the presentation of papers[1]; resolutions may also be passed but their force will expire at the end of the session[2].

Amendment of rules. The rules and standing orders may from time to time be amended. The amendments are in the first instance discussed by a Special Committee appointed by the House, of which Committee the Speaker is always a member, and are afterwards considered by a Committee of the whole House[3].

Suspension of rules. The Senate and House of Commons never permit their rules and standing orders to be suspended, except by unanimous consent though a rule may be repealed or amended by a majority of the members[4].

THE HOUSE OF COMMONS.

Commencement of the sitting. The House on days when it is in session meets at three o'clock[5]. Twenty members including the Speaker are required to constitute a quorum[6], and if on taking the chair the Speaker finds that 20 members are not present, he adjourns the House until the usual hour on the next sitting day[7]. A count-out rarely happens in Canada. Contrary to the English practice members may enter the House during the whole time the count is going on[8]. The Speaker reads a form of prayer adopted by the House in 1877, the doors are then opened and the business of the day proceeds.

Order of business. The order of routine business in the Commons is as follows[9]:—

---

[1] Burinot, p. 217.   [2] Ib.   [3] Ib. p. 214.
[4] Ib. p. 215.
[5] At 6 o'clock the Speaker leaves the chair until 7.30.
[6] B. N. A. Act 1867, ss. 35, 48.   [7] Com. S. O. 1, 2.
[8] Burinot, p. 248.   [9] Com. S. O. 19.

Presenting petitions.

Reading and receiving petitions.

Presenting reports by Standing and Select Committees.

Motions.

After the routine business come Questions, Notices of Motion, Private Bills, Government Orders, and Public Bills but the order in which these matters are taken varies. On Tuesdays and Fridays Government Notices and Orders take precedence, on Wednesdays and Thursdays Questions have the first place, whilst on Mondays the House first considers Private Bills.

On presenting a petition the member having charge Petitions. of it is allowed to state the parties from whom it comes, the number of signatures attached to it, and the material allegations it contains. He is not allowed to read it, though he may have that done by the clerk at the table. He must endorse his name on it and is answerable for its not containing any objectionable matter[1]. The petition is taken charge of by one of the clerks and after passing through the Journals' office, where it is examined so as to see that it is framed in accordance with the rules of the House, it is two days after presentation brought to the table to be read and received. Any member may oppose the reception of the petition.

By consent of the whole House a petition may be received when it is presented, but this course is only adopted in an urgent case, or where it is advisable to refer it at once to a Committee[2].

The House, following the practice of the English House Petitions for Money. of Commons[3], refuses to receive any petition involving directly a grant of money, unless it is first recommended by the Crown[4]. This does not apply to petitions which are expressed

---

[1] Com. S. O. 84—86.   [2] Burinot, p. 269.

[3] May, 613.   [4] Can. Com. J. 1867—8, 297.

in general terms and do not directly ask for public aid or which ask the House only to take the facts into its consideration or to adopt such measures as the House may think it expedient to take.

Petitions regarding Taxes. Up to 1876 petitions asking for imposition of duties were not received, but in that year it was thought advisable to alter the practice and to receive them. Petitions also are received asking for bounties for a particular industry, for remission on public grounds of taxes or duties, or for compensation for losses through legislation, but a petition in which a bounty is demanded for a particular individual, or which prays for remission of a debt due to the Crown[2] is not received.

Private Bills. Every private bill is initiated by means of a petition, and such petition is governed by the ordinary rules regulating petitions.

Opposition to private bills also is commenced by a petition.

Public Bills. A public bill may originate in either House, except when it involves an appropriation of the revenue or imposes a tax[3]. The method of procedure in the Senate differs in some respects from that adopted in the House of Commons, but both Houses have followed very closely the English practice. In the Commons a bill passes through seven stages, viz. (1) Introduction, (2) First reading, (3) Second reading, (4) Committee, (5) Report, (6) Third reading, (7) Passing.

Three readings. By the standing orders of each House the three readings are as a rule to be on separate days, except in the case of bills of an urgent nature[4].

The Senate in a case of urgency formally suspends its standing orders, but in the Commons it is sufficient for the House to declare the matter urgent[5].

---

[1] Burinot, p. 266. [2] See Burinot, p. 268.
[3] B. N. A. Act, 1867, s. 53. [4] Sen. S. O. 41, 42. Com. S. O. 43.
[5] Burinot, p. 559.

Introduction. In the House of Commons every bill is *Motion for Leave.* introduced upon motion for leave specifying the title of the bill[1], and therefore two days' notice must be given[2]; a copy of the bill must be furnished to the Speaker along with the motion in writing. It is usual for the member in charge to explain clearly the main provisions of the measure[3], but though there is no rule preventing a debate or forbidding an amendment, it is not usual to discuss the bill at this stage.

There are two classes of bills that cannot be introduced directly on motion, but which require to be first considered in committee—(1) Bills relating to Trade, and (2) Money Bills.

1. Bills relating to Trade. The 41st standing order of the House of Commons provides, that all bills relating to trade or to the alteration of the laws concerning trade must be first considered in Committee in order to give opportunity for full discussion and a wide notice to persons interested. There is no such rule in the Senate. The rule applies to bills affecting trade generally as well as those relating to a particular trade[4]. Bills relating to trade.

2. Money Bills. By order 88, it is provided Money Bills. "If any motion be made in the House for any public aid or charge upon the people, the consideration and debate thereof may not be presently entered upon but shall be adjourned until such future day as the House may think fit to appoint: and then it shall be referred to a Committee of the whole House before any resolution or vote of the House do pass thereon."

This rule requires that money bills shall first be considered as resolutions in Committee of the whole House[5].

---

[1] Com. S. O. 39.   [2] Ib. 31.   [3] Burinot, p. 517.

[4] May, 530, and see Burinot, p. 519, for cases to which the rule has been held to be applicable in Canada.

[5] Apart from this such bills must be recommended by the Governor-General, see *post* p. 164.

Money
Bills.
    If a bill contains only some clauses involving the payment of money it may be introduced on motion. The money clauses (which are not considered to be part of the bill) go before the Committee and after approval are incorporated with the bill: but this course can be adopted only if the clauses in question are a subsidiary part of the bill. "Whenever the main object of a bill is the payment of public money it must directly originate in Committee of the whole or else the proceedings will be null and void the moment objection is taken[1]."

The rule does not apply either to clauses imposing pecuniary penalties or to bills of a declaratory nature[2].

A similar rule prevails in the English House of Commons, and the principle is extended to bills, relating to Religion or altering laws relating to Religion[3].

In the Senate no notice or leave is required to bring in a bill. By standing orders 39 and 40 it is provided that

"It is the right of every Senator to bring in a bill."

"Immediately after the bill is presented it is read a first time and ordered to be printed."

This corresponds with the English practice.

First
Reading.
    First reading. After leave has been given to introduce the bill it is read a first time without amendment or debate[4]. The Speaker then proposes the formal question "when shall the bill be read a second time?" in order that the bill may be placed on the orders of the day for second reading, a motion that is usually never opposed[5].

Second
Reading.
    Second reading. On the motion for second reading the Commons discuss the principle of the measure, and it is out of order to discuss the clauses *seriatim.* The Senate has an express rule "43, the principle of a bill is usually debated at its second reading." As regards amendments the same

---

[1] Burinot, p. 524.   [2] Ib., pp. 525, 526.   [3] Anson, p. 226
[4] Com. S. O. 42.   [5] Burinot, p. 528.

practice prevails as in the English House of Commons, the second reading may be rejected or an amendment may be carried that it be read on ———— next.

If the bill be read a second time, it is then proposed "that the House go into Committee on the bill on ———— next," but in some cases it is referred to a Select Committee sessional or standing.

Committee. Three kinds of Committees have been *Committee.* established by the Canadian Parliament (1) Committees of the whole, (2) Special Committees, and (3) Joint Committees.

(1) Committees of the whole are composed of all the members and sit in the house itself.

(2) The Special Committees fall into two classes. Special Committees.

(*a*) Standing Committees appointed at the commence- (*a*) Standing Committees. ment of each session to inquire into and report on matters referred to them by the House and relating to special fixed subjects.

In the Commons these Committees are appointed on the following subjects:

(1) Privileges and Elections.
(2) Standing orders.
(3) Printing Public accounts.
(4) Expiring laws.
(5) Railway, canal and telegraph lines.
(6) Miscellaneous private bills.
(7) Banking and Commerce.
(8) Immigration and Colonization.

In the Senate similar Committees are appointed for standing orders, private bills, railways, telegraphs and harbours, and banking and commerce.

It will be observed that some of these Committees correspond to the two Grand Committees on (1) The Courts of

Law and procedure, and (2) Trade, shipping and manufactures formed by the House of Commons in 1882.

The English Grand Committees are required to consist of not less than 60, and not more than 80, members, but in Canada the standing Committees may consist of any number. The smaller Committees consist of from 30 to 40 members, whilst as many as 130 may be on the more important Committees.

(b) Other Special Committees. (b) Special Committees are often appointed to consider a particular subject, such as trade between different provinces, criminal law etc.[1] In the Commons these Committees except in special cases[2] are, as in England, limited to 15 members, but in the Senate the number is not limited[3].

The Commons maintain still the old English rule[4], that a member opposed to the principle of a bill cannot serve on a Select Committee to which such bill is referred. The 18th standing order provides—

"It shall always be understood that no member who declares against the principle or substance of a bill, resolution or matter to be committed can be nominated of such committee."

A member, who merely takes objection to some particulars of the bill, or who opposes the appointment of the Committee, is not considered as coming within the scope of the rule[5].

In England the rule no longer prevails: all that is required is that the members nominated shall be willing to serve[6].

Joint Committees. (3) Joint Committees are Committees appointed jointly by both Houses. Standing joint Committees are usually appointed to look after the Library belonging to the Houses and Government printing. Each House appoints a Committee on these subjects and authorizes it to confer

---

[1] Burinot, p. 430.   [2] Com. S. O. 78, 79.   [3] Burinot, p. 430.
[4] Lex Parl. 329, 331.   [5] Burinot, p. 435.   [6] E. S. O. 28.

with the Committee of the other House and then informs the other House by message of what it has done[1]

In some cases and always in the case of private bills, witnesses are examined before the Committees, and by the 39 Vict. c. 7, witnesses may be examined on oath if the House thinks fit. Previous to this Act it was held by the law officers of the Crown in England, that the Canadian Parliament could not by statute, vest in itself power to administer oaths where such power was not possessed by the English House of Commons at the time the British North America Act 1867 was passed. And as until the year 1871[2] the English House of Commons, except in the case of private bills[3], did not possess the power to administer an oath Canadian bills giving power to administer oaths generally were disallowed[4].

To obviate this difficulty an Act[5] was passed by the Imperial Parliament giving the Dominion Parliament the right to define by Act the powers, privileges and immunities to be enjoyed by the Senate and House of Commons, provided such powers, privileges and immunities should not exceed those enjoyed by the English House of Commons at the time of the passing of such Act by the Canadian Parliament.

Under the provisions of this Act the Canadian Parliament in 1876 passed an Act[6] giving the necessary power to examine witnesses on oath or on affirmation.

An ordinary public bill is usually referred to one of the above Committees but in some cases this course is not adopted. The Appropriation Bill is not referred to Committee in either the Commons or the Senate[7]; and in some cases where a bill was founded on resolutions passed in

Witnesses.

Appropriation Bill.

---

[1] Burinot, pp. 403, 427.　　[2] 34 and 35 Vict. (i.) c. 83.
[3] Under 21 and 22 Vict. (i.) c. 78.　　[4] Can. Com. J. 1873, Oct. sess. p. 5.
[5] 38 and 39 Vict. (i.) c. 38, see App.　　[6] 39 Vict. c. 7.
[7] Burinot, p. 549.

Committee of the whole, the Commons instead of committing the bill have had it read at length[1]. Mr Burinot[2] suggests that this practice has been followed only in a few cases where there was no wish to introduce amendments.

Assuming that the House is going into Committee on the bill the procedure is as follows.

Committee of the whole. When the order for the day for the Committee is reached, and it is desired to have any "Instructions" given to the Committee, a motion to that effect should then be made. The object of such instructions is to confer on the Committee some power it would not otherwise possess.

If no motion is made for instructions, the Speaker puts the question "that I do now leave the chair," on which a debate may ensue. When the House finally resolves itself into Committee, the Speaker leaves the chair, and there being no permanent Chairman of Committees as in England he in accordance with the standing orders calls on some member to take the chair. The bill is then considered clause by clause, the preamble and title being last considered[3]. At any time new clauses may be considered and amendments though not within the scope and title of the bill[4] may be introduced.

Report. After all the clauses have been considered the Chairman makes a report to the House.

The bill is usually taken into consideration at once, and a time is appointed for the third reading. The English practice of amending a bill at this stage is usual in the Senate but it has not been adopted in the Commons, though the bill may be recommitted with or without limitations.

Third Reading. *Third Reading.* On the third reading in the Commons the English practice is adopted of not allowing any amendment except mere verbal ones, though in former years substantial changes were sometimes introduced at this

---

[1] Can. Com. J. 1867—8, 37, 226, 314.   [2] Burinot, p. 509.
[3] Com. S. O. 45.   [4] Burinot, p. 543.

stage[1]. On the other hand the Senate constantly amends bills on the third reading without referring them back to Committee[2].

Motion, that Bill do pass. After the third reading the Passing. next question is "That this bill do pass;" and though usually this is carried *nem. con.* immediately after the third reading, it may be deferred or be postponed to a future day[3]. This seems to be the proper time for amending the title if necessary[4].

The bill being passed is reprinted and by order of the Subse- quent pro- House is communicated to the Senate through one of the ceedings. clerks, who presents it at the bar. If the Senate passes the bill without any amendment, a written message is sent to that effect, but if it is rejected no message is sent. If passed with amendments it is returned with such amendments attached to a copy of the bill. The amendments may be accepted, in which case they are read twice and agreed to forthwith, and a message returned to that effect. When the amend- ments are important, a member may propose "that they be read that day — months" and if such motion be carried, the bill is practically thrown out, or he may move that the amendments be disagreed to for certain reasons, in which case the reasons are communicated to the other House. The practice of holding a Conference is no longer resorted to[5], and if the two Houses cannot agree, the bill must drop for that session.

PRIVATE BILLS.

A Private Bill may be defined as a bill which relates to Public and Private the interests of private individuals or of corporate bodies, Bills. and does not affect the interests of the community as a whole. It is somewhat difficult to draw the line between

---

[1] Burinot, p. 550.   [2] Ib.   [3] Ib. p. 551.   [4] Ib.
[5] Ib. pp. 402, 551.

public and private bills, inasmuch as some bills may relate as much to the public interest as to individual interest. In Canada it rests with the Speaker or with the Committee to which the bill is referred to decide the class to which a bill belongs. Owing to the restrictions that have been imposed on the legislative power of Canada, it is possible for a private bill to be introduced relating to a matter not within the legislative competence of the Dominion. Sometimes the point is raised in the House itself and sometimes in Committee, and when it is clear that any provisions of the bill are "unconstitutional," they are always struck out.

Reference to Supreme Court. As a further precaution against passing an 'illegal' Act, it was provided by the Supreme and Exchequer Court Act [1], that the Supreme Court or any two of its judges should examine and report upon any private bill or petition for a private bill referred to the Court under any of the rules of either House of Parliament. A private bill is introduced by petition. As a rule previous to its introduction notice of its main provisions has to be given in the Canadian Gazette and in the local papers. Contrary to the English practice a member of the House may take charge of the bill and promote its progress. As the rules that govern ordinary petitions apply to a private bill petition, a member during the first ten days of the session presents the petition in his place, restricting himself to a statement of its prayer. It is then referred as a matter of course to the Committee on Standing Orders, who report whether the rule with regard to notice has been complied with. If there has been any informality in the notice the Committee may yet recommend the House to dispense with a regular notice, and it seems the Committee are inclined to adopt this course, where it appears that the parties interested have had sufficient notice, and that no interests are affected except those of the petitioners.

---

[1] 38 Vic. c. 11.

Where the Committee reports favourably the petition is 1st & 2nd readings. at once presented and leave given to read it a first time. On a subsequent occasion it is read a second time, and though at this or any other stage it may be opposed, it is usual to refer it without opposition to a Committee. In England Committee. the Committee on a private bill usually consists of four members nominated by a "Committee of Selection." In Canada a private bill goes before one of the large standing Committees according to its class. In the House of Commons there are four such Committees, (1) Standing Orders, 42 members, (2) Railways, Canals and Telegraph Lines, 136 members, (3) Banking and Commerce, 98 members, and (4) Miscellaneous Private Bills, 70 members. In the Senate the Committees are three in number, (1) Standing Orders and Private Bills, 36 members, (2) Railways, Telegraphs and Harbours, 32 members, and (3) Banks and Commerce, 29 members.

The Committee hears evidence for and against the bill, following the English practice, and finally makes its report to the House. If the report is favourable, the bill is read a third time.

The different stages of a private bill in the Senate In Senate. are practically the same as those in the Commons, but in the case of Divorce bills which, in accordance with the Canadian practice, are introduced in the Senate, special rules have been laid down[1].

---

[1] For a more detailed account of private bill legislation see Bourinot, pp. 584—680.

CHAPTER XV.

THE GOVERNOR-GENERAL.

Office created by Letters Patent.

THE office of Governor-General of Canada created by the Crown by Letters Patent existed prior to the Union of 1867, but after the Confederation the Letters Patent were revised, and new ones were issued in 1878. The Letters Patent create the office and declare that the person who shall fill the office shall be appointed by Commission under Sign Manual and Signet, and that he shall exercise the powers vested in him by virtue of the Letters Patent and of the Commission issued to him, according to such Instructions as may from time to time be given to him either under Sign Manual and Signet, or by Order in Council, or by Her Majesty through one of the Secretaries of State and in accordance with such laws as may be in force in the Dominion.

Changes suggested by Canada.

When the draft of these Letters Patent was submitted to the Canadian Government, it was urged by the then Minister of Justice that, as Canada possessed more extensive powers of self-government than had been conceded to any other colony, and consisted not of one province but of seven provinces, the widest powers possible consistent with the British North America Act should be conferred on the Governor-General. This principle was practically adopted by the Home Government, and on the appointment of the Marquis of Lorne several changes were introduced into the Commission and Instructions, of which the more important were as follows :—

¹ See Appendix.

The clauses (1) relating to meetings of the Privy Council, (2) authorizing the Governor to act in opposition to the advice of his ministers, (3) prescribing certain classes of bills to be reserved for Imperial consideration, (4) dealing with matters within the province of the provincial Legislatures were omitted; whilst the clause relating to the exercise of the prerogative of pardon was modified so as to draw a distinction between local cases and cases of Imperial interest[1].

The new Letters Patent[2] empower the Governor-General to keep and use the Great Seal of the Dominion; to appoint all judges, justices, and such other officers as might be appointed by Her Majesty; to remove upon sufficient cause any person appointed to any office by or under the authority of the Crown; to summon, prorogue and dissolve the Dominion Parliament, and to appoint a Deputy. The Letters Patent also make provision for appointing a Lieutenant-Governor or other person to perform the duties of the office in case of the death, incapacity, removal or absence of the Governor-General. *Powers conferred by the Letters Patent.*

The Instructions[2] require the Governor-General to take the oath of allegiance, the oath for due execution of his office, and for due and impartial administration of justice; and authorize him to administer the oath of allegiance and any other oath prescribed to all persons holding any office: they also empower him to exercise under certain conditions the prerogative of mercy, and lay down certain rules to be observed in transmitting laws to which he has assented or which he has reserved for Her Majesty's consideration. *Instructions.*

The Commission simply appoints the person selected to the office. *Commission.*

The object of the Letters Patent and Instructions is to confer on the Governor-General those powers, necessary

[1] See Todd, Chap. IV. for a detailed account of these changes.
[2] See Appendix, where Letters Patent and Instructions are set out at length.

for discharging the duties of the office, which are vested in Her Majesty, either as being part of her prerogative powers or under s. 9 of the B. N. A. Act, which declares, that "the Executive Government and Authority of and over Canada is hereby declared to continue and be vested in the Queen."

As above stated the Governor-General is appointed by the Crown by Commission[1]. He holds office during the pleasure of the Crown, but in accordance with the standing rule of the Colonial Office his term of service is limited to five or six years. His annual salary has been fixed at £10,000, and is payable out of the Consolidated Revenue Fund of Canada[2].

The Governor-General is a corporation sole, and all bonds and other instruments taken by him in his public capacity are given to him and his successors by his name of office[3].

The position of the Governor-General may be considered as regards (1) the Legislature, (2) Party Government, (3) the Executive, (4) the Judicature, (5) the Prerogatives of the Crown, (6) the Provinces, and (7) his Responsibility.

1.　Powers as regards the Dominion Legislature.

Appoints Senators.
1. He selects and summons qualified persons to the Senate[4] and fills up all vacancies[5]. He has also power to recommend the Queen to add three or six additional members representing equally Ontario, Quebec, and the Maritime Provinces of Nova Scotia and New Brunswick[6].

Appoints Speaker of Senate.
2. He appoints and may remove the Speaker of the Senate, who must however be a senator[7].

Summons House of Commons.
3. He summons and calls together the House of Commons[8].

Recommends money bills.
4. He recommends to the House of Commons the levying of taxes and the appropriation of the revenue[9].

---

[1] See Appendix for form of Commission.
[2] B. N. A. Act, s. 105.　R. S. C. c. 3, s. 2.　　[3] R. S. C. c. 3, s. 1.
[4] B. N. A. Act, s. 24.　[5] Ib. s. 32.　[6] B. N. A. Act, s. 26, see *ante*, p. 143.
[7] Ib. s. 34.　　[8] Ib. s. 38.　　[9] Ib. s. 54.

5. By a clause in the Letters Patent the Crown has conferred on the Governor-General all powers belonging to the Crown in respect of the summoning, proroguing, or dissolving of Parliament.

Summons and dissolves Parliament.

6. He assents to bills on behalf of the Crown.

Assents to bills.

The position of the Governor-General in regard to assenting to bills is governed by the 55th section of the British North America Act 1867 :—

"Where a bill passed by the Houses of Parliament is presented to the Governor-General for the Queen's assent, he shall declare according to his discretion, but subject to the provisions of this Act and to Her Majesty's Instructions, either that he assents thereto in the Queen's name or that he withholds the Queen's assent, or that he reserves the bill for the signification of the Queen's pleasure."

It will be seen from this section that "subject to Her Majesty's Instructions" three courses are open to the Governor-General "according to his discretion," he may assent to the bill, or he may veto it, or he may reserve it for the Queen's pleasure. It is therefore necessary to enquire what Instructions are usually given to the Governor-General, and how his discretion in assenting or vetoing is usually exercised. As regards the Instructions they are silent on the subject, except in so far as they require him to transmit all laws assented to or reserved by him, with explanatory observations in regard to the occasions and reasons for proposing such laws[1].

Previous to the revision of the Instructions in 1878[2] the Governor-General was expressly required not to assent to bills which related to divorce, or granted land or money to the Governor, or made paper money legal tender, or imposed differential duties, or were contrary to treaty stipulations, or infringed the discipline or control of Her Majesty's forces, or affected the Royal prerogative, or contained

---

[1] See Instructions in Appendix.   [2] See *ante*, p. 162.

provisions to which the Royal consent had once been refused, unless the bill contained a suspending clause, or unless some urgent necessity existed and the bill was not contrary to the law of England or to treaty stipulations[1]. Between 1867 and 1878 twenty-one bills, eleven of these relating to divorce, were reserved[2]; but since the last-mentioned year the Royal Instructions have not required any bill to be reserved, on the ground that it was "undesirable that they should contain anything which would be interpreted as limiting or defining the legislative powers conferred in 1867 on the Dominion Parliament[3]," and that the reserved power of disallowance possessed by Her Majesty in Council[4] was sufficient for the protection of Imperial interests.

Bills reserved.

The Governor-General may, however, under the section above quoted reserve a bill for the signification of the Queen's pleasure, in which case it does not become law until the Governor-General signifies by speech or message to each of the Houses of Parliament, or by proclamation, that it has received the assent of the Queen in Council[5].

Not bound to follow advice of ministers.

In exercising his discretionary powers in regard to legislation a Governor-General has to act on his own responsibility, and is not bound to follow the advice of his ministers, though he usually takes this course[6]. The assent of the Governor is not conclusive, as a bill, even if assented to by him, may be disallowed by the Crown[7].

But the Governor before assenting ought to satisfy himself that the bill is within the class of subjects over which the Dominion Parliament has legislative power.

It is usual for him to receive from the Minister of Justice or from the Law Officers of the Crown in the Colony a report on bills submitted for his assent, and he may, if

---

[1] Sess. J. (1873), 74; Sess. Pap. 1867—8, No 22; Burinot, p. 569.

[2] Burinot, p. 570.

[3] Despatch of Secretary for Colonies, Can. S. Pap. 1877, No. 13; Ib. 1880, No. 51.   [4] See *ante*, p. 163.   [5] B. N. A. Act, s. 57.

[6] Todd, p. 137.   [7] See *post*, c. xxi.

the matter be not of purely local concern, refer the matter to the Imperial Law Officers[1].

The British North America Act 1867 is silent both as to the place and manner of giving the Royal assent, except in the case of bills reserved, where it may be given orally, or by message or by proclamation[2]. The usual course adopted is for the Governor-General to give the Royal assent in the presence of both Houses.

Manner of giving Royal assent.

2. DUTIES AS REGARDS PARTY GOVERNMENT.

It is the duty of a Governor-General to observe strict neutrality towards the different parties in the Legislature in regard to all questions in which neither the prerogatives of the Crown nor Imperial interests are involved. In all local matters the judgment of the people expressed in their Legislatures must prevail, and a Governor-General ought always to accept and act by the advice of a Ministry prepared to give effect to such judgment.

Neutral position as regards parties.

But in all questions involving either Imperial interests or the prerogatives of the Crown, the Governor-General has to remember that he represents the Crown, and though he is expected to give due weight to the opinion of his ministers, the final decision must be made upon his own judgment and responsibility[3]. Under special circumstances he may consult Her Majesty's Secretary of State for the Colonies, care being taken that all sides of the controversy be placed before the Imperial Government. In 1874 the Governor-General consulted the Colonial Secretary as to the advisability of following the advice of his ministers where they recommended that six additional senators should be added to the Senate[4]; and in 1879 at the suggestion of the Privy Council the advice of the Home Government was sought regarding the proposed removal of M Letellier from his office of Lieutenant-Governor[5].

Imperial interests.

Consulting Home Government.

[1] Todd, pp. 134, 135.   [2] s. 57.
[3] See Todd, p. 591 and authorities there quoted.
[4] Todd, p. 161.   [5] See *post*, p. 174, Todd, p. 409.

In matters relating either to the Royal prerogative or to Imperial interests the Governor-General may, through the Secretary of State for the Colonies, consult the English Law Officers of the Crown on any question the legality of which is doubtful[1]. Such opinion has been sought as to the power of the Governor-General to create Queen's Counsel[2], and as to the power of a local Legislature to define its privileges[3].

It would not be in accordance with the usual practice for a Governor-General to take the opinion of the English Law Officers on any matter of purely local concern: in such matters he should seek the advice of the Minister of Justice, or of the person or persons who in the Dominion correspond to the Law Officers in England.

3.　FUNCTIONS AS REGARDS THE DOMINION EXECUTIVE.

The functions of the Governor-General as regards the Executive or Administration are regulated partly by Imperial Acts, partly by Dominion Statutes, and partly by the Letters Patent and Instructions already referred to. And they may be summed up by saying that he exercises in the Queen's name on her behalf the supreme Executive Power.

Appoints Ministers.　The Governor-General selects the members of the Council appointed under section 11 of the B. N. A. Act to aid and advise the Government of Canada. The members of this Council or Privy Council, as it is sometimes called, form the ministry. In accordance with the well-established principles of responsible Government the members of the Council are selected from that party which enjoys the confidence of the majority of the members of the House of Commons, and the Prime Minister nominates his colleagues.

Removal of Councillors.　The Governor-General is empowered to remove members of the Council, but in practice the ministry resign when they lose the confidence of the Legislature. By command of the

---

[1] C. O. Regulations.　　[2] Todd, p. 241, see post, p. 172.　　[3] Todd, p. 471.

Queen members of the Privy Council after their retirement are permitted to retain the title "Honourable" for life, and those who do not belong to the Cabinet for the time being may be regarded as "honourable" members of the Privy Council.

By section 15 of the B. N. A. Act, the Command-in-Chief of the land and naval militia and of all naval and military forces of and in Canada, is declared to continue and to be vested in the Queen. The Governor-General is not therefore the Commander-in-Chief of Her Majesty's forces, but he may in time of peace determine the object with which, and the extent to which, Her Majesty's forces are to be employed. *As regards the Army and Navy.*

In 1862 the Imperial House of Commons resolved, that Colonies exercising the rights of self-government ought to undertake the main responsibility of providing for their own internal order and security, and ought to assist in their own external defence, and in accordance with this resolution British troops were withdrawn from Canada and the other Colonies.

In 1868 the Dominion Parliament passed the first of a series of Militia Acts in order to provide for the defence of the Dominion. By the present Militia Act[1] the command is vested in Her Majesty, and is to be exercised either by Her Majesty personally or by the Governor-General as her representative. *Militia Act.*

The Minister of Militia is charged with the administration of Militia affairs, but power is given to the Governor-General in Council from time to time to prescribe his duties[2].

4. POWERS AS REGARDS THE JUDICATURE.

The only judicial functions that the Governor-General is called on to discharge are to hear in Council any appeal from any Act or decision of a Provincial Authority affecting any

---

[1] R. S. C. 1886, c. 41.   [2] See *post*, c. XVII.

right or privilege of a minority, whether Protestant or Roman Catholic, of the Queen's subjects in relation to education[1].

The Governor-General has, however, important duties to discharge in appointing or removing judges and in exercising the prerogative of mercy.

Appointment of Judges. The Judges of the Supreme, District and County Courts are appointed by the Governor-General, except in the case of the Courts of Probate in Nova Scotia and New Brunswick[2]. In the province of Quebec the Judges are to be taken from the bar of that province[3]; and in Ontario, Nova Scotia, and New Brunswick they are to be selected from the respective bars of those provinces until the laws relating to property and to civil rights and to the procedure of the Courts are made uniform in those provinces[4].

The Letters Patent contain a clause authorizing the Governor-General to appoint all such Judges, Commissioners and Justices of the Peace as might be lawfully appointed by the Crown.

Removal of Judges. The Judges of the Superior Courts hold office during good behaviour, but are removable by the Governor-General on address from the Senate and House of Commons[5].

Exercises right of Pardon. The power of pardoning offences is regulated by the Instructions.

"We do further authorize and empower our said Governor-General as he shall see occasion, in our name and on our behalf, when any crime has been committed for which the offender may be tried within our Dominion, to grant a pardon to any accomplice not being the actual perpetrator of such crime, who shall give such information as shall lead to the conviction of the principal offender.

"And further to grant to any offender convicted of any crime in any Court or before any Judge, Justice or Magistrate within our said Dominion, a pardon, either free or

---

[1] B. N. A. Act, s. 93. [2] Ib. s. 96.
[3] Ib. s. 98.   [4] Ib. s. 97.   [5] Ib. s. 99. R. S. C. c. 138.

subject to lawful conditions, or any respite of the execution
of the sentence of any such offender for such period as to our
said Governor-General may seem fit, and to remit any fines,
penalties, or forfeitures which may become due and payable
to us.

"Provided always, that our said Governor-General shall not Con-
ditions.
in any case, except where the offence has been of a political
nature, make it a condition of any pardon or remission of
sentence, that the offender shall be banished from or shall
absent himself from our said Dominion.

"And we do hereby direct and enjoin that our said
Governor-General shall not pardon or reprieve any such
offender without first receiving in capital cases the advice of Advice of
Privy
Council.
the Privy Council for our said Dominion, and in other cases
the advice of one at least of his ministers; and in any case in
which such pardon or reprieve might directly affect the
interests of the Empire or of any country or place beyond the
jurisdiction of the Government of our said Dominion, our
said Governor-General shall before deciding as to either
pardon or reprieve, take those interests specially into his
own personal consideration in conjunction with such advice
as aforesaid."

It will be observed that a distinction is drawn in these
Instructions between three classes of cases, (1) Capital offences,
(2) Non-capital offences, (3) Offences capital or non-capital
affecting either Imperial interests or those of any country
outside the Dominion. In cases of the first class the Governor- Capital
Offences.
General is not to act without receiving the advice of his
ministry; in cases of the second class he must consult one Non-
capital
Offences.
minister, who will usually be the Minister of Justice; whilst
in the third class, in addition to consulting his ministry or Offences
affecting
Imperial
Interests.
one minister as the case may be, he is required to take
the interests of the Empire or foreign country specially into
account.

The Instructions do not in express terms require the

Governor-General to act on the advice of his ministers. The duty of finally deciding rests on him alone, but in actual practice there is no doubt that it would be only under very exceptional circumstances that such advice would be disregarded ; and in the correspondence between Canada and the Imperial Government prior to the issue of the above Instructions, it was understood that in all cases of a merely local nature the Governor-General should act on the advice of his ministers[1].

Previous to the issue of the new Instructions, the Governor-General had felt himself at liberty to disregard the advice of his ministers, and that with the approval of the Home Government. In a despatch of Earl Carnarvon to the Governors of the Australian Colonies[2] he said, "it is true that a Governor may (and indeed must if in his judgment it seems right) decide in opposition to the advice tendered to him." In accordance with this principle, in 1861 Sir Edmund Head, Governor-General of Canada, granted a reprieve in a case of murder contrary to the advice of several ministers[3]; and in 1875 Earl Dufferin commuted a capital sentence on his own responsibility[4].

5. PREROGATIVE POWERS.

Appointment of Queen's Counsel.

As Her Majesty's representative the Governor-General may appoint Queen's Counsel. In *Lenoir* v. *Ritchie*[5] a majority of the Court expressed the opinion, that the sole right of conferring the rank of Queen's Counsel belonged to the Queen or her representative the Governor-General, and that a Province could not by a statute confer this right on a Lieutenant-Governor, inasmuch as the Crown was not a part of a provincial Legislature and therefore no provincial statute could affect its prerogatives.

[1] Can. Sess. Pap. 1879, No. 181.
[2] May 4th, 1875.
[3] *Patterson's Case*, Todd, p. 269.
[4] *Lepine's Case*, ib. p. 269.
[5] 3 Can. S. C. R. 575.

6. Powers as regards the Provinces.

Lieutenant-Governors of the Provinces are appointed by the Governor-General in Council by Commission under the Great Seal of Canada. In case of the absence, illness or other inability of the Lieutenant-Governor, the Governor-General may appoint an administrator to execute the duties of the office[1].

Appointment of Lieutenant-Governors.

By section 59 of the British North America Act a Lieutenant-Governor is not "removable within five years from his appointment except for cause assigned, which shall be communicated to him in writing within one month after the order for removal is made, and shall be communicated by message to the Senate and to the House of Commons within one week thereafter if the Parliament is then sitting, and if not, then within one week after the commencement of the next session of the Parliament." The section is silent as to the circumstances under which the removal of a Lieutenant-Governor would be justifiable, but the *Letellier case* may be taken to have established the rule that the Governor-General ought to act by and with the advice of his ministers. The facts of the case were shortly these[2]:—In 1878 the Lieutenant-Governor of Quebec, M. Letellier, dismissed his ministers on the ground that they had acted contrary to his representations, were encouraging a lavish expenditure in regard to railways, and had promoted a bill which he deemed to be an arbitrary and illegal infringement of vested rights. The subject was brought before the Governor-General by both sides, and a petition praying for the Lieutenant-Governor's dismissal was addressed to the Governor-General in Council by certain members of the dismissed ministry. The Governor-General communicated the petition and the statement of the Lieutenant-Governor to the Senate and the House of Commons.

Removal of Lieutenant-Governors.

Letellier Case.

---

[1] For form of Commission, see Can. Sess. Journ. 1878, p. 175.

[2] See Todd, p. 405, for a more detailed account.

Debates ensued in both Houses. A motion declaring the dismissal of the ministry to be at variance with Constitutional government was carried in the Senate but lost in the House of Commons. In the following year a new Parliament assembled and both Houses agreed in censuring the dismissal of the Quebec Ministry. The Cabinet thereupon advised the Governor-General to remove the Lieutenant-Governor from his office. The Governor-General stated reasons for not adopting such a course, and the ministers then advised a reference to the Home Government.

Sir M. Hicks-Beach, the Colonial Secretary, in a despatch dated the 3rd of July, 1879, informed the Governor-General that, in the removal of a Lieutenant-Governor from office, he ought to act by and with the advice of his ministers, who were responsible for the peace and good government of the Dominion to Parliament, to which the cause of removal had to be communicated. At the same time the Governor-General was requested to ask his ministry to review the case, as the spirit and intention of the B. N. A. Act 1867 required that tenure of office should as a rule endure for five years, and that the power of removal should only be exercised for grave cause.

The despatch was communicated to the ministry, who adhered to their previous decision, and by an order in Council, dated July 25, the Lieutenant-Governor was removed from office.

Disallow-ance of Provincial Bills.
By the British North America Act 1867[1] any Act passed by a provincial Legislature may be disallowed by the Governor-General within one year after its enactment. This power of disallowance is only exercised by the Governor on the advice of his ministers[2].

The course pursued in regard to all provincial Acts is governed by the principles laid down in a memorandum

[1] ss. 56, 90.
[2] Can. Sess. Pap. 1877, No. 89. See also Ib. 1876, No. 116 and Ib. 1877, No. 89.

drawn up by Sir J. A. Macdonald, the Minister of Justice in 1868, approved by the Privy Council[1], and communicated to the Legislatures of the different provinces.

"In deciding whether any acts of a Provincial Legislature should be disallowed or sanctioned the Government must not only consider whether it affects the interests of the whole Dominion or not; but also whether it be unconstitutional, whether it exceeds the jurisdiction conferred on Local Legislatures, and in cases where the jurisdiction is concurrent whether it clashes with the legislation of the General Parliament, as it is of importance that the course of local legislation should be interfered with as little as possible and the power of disallowance exercised with great caution—only in cases where the law and the general interests of the Dominion imperatively demand it, the undersigned recommends that the following course be pursued:— *Reasons for disallowance.*

"That on receipt by Your Excellency of the Acts passed in any Province they be referred to the Minister of Justice for report, and that he with all convenient speed do report as to those Acts which he considers free from objection of any kind: and if such report be approved by Your Excellency in Council that such approval be forthwith communicated to the Provincial Government.

"That he make a separate report or separate reports on those Acts which he may consider:—

1. As being altogether illegal or unconstitutional.

2. As illegal or unconstitutional in part.

3. In cases of concurrent jurisdiction, as clashing with the legislation of the general Parliament.

4. As affecting the interests of the Dominion generally: and that in such report or reports he gives his reasons for his opinions.

"That where a measure is considered only partially defective or where objectionable as being prejudicial to the general

---

[1] Can. Sess. Pap. 1869, No. 18.

interests of the Dominion, or as clashing with its legislation, communication should be had with the Provincial Government with respect to such measure, and that in such case the Act should not be disallowed if the general interests permit such a course until the Local Government has an opportunity of considering and discussing the objection taken, and the Local Legislature has also an opportunity of remedying the defects found to exist."

A report of the Privy Council in 1882, in regard to an Act of the Legislature of New Brunswick, will illustrate the course pursued.

In 1882 the Legislature of New Brunswick passed an Act authorizing the construction of a bridge over the river St. John, and indirectly power was given to interfere with the navigation of the river, so far as was absolutely necessary for the proper carrying on of the work. The Minister of Justice reported that the provincial Legislature had no power to interfere with the navigation of the river. Subsequent proceedings appear from the report.

Form of Report.

"Certified copy of a report of the Hon. Privy Council approved by His Excellency the Governor-General in Council on the 24 July, 1883.

"On a report dated the 25 July, from the acting Minister of Justice, stating with reference to the Act of the General Assembly of the province of New Brunswick passed in the year 1882, c. 69, that the grounds of objection to the Act in question are set forth at length in a report of the Minister of Justice dated the 15 Feb. 1883, and approved by Your Excellency in Council on the 6th March, 1883.

"That in conformity with the Order in Council referred to, the observations of the Minister of Justice in regard to this Act were communicated to the Lieutenant-Governor of New Brunswick for the information of his Government.

"That the attention of the Lieutenant-Governor has since been called to the previous communications had with him on the subject with a view to ascertain whether any legislation was had during the last session of the General Assembly in regard to c. 69 of 1882, and a reply had been received from the Lieutenant-Governor enclosing a memorandum of his Executive Council passed in a Council on the 30th January ult., stating that no amendment has been made in the Act nor is it in contemplation to make any amendment thereto.

"That there is no object any longer deferring action in this matter.

"The Minister recommends that under these circumstances, and for the reasons communicated in the first mentioned report, that the Act of the General Assembly of the Province of New Brunswick, passed in the year 1882, c. 69, and entitled 'an Act to incorporate the Fredericton and St Mary's Bridge Company' be disallowed; the Committee advise that the Act be disallowed accordingly."

The power of disallowance has been exercised in a comparatively small number of cases. Of the 6000 Acts passed by the provincial legislatures up to 1882 only 33 have been disallowed, viz. in Ontario 5, Quebec 2, Nova Scotia 5, Manitoba 7, British Columbia 12[1]. That the Dominion government are conscious that the power of disallowance ought to be exercised with great care and caution is evidenced by the report of the Privy Council on the disallowance of certain Acts of Manitoba in 1885.

Bills seldom disallowed.

"The Committee, whilst concurring in the report of the Minister of Justice and humbly advising your Excellency to disallow each and every of the said Acts, desire to record the expression of their constant anxiety that the action of the legislatures of the several provinces of the Dominion should be interfered with under the power of disallowance reserved to your Excellency in Council by the British North America Act 1867 as seldom as possible: but that, as in the case of these Acts, the declared policy of parliament adopted for

---

[1] Can. Sess. Pap. 1882, No. 141.

the common weal is set at naught, and local legislation enacted leading indirectly, and directly too, to its frustration, the Committee of the Privy Council conceive that they are compelled by their duty to Parliament, humbly to advise your Excellency to use the power in question[1]."

Disputes regarding disallowance. It is in regard to Acts coming under the fourth class referred to in the report of Sir J. A. MacDonald above quoted, viz. Acts affecting the interests of the Dominion generally, that difficulties have arisen and the governor's veto has been challenged. In 1881 an Act of the Legislature of Ontario was disallowed on the ground that it violated private rights without making any adequate compensation. The Government of Ontario protested, and maintained, that no Act should be disallowed which it was legally competent for a provincial legislature to pass[2]. More recently the legislature of Manitoba passed several Acts authorizing the construction of railways in the province with the object of opening up communication with the United States, and these Acts were disallowed as conflicting with the settled policy of the Dominion embodied in the agreement with the Pacific Railway, viz. that for 20 years no line should be authorized to within 15 miles of latitude 49[3] or south of the Pacific Railway except such line runs south-west.

Form of disallowance. The disallowance of an Act is notified in a form as follows :—

GOVERNMENT HOUSE, OTTAWA,
24 *July*, 1883.

" Present, His Excellency the Governor-General in Council.
" Whereas the Lieutenant-Governor of the province of New Brunswick has reported that the Legislative Council and General Assembly of that province did, on the 6th April, 1882, pass an Act which has been transmitted, intituled as follows:

[1] Can. Sess. Pap. 1885, No. 29, p. 44.
[2] Can. Sess. Pap. 1882, No. 149 a.
[3] Can. Sess. Pap. 1882, No. 166, and see *post*, c. xx.

"an Act to incorporate the Fredericton and St Mary's Bridge Company."

And whereas the said Act has been laid before the Governor-General in Council, together with a report from the acting Minister of Justice, recommending that the said Act should be disallowed, His Excellency the Governor General has thereupon this day been pleased by and with the advice of the Queen's Privy Council for Canada to declare his disallowance of the said Act and the same is disallowed accordingly. Whereof the Lieutenant-Governor of the Province of New Brunswick, and all other persons whom it may concern, are to take notice and govern themselves accordingly."

RESPONSIBILITY OF THE GOVERNOR-GENERAL.

The Governor-General is not responsible to the Dominion Parliament for either his conduct or his policy: all such responsibility must be assumed by his ministers under whose advice he is presumed to act. It would therefore be unconstitutional for a colonial legislature to pass a vote of censure upon a governor unless indeed as preliminary to an address to the Crown to remove him[1]. *To the Colony.*

The Governor-General is however responsible to the Crown, which may remove him, and to the Imperial Parliament, which may pass judgment on his acts. In 1866 the Governor of Victoria, Sir Charles Darling, was recalled on the ground that he had departed from a rigid adherence to the law, in collecting duties, in contracting a loan and in paying salaries without the sanction of law. The course pursued by the Colonial Secretary was fully approved by the Imperial Government[2]. *To the Crown and Parliament.*

Though the Governor of a Colony represents the Sovereign for many purposes, and exercises all the prerogative powers conferred either on the office by letters patent or on himself by *To Law.*

[1] Todd, p. 41.   [2] Ib. p. 105.

For State
Acts.

statute, and by the Instructions accompanying his Commission, yet he does not enjoy the privilege of complete exemption from legal liability. For all acts done under and within the limits of the authority confided to him the representative of the Sovereign is protected, "because in doing them he is the servant of the Crown and is exercising its sovereign authority[1];" and hence, where an action was brought against the Lord Lieutenant of Ireland for an alleged illegal seizure of property, the Irish Court of Common Pleas held, that as the act complained of was an act of state done by the Lord Lieutenant as such, the action would not lie[2].

On this principle the Governor of a Colony may be justified in case of rebellion, or exceptional disturbance, in resorting to a proclamation of martial law, i.e. in assuming absolute power and exercising it by military force, but such power must be exercised bonâ fide for the purpose of maintaining the safety of the colony and with reasonable moderation under the circumstances. Any abuse of such power will render the governor criminally and civilly liable[3].

For Acts
not within
his
authority.

For acts which are beyond the authority confided to him the Governor of a colony is responsible. "Such acts though the Governor may assume to do them as Governor cannot be considered as done on behalf of the Crown nor to be in any proper sense acts of State. When questions of the kind arise it must necessarily be within the province of municipal Courts to determine the true character of the acts done by a Governor, though it may be that when it is established that the particular act in question is really an act of state policy done under the authority of the Crown, the defence is complete and the Court can take no further cognizance of it[4]."

---

[1] Per P. C. in *Musgrave* v. *Pulido*, 5 App. Cas. 102, 49 L. J. P. C. 20.

[2] *Luby* v. *Lord Wodehouse*, 17 Ir. Com. L. R. 618.

[3] See *Wright* v. *Fitzgerald*, 27 St. Tr. 765. Report of *R.* v. *Eyre* by Finlason: Broom's Constitutional Law, 2nd Ed. p. 653.

[4] P. C. in *Musgrave* v. *Pulido*, 5 App. Cas. 102, 49 L. J. P. C. 20.

For acts not within his authority[1] civil or criminal[2] proceedings may be taken. By the 11 & 12 Will. III. c. 12, criminal proceedings are to be tried in the Court of King's Bench.

In the following chapter the circumstances under which the Governor-General is bound in exercising his legal powers to follow the advice of his Ministers will be more fully discussed.

[1] *Hill* v. *Bigge*, 3 Moo. P. C. 465. *Fabrigas* v. *Mostyn*, 20 St. Tr. 81 ; Cowper, 161.

[2] *R.* v. *Wall*, 28 St. Tr. 51.

CHAPTER XVI.

THE PRIVY COUNCIL.

THE B. N. A. Act, s. 11 provides for the appointment of a Council to aid and advise the Governor-General in the government of Canada. This Council corresponds to the Cabinet in England and is styled the Queen's Privy Council for Canada. A distinction is growing up in Canada between Privy Councillors, who are members of the Cabinet and Honorary Privy Councillors, who are not in the Cabinet, inasmuch as by command of the Queen, a Privy Councillor after he retires from office is entitled to be termed " Honourable " for life. Strictly speaking however these " honorary " members are not in law members of the Council.

Number.   The Privy Council in 1887 consisted of 14 members, viz.:

The President of the Council.
The Secretary of State.
The Minister of the Interior.
The Minister of Justice.
The Minister of Marine and Fisheries.
The Postmaster-General.
The Minister of Public Works.
The Minister of Railways and Canals.
The Minister of Finance.
The Minister of Customs.
The Minister of Militia and Defence.
The Minister of Agriculture.
The Minister of Inland Revenue.
One Minister without portfolio.

In 1887 Acts[1] were passed by the Canadian Parliament for the re-organization of certain departments. Under these Acts a department of Trade and Commerce presided over by a minister is to be organized : the departments of Customs and Inland Revenue are to be consolidated : and power is given to appoint a Solicitor-General.

The members of the Council are chosen by the Governor-General and may be removed by him[2]. No legal restrictions are placed on his choice, and the number of the Council is not limited. How chosen.

In practice the Governor-General in appointing Privy Councillors is guided by several important constitutional rules. The members chosen are selected from that party which possesses the confidence of the legislature, more especially of the House of Commons. The leading member of that party is requested by the Governor-General to form a ministry, and the Governor-General accepts as members of the Council those selected by him. The councillors usually have seats in the Upper or Lower House but the majority belong to the House of Commons.

There are some points in which the constitutional practice is different in Canada from what it is in England. The claims of the several provinces to representation in the Cabinet are sometimes recognised, and in the first Privy Council five representatives were assigned to Ontario, four to Quebec, two to Nova Scotia and two to New Brunswick.

Again the Attorney-General acts as Minister of Justice and sits in the Cabinet. Arguments have been brought forward in Canada and in other colonies to shew that the office ought to be non-political[3], but the necessity of having some one in the Cabinet having a special knowledge of law and of the Constitution has been so much felt in Canada, that the Attorney-General is not merely retained in the The Attorney-General.

---

[1] 50 & 51 Vic. 10. Ib. c. 11.   [2] B. N. A. Act, s. 11.   [3] Todd, p. 45.

Cabinet, but is often called upon to take the position of premier. As a rule he does not take private practice.

Each member presides over a department. To each member of the Privy Council it is usual to assign the administration of a department. But in Canada as in England there may be a minister not holding a portfolio. All the heads of Departments are not necessarily members of the Cabinet. In 1867 the number of Privy Councillors was thirteen, but since then the number has frequently varied owing to re-organization of departments.

Salary. Each Minister receives a salary of 7000 dollars per annum, and the member of the Council who holds the position of Prime Minister receives an additional sum of 1000 dollars per annum[1].

Vacation of seat on appointment. On being appointed a Privy Councillor a Senator does not vacate his seat, but a member of the House of Commons does so though he is eligible for re-election[2].

In its first session the Dominion Parliament, in order to preserve the independence of its members, re-enacted a previous act[3], disqualifying all persons holding any office under the Crown to which a salary was attached[4] from sitting in either house. Members accepting seats in the Council did not come under this rule, but they were required to be re-elected[5]. A further act was passed in 1878 in which the same principle was laid down[6]. The eligibility for re-election of a member of the Privy Council was affirmed, and it was provided in general terms that nothing in the statute should render ineligible any person holding any Cabinet office, or any office thereafter to be created to be held by a member of the Privy Council and entitling him to be a minister of the Crown, or should disqualify him from sitting or voting in the House of Commons, provided he be elected while holding such office[7].

A minister who resigns one office and accepts another

---

[1] R. S. C. c. 4, s. 3.   [2] R. S. C. c. 11, s. 9.
[3] 20 Vic. c. 22.   [4] 31 Vic. c. 25.   [5] 7 Vic. c. 65.
[6] 41 Vic. c. 5.   [7] See R. S. C. c. 11, s. 9.

within one month after his resignation does not vacate his seat, unless the ministry to which he belonged has resigned and a new administration has been formed.

It is now the rule that, on a change of ministry, all *Resignation.* outgoing ministers should resign their seats or be removed, as it is not deemed expedient that retiring ministers should retain a seat in the Council as in England, but ex-ministers have a special precedence within the Dominion and are styled " Honourable " for life[1].

Functions of the Council.

The functions of the Privy Council as regards the Governor-General are governed by two leading ideas.

First: In all prerogative matters and matters in which Imperial interests are concerned, the Governor-General, though bound to pay every consideration to the advice of his Ministers, is not bound to follow it.

Secondly: In all other matters the Governor-General is expected to follow and adopt their advice.

1. *As regards Legislation.*

(1) *Initiation of Legislation.* Two classes of legislation *Legislative Powers.* require to be distinguished, (*a*) Money bills, (*b*) Ordinary legislation.

(*a*) Bills, involving the imposition of a tax or the *Money Bills.* appropriation of the revenues, require to be recommended to the House of Commons by the Governor-General[2], and in exercising that statutory power the Governor-General adopts the constitutional practice of consulting his ministry.

(*b*) Though any bill, except a money bill, may be intro- *Other Bills.* duced into either House by any member, in Canada, as in England, the Executive controls legislation. By the standing

---

[1] Todd, pp. 42, 231.   [2] B. N. A. Act 1867, s. 54.

orders, Government measures take precedence on certain days and when necessary the Government take the whole time of the House for their own bills. The result is that Government bills have a much better chance of becoming law than have bills of private members. For all Government bills the Ministry is responsible.

Summoning Parliament.

(2) *Summoning, proroguing, and dissolving Parliament.* The Dominion Parliament is required to meet every year[1]; in appointing the time of meeting the Governor-General is guided by the advice of his Ministers. The prorogation or dissolution of Parliament being an exercise of prerogative power, the Governor-General is not bound to follow their advice. In discharging the responsibility of deciding in a particular case whether a dissolution should be granted, the Governor of a Colony "will of course pay the greatest attention to any representations that may be made to him by those who at the time are his constitutional advisers: but if he should feel himself bound to take the responsibility of not following his ministers' recommendation there can, I apprehend, be no doubt that both law and practice empower him to do so[2]."

Previous to the Confederation in 1858 the Governor of the Province of Canada declined to grant a dissolution at the request of the ministry on the grounds that a new election had lately taken place, that some measures of great importance required to be passed, and that an election would be a great inconvenience to the Province[3]. Lord Mulgrave, Governor of Nova Scotia, refused a dissolution in 1860, as he thought it was neither expedient nor for the public convenience that a dissolution should take place the year after a general election[4].

---

[1] B. N. A. Act, s. 20.
[2] Despatch of Sir M. Hicks Beach to Governor of New Zealand, quoted in Todd, p. 547.
[3] Todd, p. 528.   [4] Ib. p. 537.

(3) *Assent to Bills.* The position of the Ministry in regard to the Governor-General's assent to bills has been already referred to. The Governor-General is bound, as representing the Crown, to exercise his own discretion unfettered by any advice he may receive from his Ministers, though in practice he follows such advice.

Assent to Bills.

2. *As regards the Administration.*

The Ministry, as we have pointed out, is, unlike the English Cabinet, known to the law. The duty of the Council is stated in the Act of Union to be to "aid and advise in the government of Canada." It "aids" in the government by each member taking charge of the administration of a department, and it "advises" by suggesting to the Governor-General the course he should pursue under given circumstances.

Administrative Powers.

The Union Act and Instructions specify certain matters that are to be transacted by the Governor-General in Council or after receiving the advice of the Council, viz :—

Powers of Governor-General in Council.

1. The appointment of Lieutenant-Governors of Provinces[1].

2. The exercise of the prerogative of pardon[2].

3. The exercise of all powers which at the Union were vested in the Governors of the Provinces with the advice of the respective Executive Councils thereof[3].

4. The hearing of any Appeal under section 93 regarding the rights and privileges of the Protestant or Roman Catholic minority of the Queen's Subjects in a Province in relation to Education.

The administrative powers conferred on the Governor in Council by Canadian statutes are very numerous. Such powers are exercised by Orders in Council published in the Canadian Gazette and printed as a rule with the statutes for the year.

[1] B. N. A. Act, s. 58.   [2] See *ante*, p. 170.
[3] B. N. A. Act, s. 12.

In all matters relating to administration, such as routine business, the appointment of officials or the superintendence of state departments, the Governor-General when his concurrence is desired is expected to act on the advice of his Ministers.

3.   As regards the Provinces.

Privy Council and the Provinces.

The relation of the Privy Council to the Provinces is of importance as regards

(1)   the appointment and removal of Provincial Governor, and

(2)   the disallowance of Provincial bills.

By the B. N. A. Act, s. 58 the Lieutenant-Governors of the Provinces are to be appointed by the Governor-General in Council, but as regards their tenure of office the 59th section states that "a Lieutenant-Governor shall hold office during the pleasure of the Governor-General" without making any reference to the Council, though the cause of his removal is to be communicated to the Senate and House of Commons. The Letellier case, as has been stated, decided that the Governor-General is bound to follow the advice of his ministers as to the removal of a Lieutenant-Governor.

Disallowance of Provincial Acts.

As regards the disallowance of Provincial Acts the effect of sections 56 and 90 is to vest the power of disallowance in the Governor-General in Council. Though in practice the Governor-General invariably decides the allowance or disallowance on the advice of his ministers, the right of acting independently has been claimed for him by at least two Colonial Secretaries. In 1873 the Earl of Kimberley in a despatch referring to the proposed disallowance of certain New Brunswick Acts, said "this is a matter in which you must act on your own individual discretion and on which you cannot be guided by the advice of your responsible ministers." The Earl of Carnarvon, who succeeded Lord Kimberley as Colonial Secretary, took a similar view. The Canadian ministry, on the

other hand, strongly maintained that the power in question
was vested in the "Governor-General in Council," and that
his ministers were responsible to the Dominion Parliament
for the exercise of the power[1].

MEETINGS OF THE COUNCIL.

In the early days of responsible government in Canada Meetings
the Governor used to debate with his ministers in Council, of Council.
but this irregular proceeding was soon abandoned and the
ministers now discuss all questions of policy in private[2].
"The practice in Canada," says Mr Todd[3], "for a number of
years has been that the business in Council is done in the
absence of the Governor. On very exceptional occasions the
Governor may preside: but these would occur only at
intervals of years and would probably be for the purpose
of taking a formal decision on some extraordinary matter and
not for deliberation thereon. The mode in which business is
done is by report to the Governor of the recommendations of
the Council sitting as a Committee, sent to the Governor for
his consideration, discussed when necessary between the
Governor and the premier and made operative by being
marked 'approved' by the Governor."

RESPONSIBILITY.

Ministers are responsible to the Crown and to the Canadian Responsi-
Parliament to the same extent and in the same manner Council.
as English ministers are to the Crown and to the English
Parliament. "The responsibility of the administration for
all Acts of Government is absolute and unqualified. But it
is essentially a responsibility to the legislature and especially
to the popular chamber[4]."

---

[1] For a summary of discussion, see Todd, 335.
[2] Todd, p. 37.   [3] Ib.
[4] Todd, p. 39.

CHAPTER XVII.

The Dominion Administration.

The Administration and Government is carried on by means of fifteen departments of State exclusive of the office of the High Commissioner. All the departments are presided over by a Cabinet Minister, but two of them, viz. that charged with Public Printing and Stationery and the department of Indian affairs, are placed each under the charge of a Minister who is at the head of some other department.

Officers, how appointed.

Appointment of Officers. The Head of the Department is assisted in his duties by a Deputy Head, a chief clerk, clerks, messengers, and other employés. The number of officers and employés required for the working of a department is determined by the Governor-General in Council, but a clerkship cannot be established unless the Deputy Head reports that such an officer is necessary for the proper performance of the duties of the department, and the Head concurs in such report, and the salary has been voted by Parliament.

Civil Service Act. The appointment of all departmental officers and servants other than the Head is regulated by the Civil Service Act[1]. The Civil Service constituted by that Act includes all persons employed in the several departments of the Execu-

[1] R. S. C. c. 17.

tive Government of Canada and in the office of the Auditor-General, other than Heads of Departments and persons employed in the North-West Territories.

The Deputy Head is appointed by the Governor-General in Council and holds office during pleasure, but if a Deputy Head be removed the reasons for such removal must be laid before Parliament within the first fifteen days of the next session[1]. *Deputy Head.*

The duties of the Deputy Head are to oversee and direct, subject to the directions of the Minister, the officers, clerks and employés in the department and to have the general control of the business[2].

All appointments below that of Deputy Head in any department are as a rule made after an examination. *Other appointments.*

Two kinds of examinations are held:

(1)   The "civil service preliminary examination" which qualifies for the lower appointments such as messenger, porter, &c.

(2)   The "qualifying examination" which qualifies for a third-class clerkship.

Certain persons may be appointed to offices without examination, viz. city postmasters: inspectors, collectors and preventive officers in the customs: inspectors of weights and measures: deputy collectors and preventive officers in the Inland Revenue[3]. *Where no examination required.*

When a vacancy occurs in any department, the Head selects from the list of qualified candidates a person fitted for the vacant place. The person selected serves a probationary term of six months, after which period, if it appear that he is competent to discharge the duties of the office, he receives a permanent appointment. If rejected during the probationary period another is chosen in his stead[4].

Promotion as a rule takes place after a special examina- *Promotion.*

---

[1] R. S. C. c. 17, s. 11.   [2] Ib. s. 13.
[3] Ib. s. 37.   [4] Ib. s. 35.

tion in subjects best adapted to test the fitness of the candidates for the vacant office. The Head of the Department in selecting is to choose "the person whom he considers best fitted for the office having due reference to any special duties incident to the office, to the qualifications and fitness shown by the candidates respectively during their examination and to the record of their previous conduct in the service."

In the case of certain professional men such as barristers, attorneys, architects, actuaries, land surveyors, draughtsmen, engineers, military or civil officers of artillery in the Militia Department and graduates of a Royal Military College, the examination may be dispensed with on a report from the Deputy Head concurred in by the Head[1].

Probation.
Every promotion is subject to not less than six months probation and at any time during the first year the Head may reject the person promoted[2].

Oath of Office.
The Deputy Head and all officers, chief clerks, clerks, messengers, sorters and packers are required to take the oath of allegiance as well as the following oath.

"I (A. B.) solemnly and sincerely swear that I will faithfully and honestly fulfil the duties which devolve upon me as ———— and that I will not ask, or receive, any sum of money, services, recompense, matter, or thing whatsoever directly or indirectly in return for what I have done or may do in the discharge of any of the duties of my said office except my salary or what may be allowed me by law or by order of the Governor in Council."

The clerk of the Privy Council and all clerks under him and any officer of whom the Governor-General requires the same take the above oath with the following addition:—

"And that I will not without due authority in that behalf disclose or make known any matter or thing which comes to my knowledge by reason of my employment as ————."

_____

[1] R. S. C. c. 17, s. 4.   [2] Ib. s. 43.

The Departments of State are at present as follows, but provision has been made by two recent Acts, 50 and 51 Vic. cc. 10 and 11, for consolidating the Departments of Customs and of Inland Revenue in one, to be placed under the Minister of Trade and Commerce or under a Minister of Finance :—

Departments of State.

1. Secretary of State.
2. Public Printing and Stationery.
3. Interior.
4. Inland Revenue.
5. Customs.
6. Finance.
7. Public Works.
8. Railways and Canals.
9. Post-Office.
10. Justice.
11. Agriculture.
12. Marine and Fisheries.
13. Militia and Defence.
14. Indian Affairs.
15. High Commissioner.

1. DEPARTMENT OF SECRETARY OF STATE.

This department was constituted by the 31 Vic. c. 42. It is presided over by the Secretary of State, who is assisted in the discharge of his duties by an Under-Secretary.

The department has charge of the state correspondence and keeps all state records and papers not specially transferred to other departments.

General Duties.

A special branch of the department called the Register Branch is charged with the registration of all writs of summons, proclamations, commissions, letters patent, letters patent of land, writs and other instruments and documents issued under the Great Seal, and all bonds, warrants of

Register Branch.

M.   13

extradition, warrants for the removal of prisoners, leases, releases, deeds of sale, surrenders and all other instruments requiring registration.

The Secretary of State is Registrar-General, but the Deputy Registrar may sign and certify the registration of all instruments and documents required to be registered and of copies thereof.

2. DEPARTMENT OF PUBLIC PRINTING AND STATIONERY.

Up to 1866 the supplying of stationery to the different departments of state fell within the duties of the Secretary of State, but by the 49 Vic. c. 22 a new department was constituted to deal specially with printing and the supply of stationery.

The department is presided over by the Secretary of State or by such other member of the Privy Council as the Governor-General in Council shall direct. The Minister is assisted in his duties by the Queen's Printer, who is Deputy Head, by a Superintendent of printing and by a Superintendent of stationery.

Duties. The following matters must always be transacted through this department :—

1. Printing, stereotyping or electrotyping, lithography or binding work, required for the use of the Senate, the House of Commons, and the several departments of state.

2. The purchase and distribution of all paper, books and all other articles of stationery.

3. The distribution and sale of all books or publications issued by order of either House or of any department.

4. The auditing of all accounts for advertising required for the public service.

Printing. All printing, electrotyping, stereotyping, lithography and binding required for the service of the Parliament or Government of Canada is done at the Government Printing-office at Ottawa under the direction of the Superintendent of printing appointed by the Governor-General in Council.

A branch of the department called the Stationery Office Station is under the management of the Superintendent of stationery, cry. an official appointed by the Governor-General in Council. He is authorized to purchase all paper or stationery required for printing, or for Parliament, or for the departments. In the case of paper necessary for Parliamentary printing, or for printing either the Canada Gazette or the departmental reports, purchases are made in accordance with contracts entered into, after tenders have been called for. In other cases the purchases are made by the Superintendent after approval by the Minister or the Queen's Printer.

The Superintendent of stationery supplies all articles of stationery to the different departments of state upon requisition signed by the Deputy Head, and to either House of Parliament upon the requisition of a Clerk of the House.

He also has charge of both the sale of all official publications and the distribution of all public documents and papers. All moneys received by him are paid over to the Consolidated Fund.

3. DEPARTMENT OF THE INTERIOR.

In 1879 a portion of the duties, up to that year performed by the Department of Public Works, was assigned to a new department called the Department of the Interior[1], to be presided over by the Minister of the Interior.

The statutory duties assigned to the department are :—

(1) The management and control of the affairs of the Duties. North-West Territories. The grant of a constitution to these Territories has to a large extent relieved the department of this duty.

(2) The control and management of all Crown lands being the property of the Dominion, including those known as ordnance and admiralty lands, and all other public lands

[1] 36 Vic. c. 4.

excepting (1) those either under the control of the Department of Public Works or that of Militia and Defence, and (2) Marine Hospitals and Lighthouses, and lands connected therewith, and (3) St Paul's, Sable and Portage Islands.

Geological Survey. A Geological and Natural History Survey Office is attached to the department[1]. This branch is in charge of the Director of the Geological Survey, who is assisted by the necessary officials. The objects of the Survey are "to elucidate the geology and mineralogy of Canada, and to make a full and scientific examination of the various strata, soils, ores, coals, oils, and mineral waters and of its recent *fauna* and *flora*, so as to afford to the mining, metallurgical and other interests of the country correct and full information as to its character and resources."

Duties of Persons in Charge. The persons in charge of the Survey are required

1. To collect, classify and arrange such specimens as are necessary to ensure a complete and exact knowledge of the mineralogical resources of the several provinces and territories of Canada; to carry on palæontological investigations; to study and report upon the *fauna* and *flora* of Canada, and to make such other researches as will best tend to ensure the carrying into effect the object and purpose of the Act.

2. To collect the necessary materials for a Canadian Museum of Natural History, Mineralogy and Geology.

3. To report from time to time their proceedings, and to furnish proper maps and diagrams, drawings and collections of specimens to illustrate the same.

Yearly Report. Every year the Director is required to make a full report to the Minister of the proceedings and work of the Survey during the preceding year.

4. DEPARTMENT OF INLAND REVENUE.

This department was constituted by the 31 Vic. c. 49. It is presided over by the Minister of Inland Revenue, who

---

[1] R. S. C., c. 23.

is assisted by (1) a commissioner and an assistant commissioner, who hold office during pleasure and perform such duties as may be assigned to them by the Governor-General or by the Minister[1], and (2) certain other officers appointed by the Governor-General.

The duties assigned to the department by statute are defined to be:— Duties.

(1) The control and management of

    a. the collection of all duties of Excise,

    b. the collection of stamp duties and the preparation and issue of stamps and stamped paper, except postage stamps,

    c. all internal taxes,

    d. standard weights and measures.

(2) The administration of the laws affecting the cutting and measurement of timber, masts, spars, deals, staves, and other articles of a like nature, and the collection of slidage and boomage dues.

(3) The collection of bridge and ferry tolls and rents, and of tolls on the public canals and the control of matters incident thereto.

Provision has been made for the transfer of this department to the newly-created Department of Trade and Commerce[2].

5. DEPARTMENT OF CUSTOMS.

This department was established by the 31 Vic. c. 43, and is presided over by the Minister of Customs. The Minister is assisted by a commissioner and an assistant commissioner, who have such powers and perform such duties as may be assigned to them by the Governor-General or by the Minister.

The department has the control and management of Duties. the collection of customs, duties and all matters incident

[1] R. S. C., c. 31.   [2] See *ante*, p. 193.

thereto, and of the officers and persons employed in that service[1].

By the 50 and 51 Vic. c. 11 this department is to be transferred to the Minister of Trade and Commerce or to the Minister of Finance[2].

6. DEPARTMENT OF FINANCE.

This department was constituted by the 32 and 33 Vic. c. 4, and has the supervision, control and direction of all matters relating to such financial affairs, public accounts, revenue and expenditure of the Dominion, as are not or in so far as they are not by law or by order of the Governor in Council assigned to any other department of the Civil Service, as well as such other duties as may be from time to time assigned to it by the Governor in Council.

By a subsequent Act[3] the office of Receiver-General was abolished and the duties of that official were transferred to the Minister of Finance.

Two important branches of the department are the Treasury Board and the Audit Office.

The Treasury Board.
The Treasury Board, formed of the Minister of Finance, and five Ministers nominated by the Governor in Council[4], acts as a committee of the Privy Council in all matters of finance which are referred to it by the Council or to which it thinks it necessary to call the attention of the Council. It is empowered to direct that books and accounts be kept by any officer engaged in the revenue department, and to prescribe how accounts are to be kept by the various branches of the public service[5].

It directs how each department is to prepare its appropriation account.

The Audit Office.
The Audit Office is under the charge of the Auditor-General, who is appointed by the Governor-General under the

---

[1] R. S. C. 1886, c. 32, s. 5.   [2] See ante, p. 193.   [3] 42 Vic. c. 7.
[4] 50 and 51 Vic. c. 13.   [5] R. S. C., c. 28.

Great Seal. The Auditor-General's assent is required before any cheque can be issued for the payment of public moneys. He is required to audit the state accounts every year, and may be called on by the Minister of Finance to audit the accounts forming the Consolidated Revenue Fund, the accounts current with the banks and fiscal agents of Canada, the accounts relating to the issue of loans, the accounts with the Indian tribes, the accounts with the provinces, and the accounts with the Government of the United Kingdom.

The Deputy of the Minister keeps the accounts with the financial agents of Canada in England, and with the bank or banks receiving or paying public moneys, and the accounts of moneys paid for interest on Canadian Stock, debentures or other Canadian securities[1]. He also classifies all appropriations of public moneys in the appropriation book, and enters the amount drawn on account of such appropriation, and generally keeps the public accounts of Canada. *Duties of the Deputy.*

The ordinary revenue of Canada is derived from various sources, and may be classified under the heads of (1) Taxation, (2) Other sources. The revenue raised by taxation consists solely of Customs and Excise duties, that from other sources consists of money derived from the post-office, Government railways and works, interest on investments &c. The income in the year 1887—8 amounted to 35,908,463 dollars. *The Revenue.*

Taxation.		$
	Customs	22,105,926
	Excise	6,071,486
		28,177,412
Other sources.	Public Works	3,556,100
	Dominion Lands	217,083
	Post-office	2,379,241
	Various	1,578,627
		35,908,463

The above revenue forms the Consolidated Fund out of

[1] R. S. C., c. 28, s. 5.

which is paid the ordinary expenditure. The charges on this
Fund in the year 1887—8 were as follows :—

	$
Charges for the Public Debt	11,105,981
Ordinary Expenditure	16,822,749
Collection of Revenue	8,789,764
	36,718,495

In addition to the above revenue and expenditure the
Dominion receives and expends a large amount of moneys
every year. This may be illustrated by the following table
for the year 1887—8.

Receipts.		*Expenditure.*	
	$	Ordinary Expendi-	$
Ordinary Revenue	35,908,463	ture	36,718,495
Loans	11,335,793	Redemption of Pub-	
Savings Bank	13,059,846	lic Debt	3,185,726
Investments	3,525,179	Savings Banks	12,521,064
Trust Funds (Indians		Railway Subsidies	1,027,041
and Widows)	294,038	Investments	5,200,769
Dominion Notes	1,189,482	Trust Funds (Indian)	276,230
Miscellaneous	2,715,114	Province Accounts	115,775
		Railways and Canals	2,798,704
		Public Works	963,778
		Transfers to Con-	
		solidated Fund	2,881,127
		Miscellaneous	2,339,206
	68,027,915		68,027,915

Payments
of Moneys.
When a sum of money is granted to Her Majesty by
resolution of the House of Commons or by Act of Parliament,
the Governor-General from time to time under his sign
manual, countersigned by a member of the Treasury Board,
authorizes and requires the Minister of Finance to issue out
of the moneys appropriated for defraying the expense of such
services and in the hands of the Receiver-General, the sums
required from time to time not exceeding the amount of the
sums so voted[1].

[1] R. S. C., c. 29, s. 29.

The Minister of Finance then causes to be issued in favour of the Deputy Head or other person connected with the departments or service charged with the expenditure credits on some bank authorized to receive the public moneys.

A statement of moneys drawn under such credits and the cheques paid by the banks is furnished to the Auditor-General, and the Minister of Finance and the Auditor-General if satisfied of the correctness of the statement, may request the Minister of Finance to cause cheques to be prepared to reimburse the bank for the advances: such cheques to be signed by the Minister of Finance and countersigned by the Auditor-General[1].

The Auditor-General must always satisfy himself, that no cheque issues for the payment of any public money, for which there is no direct parliamentary appropriation, and he is required to report to the Governor in Council any case, in which money is expended for any purpose, for which there is no legislative authority[2].

In three exceptional cases it is provided that a cheque may issue without the certificate of the Auditor-General that there is parliamentary authority for the expenditure :— *Exceptional Cases.*

1. Where a Law-officer of the Crown gives a written opinion that there is authority to issue the cheque.

2. Where special unforeseen cases during the recess of Parliament require expenditure for the public good, in which cases the Governor-General in Council issues a special warrant signed by himself for the issue of the amount required.

3. Where the Treasury Board after receiving a report from the Auditor-General and the Deputy Minister of Finance overrides the objection.

In all the above cases a report thereon must be laid before Parliament by the Auditor-General.

If the moneys are required for work performed or materials

---

[1] Ib. s. 30.   [2] Ib. s. 31.

supplied, no payment is to be authorized until the person in charge of such work or materials has certified to the Auditor-General that the work has been performed or the materials supplied[1].

In every case the moneys can be paid only out of the sum appropriated by Parliament for the specific purpose mentioned.

Consolidated Fund.

All the moneys and revenue over which the Parliament of Canada has power of appropriation form the Consolidated Fund; and it has been provided by statute that such moneys are to be appropriated in the following order:—(1) expenses of collection, (2) the interest on the public debt, (3) the salary of the Governor-General, (4) moneys borrowed in connexion with the Pacific Railway, (5) moneys borrowed in connexion with the Hudson Bay Co. and Rupert's Land, (6) moneys borrowed for Public Works, (7) salaries of the judges.

Accounts.

Each department of state is required to prepare an account of the moneys appropriated for the expenses of the department and of the moneys actually expended. After such account is audited by the Deputy Head or other person charged with the expenditure, it is transmitted to the Auditor-General, who again audits the account before it is laid before Parliament.[2]

In addition to the above accounts, the Minister of Finance prepares an account of all sums expended out of the Consolidated Fund for the financial year which ends on the 30th June: such account with the report of the Auditor-General thereon is laid before Parliament[3].

7. DEPARTMENT OF PUBLIC WORKS.

This department was constituted by the 31 Vic. c. 52. In 1879 some of its functions were transferred to the newly-created Department of the Interior. It is now regulated by the Public Works Act[4].

[1] R. S. C., s. 33. [2] Ib. c. 29. [3] Ib. [4] Ib. c. 36.

The Minister of Public Works is assisted by a Deputy, a Secretary, an Engineer and other officials.

The department has charge of the construction, manage- Duties.
ment and direction of all public works and property, except those transferred to a province or municipality or placed under some other department. No expenditure can be incurred without the sanction of Parliament except for repairs and alterations required by the necessities of the public service. As a rule tenders are to be invited for the execution of all works, and security is to be taken for the due performance of every contract.

The power to impose tolls on public works, to frame regulations for the use and protection of public buildings, and to transfer public roads and bridges to the local authorities, is vested in the Governor in Council, and not in the Minister.

The Secretary has the following statutory duties to per- The
form[1]:—   Secretary.

To keep separate accounts of the moneys appropriated for, and expended on, each public work.

To submit accounts to be audited.

To take charge of all plans, contracts, estimates, documents, and titles.

To keep proper accounts with each contractor employed.

To see all contracts properly drawn out and executed.

To prepare all certificates upon which a warrant is to issue.

To keep minutes of all proceedings of the department.

To prepare reports and to conduct under the direction of the Minister the correspondence of the department.

The Engineer is required[2] to prepare maps, plans and Engineer.
estimates for all public works to be constructed, altered or repaired; to report for the information of the Minister on any question relating to any such public work; to examine and

---

[1] Ib. s. 5.   [2] Ib. s. 6.

revise plans, estimates and recommendations of other engineers, architects, and officers touching any public work, and generally to advise the Minister on all engineering or architectural questions affecting any work.

Official Arbitrators.

By the Expropriation Act[1] very extensive powers are given to the Minister to take public lands required for any public work. The compensation to be paid for such land is fixed by official arbitrators appointed by the Governor[2].

8. DEPARTMENT OF RAILWAYS AND CANALS.

The Department of Railways and Canals was constituted by the 42 Vic. c. 7. The Minister of Railways and Canals presides over the department.

The Minister of Railways and Canals has the management, charge and direction of all Government railways and of all canals, and of works or property appertaining or incident thereto.

The powers and duties of the Minister in respect to railways and canals are practically the same as those of the Minister of Public Works regarding public works.

9. DEPARTMENT OF THE POST-OFFICE.

This department was established by the 31 Vic. c. 10, but it is now regulated by the Post-Office Act[3]. Previous to the Confederation each province managed its own postal system.

Officers.

The chief officers of the department are the Postmaster-General, the Deputy, and the Inspectors, who are all appointed by the Governor-General. Postmasters in cities and towns having permanent salaries are also appointed by the Governor-General, all other postmasters are appointed by the Postmaster-General.

The Post Master-General.

The powers of the Postmaster-General are very wide and

[1] R. S. C., c. 39.   [2] Ib. c. 40.   [3] Ib. c. 35.

varied. He is authorized by statute[1] to exercise the following powers :—

1. to establish and close post-offices and post routes,

2. to appoint postmasters, other than those appointed by the Governor-General, and other officers and servants, and to remove or suspend any postmaster or other officer or servant,

3. to enter into and enforce mail contracts,

4. to make regulations as to what is mailable matter; to restrict the weight and dimensions of letters and packets sent by post; and to prevent the sending of explosive, dangerous, contraband or improper articles, or obscene or immoral publications,

5. to establish rates of postage for mailable matter not being letters, and to prescribe the conditions on which such articles will be received,

6. to prepare and distribute postage stamps and stamped envelopes,

7. to make postal arrangements with other countries,

8. to make arrangements for refunding postage on H. M. Military or Naval Service,

9. to make regulations regarding money orders,

10. to make regulations regarding registered letters,

11. to decide what is to be decreed a letter,

12. to sue for money due,

13. to provide street boxes,

14. to grant licenses for sale of stamps,

15. to impose pecuniary penalties not exceeding $200 for contravention of regulations,

16. generally to make regulations for carrying on the work of the department.

In addition to the above powers relating to the ordinary business of a post-office the Postmaster-General has also power to establish a parcel post[2], and with the consent of the Governor-General a system of post-office savings banks[3].

---

[1] Ib. s. 9.   [2] Ib. s. 41.   [3] Ib. s. 65.

Inspec-
tors.

The statutory duties of the Inspectors are[1] to

a. superintend the performance of the mail service,

b. instruct new postmasters in their duties,

c. keep postmasters to their duty of rendering accounts and paying over moneys,

d. inspect every post-office from time to time,

e. inquire into complaints and suspected cases of misconduct,

f. and generally to do all they are required to do by
the Postmaster-General.

Postal
Union.

The Dominion entered into a postal agreement with the
United States in 1875 by which a common rate of postage
was adopted for the two countries, each country to return all
money collected. At the second Congress of the General
Postal Union held at Paris in May 1878, Canada was admitted into the Postal Union.

The Postal Union was in 1874 replaced by the Universal
Postal Union formed at Berne, which now embraces all
British Possessions except the Australian Colonies and South
Africa.

10. DEPARTMENT OF JUSTICE.

By the 31 Vic. c. 39 a Department of Justice was constituted to be presided over by the Minister of Justice, who
for the time being is to be *ex officio* Her Majesty's Attorney-
General for Canada. The Governor-General has power to
appoint a Deputy and, subject to the Civil Service Acts, to
appoint clerks and other officers in the department. A recent
Act 50 and 51 Vic. c. 14 has made provision for the appointment of a Solicitor-General to assist the Minister of Justice.

Duties of
Minister
as such.

The Minister of Justice as such is the official legal adviser
of the Government, and is required to advise the Crown upon
all matters referred to him by the Crown. It is his duty to
see that the administration of public affairs is in accordance

[1] R. S. C., s. 11.

with law, and to superintend all matters connected with the administration of justice in Canada and not falling within the jurisdiction of any province. He advises upon all legislative acts and proceedings of the Legislatures of the different provinces of Canada, and is charged with all duties assigned to him by the Governor-General in Council[1].

As Attorney-General his powers and duties are as follows:— *Duties as Attorney-General.*

(1) He is entrusted with the powers and charged with the duties, which by law or usage belong to the office of Attorney-General in England so far as the same powers and duties are applicable to Canada.

(2) He is entrusted with the powers and duties that by the laws of the several provinces belonged to the office of Attorney-General in each province up to the time when the British North America Act 1867 came into force, which laws under the provisions of such Act are administered and carried into effect by the Government of the Dominion.

(3) He has to advise the Heads of the several Departments of the Government upon all matters of law connected with such departments.

(4) He is charged with the settlement and approval of all instruments issued under the Great Seal of Canada.

(5) He has the superintendence of penitentiaries and of the prison system of the Dominion.

(6) He has the regulation and conduct of all litigation for or against either the Crown or any public department in respect of any subjects within the authority and jurisdiction of the Dominion.

(7) He is charged generally with such other duties as may at any time be assigned to him by the Governor-General.

A police force has been constituted for the North-West Territories, and at the present time it is under the control and management of the Minister of Justice. The force is *North-West Mounted Police.*

[1] R. S. C., c. 21.

limited to 1000 men, and all appointments are made by the Governor in Council. It is under the command of a commissioner and assistant commissioners, who exercise all the powers of stipendiary magistrates. The Lieutenant-Governor of Keewatin has the local disposition of the force in that district subject to any order of the Governor-General, and the Governor-General is authorised to make arrangements with any province for the employment of the force in such province[1].

11.   DEPARTMENT OF AGRICULTURE AND STATISTICS.

This department was constituted by the 31 Vic. c. 53 and is presided over by the Minister of Agriculture. He is assisted in carrying on the work of the department by a Deputy and a staff of officers and clerks appointed by the Governor-General.

The Minister. The duties and powers of the Minister extend to the execution of the laws of the Parliament of Canada and of the Orders of the Governor in Council relating as well to the following subjects as to the direction of all public bodies, officers and servants employed in the execution of such laws and orders[2]:—

1. Agriculture.
2. Immigration and Emigration.
3. Public Health and Quarantine.
4. Marine and Emigrant Hospitals of Quebec.
5. Arts and Manufactures.
6. Census Statistics and the registration of Statistics.
7. Patents of Invention[3].
8. Copyright[3].
9. Industrial Designs and Trade-marks[3].
10. Experimental Farm stations.

[1] See R. S. C., c. 45.   [2] Ib. c. 24.
[3] By the 50 & 51 Vic. c. 12, patents and copyrights may be transferred to the Department of the Secretary of State, and Industrial Designs and Trademarks to the new Department of Trade and Commerce.

Subject to the Minister, the Deputy has authority to The Deputy. oversee and direct the officers and servants of the department: he has such powers and duties as are assigned to him by the Governor in Council, and in the absence of the Minister may suspend any officer or servant who neglects or refuses to obey his directions[1].

12. DEPARTMENT OF MARINE AND FISHERIES.

This department was constituted by the 31 Vic. c. 57. It is presided over by the Minister of Marine and Fisheries, who is assisted by officers appointed by the Governor-General.

The department has, subject to the Acts of the Parliament Duties. of Canada and of the Provincial Legislatures, the control, management and supervision, as well as the execution, of laws regulating the following matters[2]:—

1. Sea, coast, and inland fisheries and the management, regulation and protection thereof and anything relating thereto.

2. Pilots and pilotage and decayed pilots' funds.

3. Beacons, buoys, lights, and lighthouses and their maintenance.

4. Harbours, ports, piers and wharves, steamers and vessels belonging to the Government of Canada, except gunboats or other vessels of war.

5. Harbour commissioners and harbour masters.

6. Classification of vessels and examination of, and granting certificates to, masters and mates and others in the merchant service.

7. Shipping masters and shipping officers.

8. Inspection of steamboats and boards of steamboat inspection.

9. Inquiries into the causes of shipwrecks.

[1] R. S. C. c. 24, s. 3. [2] Ib. c. 25.

10. Establishment, regulation, and maintenance of marine and seamen hospitals and care of distressed seamen.

11. Generally such Canadian matters as refer to marine and navigation.

Officers.

In order to discharge the above very varied duties the department has organized the following special offices or branches :—

A Board of Examiners for Masters and Mates.

A Board of Steamboat Inspectors.

A Board of Lights.

A Board of Fisheries.

A Board of River and Harbour Police.

A Meteorological Office.

13. DEPARTMENT OF MILITIA AND DEFENCE.

The department of Militia is now presided over by the Minister of Militia and Defence.

Duties of Minister.

The Minister is charged with and is responsible for the administration both of Militia affairs, including all matters involving expenditure, and of the fortifications, gunboats, ordnances, ammunition, arms, armouries, stores, munitions and habiliments of war belonging to Canada. The initiative in all Militia affairs involving expenditure belongs to him.

The Governor in Council may from time to time prescribe what duties he is to discharge.

Command-in-Chief.

In accordance with the provisions of the 15th section of the B. N. A. Act 1867 the Canadian Act[1] declares the Command-in-Chief of the land and naval Militia to be vested in Her Majesty or in the Governor-General as her representative. As a rule the Crown appoints a Major-General to take command of the forces.

Persons liable to serve.

All male inhabitants of Canada between the ages of 18 and 60, being British subjects, and not exempted or disquali-

[1] R. S. C. c. 41.

fied by law, are liable to serve in the Militia, but power is given to Her Majesty to require the services of all male inhabitants of the Dominion capable of bearing arms in case of a *levée en masse*[1].

The following persons between the ages of 18 and 60 are at all times exempt from enrolment and actual service[2]:— Persons exempt from Service.

> Judges of all Courts of Law.
>
> Clergy and Ministers of all denominations.
>
> Professors in Colleges, and Universities.
>
> Teachers in religious orders.
>
> Keepers of penitentiaries and asylums.
>
> Persons disabled by bodily infirmity.
>
> The only son of a widow being her only support.

Except in case of war, invasion or insurrection the following though enrolled are exempt from actual service :—

> Halfpay and retired officers.
>
> Sailors employed in their calling.
>
> Pilots during the season of navigation.
>
> Masters of public and common schools engaged in teaching.

Quakers or other persons, who from the doctrines of their religion are personally averse to bearing arms, are exempt under such regulations as the Governor in Council may prescribe.

In every case the exemption must be claimed by affidavit of the ground alleged for exemption, and such ground must be proved[3]. Claim of Exemption.

For military purposes Canada is divided into 12 military districts; each district into regimental and brigade divisions, and each regimental division into company divisions[4]. Division into Military Districts.

The captain of each company division has by actual inquiry at each house in his division to ascertain the persons liable to serve, and must compile a roll accordingly[5].

---

[1] Ib. s. 10.   [2] Ib. s. 11.   [3] Ib. s. 21.   [4] Ib. s. 16.   [5] Ib. s. 20.

Militia, how classified.

The men are divided into four classes[1] :—

1. Those between 18 and 30 who are unmarried or are widowers without children.

2. Those between 30 and 45 who are unmarried or are widowers without children.

3. Those between 18 and 45 who are married or are widowers with children.

4. Those between the age of 45 and 60.

Company, how made up.

When the Militia is called out, each company has to furnish its quota of the number fixed, and if a sufficient number of men do not volunteer the men enrolled in the first class settle by ballot who are to serve: if more than the whole number in the first class are required, then the second class ballot to make up the deficiency and so on[2].

Substitutes.

When a man is chosen by ballot, he may provide a substitute, and provided the substitute does not himself become liable[3] he remains exempt from service until his time again comes to serve.

The Active Militia and the Reserve.

The whole force is divided into[4]

1. The Active Militia, which is subdivided into the land force and the marine force.

    (a) The land force consists of corps raised by voluntary enlistment, or by ballot as above described.

    (b) The marine force is composed of seamen, sailors and persons whose usual occupation has been in a steam or sailing craft navigating the waters of the Dominion.

2. The Reserve Militia, which is composed of the whole of the men not serving in the Active Militia.

Period of Service.

For the Active Militia the period of service in time of peace is three years[5], in time of war it is one year[6].

The Reserve Militia may be called out every year by Her

---

[1] R. S. C. c. 41, s. 11.   [2] Ib. s. 30.   [3] Ib. s. 32.   [4] Ib. s. 12.
[5] Ib. s. 13.   [6] Ib. s. 80.

Majesty for a period of not less than eight days and not exceeding 16 days[1].

The Active Militia may be called out as follows :— Calling out Militia.

1. By Her Majesty in the case of war, invasion, or insurrection.

2. By the Lieutenant-Governor of Manitoba, if a notable disturbance of the peace or other emergency occurs in the North-West Territories or Keewatin.

3. The officer commanding any military district or division upon any sudden emergency of invasion or insurrection or imminent danger of either may call out the whole of the Militia under his command[2].

4. The officer in any district may call out the Active Militia under his command in aid of the civil power when a riot, disturbance of the peace or other emergency requiring such service occurs or is in the opinion of the civil authorities likely to occur[3].

5. The Active Militia may be called out also by order in Council to serve as guards of honour, as escorts, or as guards and sentries at the opening or closing of Parliament, to attend the Governor-General or any member of the Royal Family in Canada, or to guard armouries.

14. DEPARTMENT OF INDIAN AFFAIRS.

By the Act constituting a Department of Indian Affairs[4] the Minister of the Interior was made Superintendent of Indian Affairs, but a subsequent Act[5] repealed that provision, and enacted that the Superintendent of Indian Affairs should be either the Minister of the Interior or the head of some other department appointed for that purpose by Order in Council. The President of the Council is now (1887) the Superintendent.

---

[1] Ib. s. 59.   [2] Ib. s. 78.   [3] Ib. s. 31.   [4] 43 Vic. c. 28.
[5] 46 Vic. c. 6.

Indians in Canada fall into two classes, (1) Enfranchised Indians and (2) Unenfranchised Indians. Those of the former class practically enjoy the same rights and privileges as other subjects of the Crown in Canada, whilst those of the latter class possess a special status, that is, they have special rights and are under special disabilities.

Enfran- chised Indians. An enfranchised Indian is defined by the Indian Act as follows :—"Any Indian, his wife, or minor unmarried child who has received letters patent granting to him in fee simple any portion of the reserve which has been allotted to him or to his wife and minor children by the band to which he belongs, or any unmarried Indian who has received letters patent for an allotment of the reserve[1]."

The effect of enfranchisement is, that the person enfranchised is no longer deemed an Indian except as regards his right to participate in the annuities and interest moneys, rents and councils of the band to which he belongs.

The general management of all matters relating to Indians is placed under the control of this department. Subject to the provisions of the Indian Act the Superintendent locates Indians on reserves, removes trespassers, registers sales of land, decides disputes regarding descent of property, sees that bridges and roads are kept in repair, grants licences to cut timber, and grants certificates of enfranchisement.

In order to carry out the duties of the department the Superintendent is assisted by a Deputy, and the Governor-General has power to appoint Indian Commissioners and Assistant Indian Commissioners for Manitoba, the North-West Territories and British Columbia.

15. THE HIGH COMMISSIONER.

The High Commissioner for Canada is appointed by the Governor-General and holds office during pleasure[2].

---

[1] R. S. C. c. 43, s. 2 (j).   [2] Ib. c. 16.

His duties are[1]:—

1. To act as the resident agent of the Dominion in the United Kingdom and in that capacity to execute such powers and perform such duties as may from time to time be conferred upon or assigned to him by the Governor-General in Council.

2. To take charge of and supervise the Emigration officers and agencies in the United Kingdom under the Minister of Agriculture.

3. To carry out such instructions as he may from time to time receive from the Governor-General respecting the commercial, financial, and general interests of the Dominion in the United Kingdom and elsewhere.

The salary attached to the office is 10,000 dollars a year.

[1] R. S. C. c. 16, s. 2.

CHAPTER XVIII.

THE DOMINION JUDICATURE.

THE relation of the Dominion to the administration of Justice may be considered under three heads, (1) the establishment of Courts, and (2) the appointment of Judges, and (3) appeals to the Privy Council.

1. ESTABLISHMENT OF COURTS.

Powers under B. N. A. Act.

By section 101 of the B. N. A. Act 1862 the Parliament of Canada was authorized "from time to time to provide for the constitution, maintenance and organization of a general Court of Appeal for Canada and for the establishment of any additional courts for the better administration of the laws of Canada." And by section 41 power was given to the Parliament to provide for the trial of controverted elections. Under these provisions the following courts have been established, viz. the Supreme Court, the Court of Exchequer, Courts for the trial of controverted elections and a Maritime Court.

i. *The Supreme and the Exchequer Courts.*

In 1875 an Act was passed[1] establishing an Exchequer Court and a Supreme Court, which are now regulated by c. 135 of the Revised Statutes of 1886, and the 50 and 51 Vic. c. 16.

Court of Exchequer.

Under the latter Act the causes in the Exchequer Court are heard before one judge.

[1] 38 Vic. c. 11.

The Exchequer Court possesses an exclusive and a concurrent jurisdiction.

1. It has exclusive jurisdiction in,

(a) All cases in which relief is sought, which might in England be a subject of a suit or action against the Crown.

(b) Claims against the Crown for property taken for any public purpose.

(c) Claims against the Crown for damage to property.

(d) Claims against the Crown arising out of death or injury to person or property in any public work, resulting from the negligence of any officer or servant of the Crown acting within the scope of his duties or employment.

(e) Claims against the Crown arising under either any law of Canada or any regulation made by the Governor in Council.

(f) Every set-off, counterclaim, claim for damages or other demand on the part of the Crown against any person making a claim against the Crown.

2. The Court has a concurrent jurisdiction,

(a) In all cases relating to the revenue.

(b) In all cases in which at the instance of the Attorney-General it is sought to impeach any patent of invention or any patent, lease or other instrument respecting lands.

(c) In all cases where relief is sought against any officer of the Crown for anything done or omitted to be done in the performance of his duty.

(d) In all actions or suits in which the Crown is plaintiff or petitioner.

An appeal lies from the Exchequer Court to the Supreme Appeal. Court, if the actual amount in controversy exceeds 500 dollars, but where the amount does not exceed that sum

no appeal lies except the question (1) involves the validity
of an Act of Canada or of a Provincial Act, or (2) relates to
any fee of office, duty, rent, revenue or sum of money payable
to Her Majesty; or to any title to lands or tenements, annual
rents or such like matters or things where rights in future
might be bound, and even in these cases leave to appeal must
be obtained from a judge of the Supreme Court.

The Supreme Court. The Supreme Court consists of a Chief Justice and five
puisne justices, and exercises an appellate civil and criminal
jurisdiction throughout the Dominion.

In all final judgments, judgments upon special cases,
points reserved, motions for new trials, decrees in equity,
motions to set aside awards, proceedings for a writ of Habeas
Corpus, an appeal lies from a Supreme Provincial Court to
the Supreme Court of Canada.

It has also an appellate jurisdiction in criminal cases,
maritime causes from Ontario, controverted elections and
the winding-up of companies[1].

An appeal also lies to the Supreme Court from the
Exchequer Court[2].

Consultation of Court by Privy Council. In England the House of Lords has the power of consulting the judges; a similar power has been conferred on
the Canadian Privy Council. The Governor-General in
Council may refer to the Supreme Court for hearing or
consideration any matter which he thinks fit to refer, and the
Court is required to certify its opinion to the Governor in
Council.

The Senate and House of Commons are empowered to
refer to the Court or to any two judges thereof, any private
bill or petition for a private bill, and the Court is to examine
and report upon the same[3].

Controversies between Dominion and Provinces. In the case of those provinces that passed a law to such
effect, provision was made for conferring a special jurisdiction
on the Supreme and Exchequer Courts in controversies

[1] R. S. C. c. 135. ss. 23—31.   [2] Ib. s. 70.   [3] Ib. s. 38.

between the Dominion and a province, or between provinces, or relating to the validity of provincial laws.

"When the Legislature of any province forming part of Canada shall have passed an Act agreeing and providing that the Supreme Court and Exchequer Court or the Supreme Court alone shall have jurisdiction in any of the following cases—

"(1) Controversies between the Dominion of Canada and such province.

"(2) Controversies between such province and any other province or provinces which may have passed a like Act.

"(3) Suits, actions, or proceedings in which the parties thereto by their pleadings shall have raised the question of the validity of an Act of the Parliament of Canada when in the opinion of the judge of the court in which the same are pending such question is material.

"(4) Suits, actions, or proceedings in which the parties thereto by their pleadings shall have raised the question of the validity of an act of the Legislature of such province when in the opinion of the judge of the court in which the same are pending such question is material, then this section of the Act is to be in force in the class of cases in respect of which such Act may have been passed."

In (1) and (2) the proceedings are to be in the Court of Exchequer, with an appeal to the Supreme Court. In (3) and (4) the judge who decides that the question is material, is to order the case to be removed into the Supreme Court for the decision of such question[1].

British Columbia in 1882 passed an Act[2] to give these provisions force within the province, and Ontario and Nova Scotia have now passed similar Acts[3].

The process of the Supreme Court and of the Exchequer Court runs throughout Canada, and the provincial sheriffs of *Process of Court runs in the Provinces.*

---

[1] R. S. C. c. 135, ss. 72—74. [2] B. C. 45 Vic. c. 2.
[3] O. R. S. 1887, c. 42. N. S. R. S. 1884, c. 111.

counties are *ex officio* officers of the Supreme and Exchequer Courts.

" The process of the Supreme Court and the process of the Exchequer Court shall run throughout Canada and shall be tested in the name of the Chief Justice, or in case of a vacancy in the office of Chief Justice in the name of the senior puisne judge of the court, and shall be directed to the sheriff of any county or other judicial division into which any province is divided: and the sheriffs of the said respective counties or divisions shall be deemed to be taken to be *ex officio* officers of the Supreme and Exchequer Courts respectively and shall perform the duties and functions of sheriffs in connection with the said courts : and in any case when the sheriff is disqualified such process shall be directed to any of the coroners of the county or district[1]."

ii.   *Courts for the trial of Controverted Elections.*

An account has already been given of the provisions of the Act which assigns the trial of election petitions to certain courts of the provinces[2]. The judges of these courts when sitting for the purpose of trying election petitions form a Dominion and not a Provincial Court, and therefore it is within the power of the Dominion to prescribe the procedure to be observed.

iii.   *Maritime Court of Ontario.*

In 1877 the Dominion Parliament constituted a court of Maritime Jurisdiction for the province of Ontario.

The court has jurisdiction in matters arising out of or connected with navigation, shipping, trade or commerce on any river, lake, canal, or inland water of which the whole or part is in the province of Ontario[3].

An appeal lies to the Supreme Court from all decisions having the force of a final order.

---

[1] R. S. C. c. 135, ss. 66 & 75.   [2] See *ante*, p. 137   [3] R. S. C. c. 137, s. 11.

2.   APPOINTMENT OF JUDGES.

The judges of the Supreme, District, and County Courts (except the Courts of Probate in Nova Scotia and New Brunswick) are appointed by the Governor-General, and their salaries are paid by the Dominion[1].

The judges of the Supreme Courts hold office during good behaviour, but they are removeable by the Governor-General on address of the Senate and House of Commons[2].

Judges of the County Courts also hold office during good behaviour, and during residence within their districts[3].

They may be removed by Order in Council for (a) inability or old age or ill health, (b) incapacity or misbehaviour. An inquiry must be held before removal, and reasonable notice be given to the judge of such inquiry. The inquiry is to be held by a Commission, which may consist of the judges of the Supreme Courts either of Canada or of any province[4].

3.   APPEALS TO THE PRIVY COUNCIL.

An appeal lies from the Supreme Court of Canada to the Judicial Committee of the Privy Council, by permission of the Judicial Committee. The Canadian Act establishing the Supreme Court enacted that the judgment of the Court should be final and conclusive "saving any right which Her Majesty may be graciously pleased to exercise by virtue of her royal prerogative[5]." These last-mentioned words were held to leave entirely untouched and to have preserved Her Majesty's prerogative to allow an appeal[6].

---

[1] B. N. A. Act, 1867, ss. 96—100. R. S. C. c. 138.
[2] B. N. A. Act, s. 99.   [3] R. S. C. c. 138.   [4] Ib.
[5] R. S. C. c. 135, s. 71.   [6] *Johnston* v. *Minister and Trustees of St Andrew's Church*, L. R. 3 App. Cas. 159.

By the Canadian Insolvency Act[1] it was enacted, that the court to which an appeal could be made under the Act should be final, no saving clause being inserted regarding the prerogative but on the ground that the rights of the Crown could be taken away only by express words, and as there were no words in the Act that could be held to derogate from the prerogative of the Crown, the Judicial Committee held that Her Majesty's right to allow appeals as of grace in insolvency matters was not affected[2].

There is however no prerogative right in the Crown to review the judgment of a Supreme Court in Canada upon an election petition. The subject-matter of the jurisdiction delegated to courts in regard to elections to a Legislative Assembly is of a special nature, and the transfer of such jurisdiction from the Legislature itself to a court of law does not imply that the final decision should belong to the Queen in Council[3].

In advising Her Majesty whether to allow an appeal or not, the Judicial Committee will have regard not merely to the amount in dispute but to the importance of the questions involved.

---

[1] 38 Vic. c. 16.　　[2] *Cushing* v. *Dupuy*, 5 App. Cas. 409.
[3] *Théberge* v. *Landry*, 2 App. Cas. 102.

CHAPTER XIX.

Division of Legislative Power.

LEGISLATIVE power over Canada is shared amongst the following authorities: (1) the Lieutenant-Governors and the Provincial Legislatures, (2) the Governor-General and the Dominion Parliament, and (3) the Crown and the Imperial Parliament. The provinces can legislate on matters which are either specifically enumerated or are governed by general clauses; the Imperial Parliament has an implied exclusive jurisdiction on matters expressly or impliedly reserved: the balance of legislative power belongs to the Dominion. But even in those matters committed to the Dominion and the provinces the Imperial Parliament retains a concurrent jurisdiction.

It is difficult to refer the distribution of legislative power to any one principle. The provisions of the Union Act of 1867 were based on certain resolutions agreed to by the Imperial Government and the Canadian provinces, and it is not surprising to find a singular want of principle in the framework of the Act. An attempt has been made in it to enumerate the respective powers assigned to the Dominion and to the provinces, but the impossibility of enumerating all the possible subjects on which legislation might be required forced the framers to insert two general clauses, one giving power to the provinces to legislate on "all matters of a merely local or private nature in the province," and the other conferring on the Dominion power to legislate "for the peace, order and good government of Canada in relation to all matters" not assigned to the provinces. The result is that the interpretation of the Union Act is much more difficult than the interpretation of the constitution of the United States. The following remarks of the Judicial Committee of the Privy Council in the *Citizens Insurance Co.* v. *Parsons*[1] shew the view that has been taken by the courts as to the relation of the important sections containing the enumeration of the chief legislative powers of the Dominion and the provinces.

"The scheme of this legislation as expressed in the first branch of sect. 91 is to give to the Dominion Parliament authority to make laws for the good government of Canada in all matters not coming within the classes of subjects assigned exclusively to the Provincial Legislature. If the 91st section had stopped here and if the classes of subjects enumerated in sect. 92 had been altogether distinct and different from those in sect. 91, no conflict of legislative authority could have arisen. The Provincial Legislatures would have had exclusive legislative power over the 16 classes of subjects assigned to them, and the Dominion Parliament exclusive power over all other matters relating to the good government of Canada.

"But it must have been foreseen that this sharp and definite distinction had not been and could not be attained, and that some of the classes of subjects assigned to the Provincial Legislatures unavoidably ran into and were embraced in some of the enumerated classes of subjects in sect. 91 : hence an endeavour appears to have been made to provide for cases of apparent conflict: and it would seem that with this object it was declared in the second branch of the 91st section "for greater certainty but not so as to restrict the generality of the foregoing terms of this section" that (not-

---

[1] L. R. 7 App. Cas. 96.

withstanding anything in the Act) the exclusive legislative
authority of the Parliament of Canada should extend to all
matters coming within the classes of subjects enumerated in
that section. With the same object apparently the paragraph at the end of sect. 91 was introduced, though it may
be observed that this paragraph applies in its grammatical
construction to No. 16 of sect. 92.

" Notwithstanding this endeavour to give pre-eminence to
the Dominion Parliament in cases of a conflict of powers, it is
obvious that in some cases where this apparent conflict exists,
the Legislature could not have intended that the powers exclusively assigned to the provincial Legislature should be
absorbed in those given to the Dominion Parliament. Take
as one instance the subject 'marriage and divorce,' contained in the enumeration of subjects in sect. 91: it is evident
that solemnization of marriage would come within this
general description; yet 'solemnization of marriage in the
province' is enumerated among the classes of subjects in
sect. 92, and no one can doubt, notwithstanding the general
language of sect. 91, that this subject is still within the
exclusive authority of the Legislatures of the provinces. So
'the raising of money by any mode or system of taxation'
is enumerated among the classes of subjects in sect. 91 : but
though the description is sufficiently large and general to
include 'direct taxation within the province in order to the
raising of a revenue for provincial purposes' assigned to provincial Legislatures by sect. 92, it obviously could not have
been intended that in this instance also the general power
should override the particular one. With regard to certain
classes of subjects, therefore, generally described in sect. 91,
legislative power may reside as to some matters falling
within the general description of these subjects in the Legislatures of the provinces. In these cases it is the duty of the
Courts, however difficult it may be, to ascertain in what
degree, and to what extent, authority to deal with matters

falling within these classes of subjects exists in each Legislature, and to define in the particular case before them the
limits of their respective powers. It could not have been
the intention that a conflict should exist ; and in order to
prevent such a result the two sections must be read together,
and the language of the one interpreted, and where necessary
modified, by that of the other. In this way it may in most
cases be found possible to arrive at a reasonable and practicable construction of the language of the sections so as
to reconcile the respective powers they contain and give
effect to all of them. In performing this difficult duty it
will be a wise course for those on whom it is thrown to
decide each case which arises as best they can, without
entering more largely upon the interpretation of the statute
than is necessary for the decision of the particular question
in hand."

Before attempting to arrange or discuss the various
legislative powers, attention may be called to some general
principles that ought to be borne in mind, and which are
suggested either by the Act itself or by judicial decisions of
the Judicial Committee and of the Canadian Courts.

Co-ordinate power of Imperial Parliament. 1.   Though the 91st section of the Act professes to give
" exclusive " legislative authority to the Dominion Parlia-
ment on the matters specified, such authority is " exclusive "
only of provincial Legislatures, and does not affect the supreme
legislative power possessed by the Imperial Parliament over
all the dominions of the Crown. In other words, the Imperial
Parliament still retains co-ordinate legislative power in all
matters assigned to either the Dominion or the provincial
Legislatures[1].

Conflict of Imperial and Colonial Legislation. 2.   By the Imperial Act 28 and 29 Vic. c. 63, intituled
" An Act to remove Doubts as to the validity of Colonial
Laws," it is enacted that any Colonial law " repugnant to
the provisions of any Act of Parliament extending to the

---

[1] See for a fuller discussion of this point *post* c. xxi.

colony to which such law may relate, or repugnant to any order or regulation made under authority of such Act of Parliament, or having in the colony the force and effect of such Act, shall be read subject to such Act, order or regulation, and shall to the extent of such repugnancy " be void.

In the case of *The Farewell*[1] the judge of the Quebec Vice-Admiralty Court applied the above statute, and held that a clause of the Merchant Shipping Act of 1854 superseded the Dominion Pilotage Act of 1873.

3. The provincial Legislatures "are in no sense delegates of or acting under any mandate from the Imperial Parliament. When the British North America Act enacted that there should be a Legislature for Ontario, and that its Legislative Assembly should have exclusive authority to make laws for the province and for provincial purposes in relation to the matters enumerated in sect. 92, it conferred powers not in any sense to be exercised by delegation from or as agents of the Imperial Parliament, but authority as plenary and as ample within the limits prescribed by sect. 92 as the Imperial Parliament in the plenitude of its power possessed and could bestow. Within these limits of subjects and area the local Legislature is supreme, and has the same authority as the Imperial Parliament or the Parliament of the Dominion would have had under like circumstances to confide to a municipal institution or body of its own creation authority to make by-laws or resolutions as to subjects specified in the enactment, and with the object of carrying the enactment into operation and effect[2]."

Provincial Legislatures supreme within limits of legislative power.

4. Power to legislate on a particular subject implies the right to legislate on incidental subjects necessary to an exercise of such power.

Implied power of Legislation.

" We consider as a proper rule of interpretation in all these cases that when a power is given either to the

[1] 7 Quebec L. R. 380, 2 Cart. 378.
[2] P. C. in *Hodge* v. *The Queen*, L. R. 9 App. Cases, at p. 132.

Dominion or to the provincial Legislatures to legislate on certain subjects coming clearly within the class of subjects which either Legislature has a right to deal with, such power includes all the incidental subjects of legislation which are necessary to carry on the object which the B.N.A. Act declared should be carried on by that Legislature. The determining of the age or of other qualifications required by those residing in the province of Quebec to manage their own business, or to exercise certain professions or certain branches of business attended with danger or risk for the public, are local subjects in the nature of internal police regulations; and in passing laws upon those subjects, even if those laws incidentally affect trade and commerce, it must be held that this incidental power is included in the right to deal with the subjects specially placed under their control, the exercise of which cannot be considered to be unconstitutional[1]."

General powers of Dominion.   5. If a matter does not fall within any of the classes of subjects assigned exclusively to the Legislatures of the provinces, then it is within the general power given to the Parliament of Canada " to make laws for the peace, order, and good government of Canada." On this ground an Act of the Canadian Parliament introducing throughout the Dominion uniform legislation for the promotion of temperance by prohibiting the sale of liquors, except under certain restrictions, where the inhabitants of a county or city adopted its provisions, is not *ultra vires*[2]. This principle must however be taken subject to the qualification that the matter in question does not fall within any of the restrictions imposed by the Act on the powers of the Dominion Parliament. The Dominion Parliament cannot for instance change

---

[1] Dorion, C. J., in *Bennett* v. *Pharmaceutical Association of Quebec*, 1 Dorion Quebec Appeals 336, 2 Cart. 250. See also *Ex parte Lereillé.* Q. 2 Stephens Dig. 445, 2 Cart. 349.

[2] *Russell* v. *the Queen*, 46 L. T., N. S. 889.

the seat of government[1], nor alter the constitution of the
Senate, except by providing for the representation of new
provinces[2], nor alter the constitution of a new province[3],
nor impose protective duties as between provinces, nor increase its own powers; all these matters are within the
exclusive jurisdiction of the Queen and English Parliament.

6. The Courts in deciding upon the relative powers of the Dominion and provincial Legislatures will have regard to the powers of the provinces at the time of the Con-federation[4]. Former powers of Provinces.

7. When the validity of an Act is in question the first point to be decided is this: does the subject-matter fall within any of the matters assigned to the provinces? If it does not and it is a provincial Act, then such Act is *ultra vires*; but if it *prima facie* falls within one of such classes, then the further question arises, viz. "whether, notwithstanding this is so, the subject of the Act does not also fall within one of the enumerated classes of subjects in sect. 91, and whether the power of the provincial Legislature is not thereby over-borne?" Method of interpreta-tion.

Instead of following the order in which the legislative
powers are expressly or impliedly mentioned in the Act, the
following attempt is made to group the various powers
under definite heads.

1. AMENDMENT OF THE CONSTITUTION.

Certain important but limited powers are given to the
Dominion Parliament and to the provincial Legislatures to
enable them from time to time to amend their Constitutions.

---

[1] B. N. A. Act, s. 16. [2] 31 & 35 Vic. (i.) c. 28. s. 2. [3] Ib. s. 6.
[4] *The Corporation of Three Rivers* v. *Sulte*, Q. 5 Legal News, 330.
[5] *Citizens' Insurance Co.* v. *Parsons*, 45 L. T., N. S. 721, Cart. 265; *Dobie*
v. *The Temporalities Board*, 7 App. Cas. 136, 1 Cart. 351; *Bank of Toronto*
v. *Lambe*, L. R. 12 App. Cas. 575.

The Governor-General and Lieutenant-Governors.

The Governor. The salary of the Governor-General may be varied by the Dominion Parliament[1], but otherwise the Parliament has no legal control over his office. The salaries of the Lieutenant-Governors are fixed and provided for by Parliament[2]. The provinces have no legal control over the office of Lieutenant-Governor[3], but the Governor-General is by constitutional custom required to rely on the advice of his ministers in making or revoking an appointment[4].

The Upper House.

The Senate. The only powers conferred on the Dominion Parliament over the Senate are those for varying the number necessary to form a quorum[5] and of hearing and determining any question that arises relating to the qualification of a senator or to a vacancy in the Senate[6]. The Parliament cannot abolish the Senate, nor alter the number of members[7], except by providing for the representation of new provinces or of territories not in a province[8]; nor prescribe what qualifications a senator should possess: all these matters are settled by the Act of Union and subsequent Acts, and can only be altered by the Imperial Parliament.

The Provincial Legislative Council.

The Legislative Council. The provinces, on the other hand, have power not only to alter the constitution of the Legislative Council but even to abolish it[9]. By section 92 a provincial Legislature may amend from time to time the constitution of the province notwithstanding anything in the Act. The only legislative Council constituted in detail in the Union Act is that of Quebec, as the constitutions of the Legislative Councils in Nova Scotia and New Brunswick were continued as they existed at the time the Act passed. Manitoba has taken advantage of the above power and abolished its upper House[10].

The Lower House.

The House of Commons. As regards the House of Com-

---

[1] B. N. A. Act, s. 105.   [2] Ib. s. 60.   [3] Ib. s. 92 (1).
[4] See *ante*, p. 187.   [5] B. N. A. Act. s. 35.   [6] Ib. s. 33.
[7] 34 & 35 Vic. (i.) c. 28.   [8] 49 & 50 Vic. c. 35.
[9] B. N. A. Act. ss. 72, 88, 92 (1).   [10] Man. 39 Vic. c. 28.

mous the Dominion Parliament has power to legislate on the following subjects:—

The distribution of seats,

the qualifications and disqualifications of members,

the voters at elections,

the oaths to be taken by voters,

returning officers, their powers and duties,

proceedings at elections[1],

periods during which elections may be continued,

trial of controverted elections[2],

vacating of seats of members,

execution of new writs in case of seats vacated otherwise than by dissolution[3].

The number of members may be increased every decennial census subject to the conditions specified in section 51.

Parliament may also make provision for the absence of the Speaker of the House of Commons[4].

The Legislative Assembly. The provincial Legislatures possess the same powers for altering the constitution of the Assembly that they have for altering the constitution of the Legislative Council, except that where the Legislative Assembly is the only House it cannot be abolished. It is true that there is no express provision in the Act against the abolition of a provincial Assembly, but in such a case it must be remembered not only that such an abolition would be inconsistent with the provisions of the Act, but that the power of a province to affect its constitution is a power to "amend" not to "abolish." The Union Act implies a Legislature of some kind in each province. The Provincial Lower House.

Privileges. The Dominion Parliament has power from time to time to define by Act the privileges, immunities and powers to be enjoyed by the Senate and House of Commons, and by the members thereof respectively, but the privileges Privileges of Parliament.

[1] As to punishment of bribery at elections, see *Doyle* v. *Belle*, 11 Ont., App. Rep. 32.   [2] See *ante*, p. 137.   [3] B. N. A. Act, ib. s. 41.   [4] Ib. s. 47.

immunities and powers so conferred are not to exceed those enjoyed by the English House of Commons at the time of the passing of such Act[1].

Privileges of Provincial Legislatures. No express power was given to the provincial Legislatures to define their privileges, but Acts for that purpose have been passed by Ontario, Quebec, Manitoba and British Columbia[2].

Powers of Parliament. Neither the Dominion Parliament nor the provincial Legislatures can increase or vary the powers expressly or impliedly conferred on the Dominion and the provinces respectively by the Imperial Parliament.

Dominion cannot alter Provincial Constitution. The Dominion Parliament has no power to alter the constitution of any of the provinces admitted into the Union. And by the Imperial Act 34 Vic. c. 28, s. 6, it is not for instance competent for the Parliament to alter the 32 and 33 Vic. c. 3, providing a constitution for Manitoba, or any other Act establishing new provinces in the Dominion.

The Parliament of Canada may with the consent of the Legislature of a province alter the limits of a province upon the terms and conditions agreed on by such Legislature, 34 Vic. (i), c. 28.

The 34 Vic. (i.), c. 28, conferred on the Parliament of Canada power to make provisions from time to time for the administration, peace, order, and good government of any territory not for the time being included in any province. A clause in the order in Council surrendering the North-West Territory and Ruperts-land to the Dominion confers a similar power as regards these Territories, but the same order in Council[3] imposes certain conditions, relating chiefly to the Hudson's Bay Company, that are binding on the Dominion Parliament and cannot be altered by it.

2. NEW PROVINCES AND TERRITORIES.

At the time of the incorporation of the North-West

---

[1] 38 & 39 Vic. (i.) c. 38, s. 1.   [2] See *ante*, p. 67.
[3] See Appendix.

Territory, a doubt arose as to whether the Dominion had power to establish new provinces. To set the matter at rest the Imperial Act 34 Vic. c. 28 was passed, conferring power on the Dominion Parliament to establish new provinces in territory not included in any province, to make provision for the constitution and administration of the province, to pass laws for the peace, order, and good government of such province, and to provide for its representation in the Dominion Parliament.

3. TREATY OBLIGATIONS.

The power of entering into treaties has not been con- ferred on the Dominion, but the Parliament of Canada has " all powers necessary or proper for performing the obligations of Canada or of any province thereof as part of the British Empire towards foreign countries arising under treaties between the Empire and such foreign countries[1]."

4. PUBLIC PROPERTY.

Dominion Powers.	*Provincial Powers.*
The Public Property. s. 91 (1).	The Management and Sale of the Public Lands belonging to the province, and of the timber and wood thereon. s. 92 (5).

By sect. 108 of the B.N.A. Act it was enacted that the following public works and property in each province were to be the property of the Dominion Government :—

1. Canals, with lands and water power connected therewith.

2. Public harbours.

3. Lighthouses and piers and Sable Island.

4. Steam boats, dredges, and public vessels.

5. Rivers and lake improvements.

[1] B. N. A. Act, s. 132.

6. Railways and railway stocks, mortgages, and other debts due by railway companies.

7. Military roads.

8. Custom Houses, Post Offices, and all other public buildings, except such as the Government of Canada appropriate for the use of the provincial Legislatures and Governments.

9. Property transferred by the Imperial government and known as Ordnance property.

10. Armouries, drill sheds, military clothing and munitions of war, and lands set apart for general public purposes.

Debts of Provinces. The Act also by sect. 102 imposed upon the Dominion the charge of the general public debts of the several provinces, and vested in the Dominion the general public revenues as then existing of the provinces. But this provision was made subject to certain exceptions contained in sect. 126, viz. (1) such portions of the pre-existing duties and revenues as were by the Act "reserved to the respective Legislatures of the provinces;" and (2) such duties and revenues as might be "received by them in accordance with the special powers conferred on them by the Act." As regards the first exception the only duties and revenues reserved to the provinces are specified in section 109, which enacted that all lands, mines, minerals and royalties belonging to the several provinces at the time of the Union were to remain vested in the provinces[1]; and it was provided that the several provinces should retain all their respective public property not otherwise disposed of by the Act, subject to the right of Canada to reserve any lands or public property required for fortifications or for the defence of the country[2].

The right of the provinces to the above land includes the right to the banks and beds of rivers and streams in each province, and therefore it has been held[3] that the Dominion

---

[1] B. N. A. Act, s. 109.   [2] Ib. s. 117.
[3] *Regina* v. *Robertson*, 6 Can. S. C. R. 52; 2 Cart. 65.

Parliament cannot grant a lease of a bed of a provincial river, or even a license to fish, as a franchise or right apart from the ownership of the soil.

In 1883 arose the important question[1] whether lands escheated to the Crown for want of heirs belonged to the Dominion or to the province; and it was held by the Judicial Committee of the Privy Council that the words used in section 109 were wide enough to cover escheated lands, and that such lands belonged to the province.

5. PUBLIC DEBT AND TAXATION.

Dominion Powers.

The public debt. s. 91 (1).

The borrowing of money on the public credit. s. 91 (4).

The raising of money by any mode or system of taxation. s. 91 (3).

Provincial Powers.

The borrowing of money on the sole credit of the province. s. 92 (3).

Direct taxation within the province in order to the raising of a revenue for provincial purposes. s. 92 (2).

Shop, saloon, tavern, auctioneer and other licenses in order to the raising of a revenue for provincial, local or municipal purposes. s. 92 (9).

The alteration of the Customs and Excise laws of each province, subject to the provisions that "all articles of growth, produce or manufactures of any one of the provinces shall from and after the Union be admitted free into each of the other provinces," (ss. 121, 122).

No land or property belonging to Canada or any province shall be liable to taxation. s. 125.

Public Debt.

Borrowing of money.

Licences.

Customs and Excise.

Public Property.

---

[1] *A. G. of Ontario* v. *Mercer*, 8 App. Cas. 767.

The above powers may be classified under the heads of (1) Public Debt, (2) Direct Taxation, and (3) Indirect Taxation.

Public Debt, Canada.

Public Debt.   The Public Debt of the Dominion is under the exclusive jurisdiction of the Dominion Legislature.   By section 111 of the B.N.A. Act, Canada was made liable for the debts and liabilities of each province existing at the Union, and on the admission of British Columbia and Prince Edward Island the debts of these two provinces were taken over.

The provinces, however, were made liable to Canada for the amount by which their respective debts at the time of the Union exceeded the respective sums mentioned in the Act; and on such sums five per cent. interest is payable[1]; and on the other hand Canada undertook to pay British Columbia interest on the difference between its indebtedness and the indebtedness of Nova Scotia and New Brunswick, and to pay Prince Edward Island the difference between its indebtedness and a certain amount specified in the order in Council.

Direct Taxes.

Direct Taxation.   A province may raise a revenue by direct taxes for provincial purposes.

A. G. for Quebec v. Queen Insurance Co.

The meaning of " direct taxation" was discussed in *A. G. for Quebec v. Queen Insurance Co.*[2]

In 1875 an Act was passed by the Legislature of Quebec[3] which enacted that every assurer carrying on in the province of Quebec, any business of assurance other than that of marine assurance should take out a license every year, and should pay for such license a certain percentage of every premium by means of an adhesive stamp affixed to the policy or receipt.   In an action for penalties for not complying with the terms of the statute, it was contended, that the above Act was not within the powers conferred on the Legislature of Quebec, as the tax imposed by the Act was neither a

---

[1] B. N. A. Act, ss. 110–116.   [2] L. R. 3 App. Cas. 1090 ; 1 Cart. 117.
[3] 39 Vic. c. 7.

direct tax within the meaning of sect. 92, subsect. 2, nor a license within the meaning of subsect. 9. This view was taken by the Canadian Court, and was upheld by the Privy Council. Stress was laid on the fact that the Act did not require any payment to be made for the license, nor did it impose any penalty for not taking out the license—the penalty being incurred only if a policy was issued without the stamp. The Act was therefore a Stamp Act, and not a Licensing Act. Being a Stamp Act it was a method of indirect and not of direct taxation.

On the other hand a duty or stamp on exhibits filed in a Court in an action is an indirect tax, as the litigant, who in the first instance pays it, is not necessarily the person on whom the burden may ultimately fall[1].

In a more recent case[2] the Judicial Committee held that a Quebec Act imposing a tax on banks and insurance companies, varying in the case of banks in proportion to paid-up capital, and based in the case of insurance companies on a sum specified in the Act, was valid, on the ground that looking at the Act in question it was evident that it was the intention of the Legislature that the corporations from whom the tax was demanded should pay and finally bear it. Mill's definition was taken as a fair test of a direct tax, viz. "a direct tax is one which is demanded from the very persons who it is intended or desired should pay it. Indirect taxes are those which are demanded from one person in the expectation and intention that he shall indemnify himself at the expense of another." It was also held in the same case that a province may levy a tax on a business in the province though some of the persons on whom the tax would fall were domiciled elsewhere, as sect. 92 (2) did not require the persons taxed to be domiciled in the province.

Taxes on banks.

---

[1] *A. G. of Quebec* v. *Reed*, 10 App. Cas. 141.
[2] *Bank of Toronto* v. *Lambe*, L. R. 12 App. Cas. 575.

It was suggested in *Dow* v. *Black*[1] that the clause only authorized direct taxation for the purpose of raising a revenue for general provincial purposes, that is, taxation incident on the whole province for the general purposes of the whole province. The Judicial Committee refused to adopt this view, and held that the clause was sufficiently wide to enable a provincial Legislature, whenever it should see fit, to impose direct taxation for a local purpose upon a particular locality within the province.

Tax on Dominion Officers.

A provincial Legislature has no power either to impose itself or to authorize a municipality to impose a tax on the incomes of officers of the Dominion Government residing in the province. Such a power would conflict with the right given to the Dominion Government to fix and provide the salaries of the civil and other officers of the Government of Canada conferred by s. 91 (8) of the Act of 1867, inasmuch as a provincial tax would mean a reduction in the salaries fixed[2].

Indirect Taxation. Except in the case of certain licenses a province has no power to levy an indirect tax. The Dominion Parliament may impose indirect taxation, subject to the proviso that no protective duty can be imposed as between the different provinces.

Licenses.

The licenses above referred to as within provincial jurisdiction are "shop, saloon and other licenses in order to the raising of a revenue for provincial, local or municipal purposes."

"Shop licenses" refer to licenses for the retail of liquors in quantities not less than one quart in shops other than places of public entertainment; whilst "saloon" and "tavern" licenses apply to places of public entertainment.

The power given by this subsection is, notwithstanding the use of the words "and other licenses," limited to licenses

---

[1] L. R. 6 P. C. 272; 1 Cart., p. 95.

[2] *Lephrohon* v. *City of Ottawa*, 2 App. Rep. (Ont.) 522; 1 Cart. 592, and see *Evans* v. *Hudon*, O. 22 L. C. Jurist, 268; 2 Cart. 346.

for objects strictly municipal or local in character, and does not extend to licenses on manufactures, such as brewers' licenses[1].

A license is to a certain extent an interference with "trade and commerce," but such right of interference is implied, and therefore a license tax on butchers keeping stalls in the city of Montreal elsewhere than in the public market was held valid[2]. *Licenses an interference with "trade and commerce."*

But to require a license from the person authorized by the Dominion Parliament to sell goods under the Dominion Insolvency Act was regarded as an interference with the Dominion's power over "bankruptcy and insolvency[3]." *Interference with "bankruptcy and insolvency."*

In the earlier cases it was suggested that a province could legislate only in regard to licenses for the purpose indicated in clause 9; viz. the raising of a revenue, but in *Regina* v. *Frawley*[4] it was pointed out by Spragge, C. J., that clause 9 was cumulative to clause 8, relating to municipal institutions, and that a province had therefore power to legislate for the prevention of intemperance, the preservation of order, and other matters of police, and such legislation might be carried into effect by means of licenses.

6. ADMINISTRATION.

Under this head may be classified matters relating to (1) Public Safety, (2) Public Works and Means of Communication, (3) Marine Matters, (4) Matters of State Management, and (5) the Civil Service.

1. *Public Safety.*—The Dominion has sole jurisdiction over *Public Safety.*

(*a*) The militia, military, and naval service and defence. s. 91 (7).

(*b*) Quarantine. s. 91 (11).

[1] *Severn* v. *The Queen*, 2 Can. S. C. R. 70 ; 1 Cart. 414.
[2] *Angers* v. *City of Montreal*, Q. 24 L. C. Jurist, 259 ; 2 Cart. 335.
[3] *Coté* v. *Watson*, 3 Quebec L. R. 157 ; 2 Cart. 343.
[4] O. 7, App. Rep. 246.

Public
Works.

2. *Public Works and Means of Communication.*—The Dominion has jurisdiction in all works that fall within any of the following classes :—

(*a*) Ferries between a province and any British or foreign country or between two provinces. s. 91 (13).

(*b*) Beacons, buoys, lighthouses, and Sable Island. s. 91 (9).

(*c*) Establishment and maintenance of marine hospitals. s. 91 (11). But each province has committed to it "the establishment, maintenance and management of hospitals, asylums, charities, and eleemosynary institutes as and for the province other than marine hospitals." s. 92 (7).

(*d*) The postal service. s. 91 (5).

(*e*) Lines of steam or other ships, railways, canals, telegraphs and other works and undertakings connecting the province with any other or others of the provinces, or extending beyond the limits of the province. s. 92 (10).

(*f*) Lines of steam ships between the province and any British or foreign country. s. 92 (10).

(*g*) Such works as, although wholly situate within the province, are before or after their execution declared by the Parliament of Canada to be for the general advantage or for the advantage of two or more provinces. s. 92 (10).

Marine.

3. *Marine Matters.*—To the Dominion is committed :—

(*a*) Navigation and Shipping. s. 91 (10).

This clause gives power to confer jurisdiction on Admiralty Courts, but such jurisdiction must be restricted to the territorial limits of the Dominion, i.e. to within three marine miles from the coasts [1].

The Supreme Court of Canada held that this clause excludes a province from conferring on a boom company power to obstruct a tidal navigable river [2].

[1] *The Farewell*, 7 Quebec L. R. 380 ; 2 Cart. 378.

[2] See *Queddy Boom Co.* v. *Davidson*, 10 C. S. C. 222. In *McMillan* v. *South-west Boom Co.* N. B., Pugsley & Burbidge, 715 ; 2 Cart. 542, the opposite view was laid down.

(b)   The Sea-coast.   s. 91 (12).   Sea-coast.

(c)   Inland Fisheries.   Fisheries.

The meaning of "inland fisheries" was discussed in *The Queen v. Robertson*[1]. "I am of opinion," said Ritchie, C. J. "that the legislation in regard to inland and sea fisheries contemplated by the B. N. A. Act was not in reference to 'property and civil rights,' that is to say, not as to the ownership of the beds of the rivers or of the fisheries or the rights of individuals therein, but to subjects affecting the fisheries generally, tending to their regulation, protection, and preservation, matters of a national and general concern and important to the public, such as the forbidding fish to be taken at improper seasons in an improper manner, or with destructive instruments, laws with reference to the improvement and increase of the fisheries : in other words, all such general laws as enure as well to the benefit of the owners of the fisheries as to the public at large who are interested in the fisheries as a source of national and provincial wealth: in other words, laws in relation to the fisheries such as those which the local Legislatures were, previously to and at the time of Confederation, in the habit of enacting for their regulation, preservation and protection, with which the property in the fish or the right to take the fish out of the water to be appropriated to the party so taking the fish has nothing whatever to do, the property in the fishing or the right to take the fish being as much the property of the province or the individual as the dry land or the land covered with water." The grant by the Dominion Minister of Marine and Fisheries of a right to fish in a provincial river was therefore held invalid.

4.   *Matters of State Management.*   The Dominion has exclusive jurisdiction in regard to :—

(a)   The Census.   s. 91 (6).   Census.

---

[1] 6 Can. S. C. R. 52; 2 Cart. 65.

Statistics.   (*b*)   Statistics.   s. 91 (6).
Weights
and   (*c*)   Weights and Measures.   s. 91 (17).
Measures.
Civil   5.   *The Civil Service.*   For carrying on the necessary de-
Service. partments of state the Dominion has the following powers:—

1.   The fixing of and providing for the salaries of the Governor-General (s. 105) and of the Lieutenant-Governors. s. 60.

2.   The fixing of and providing for the salaries, allowances and pensions of the judges of the Superior, District, and County Courts (except the Courts of Probate in Nova Scotia and New Brunswick) and of Admiralty Courts in cases where the judges are paid by salary.   s. 100.

3.   The fixing of and providing for the salaries and allowances of civil and other officers of the Government of Canada.   s. 91 (8).

The provinces have also powers regarding " the establishment and tenure of provincial officers and the appointment and payment of provincial offices."   s. 92 (3).

7. ADMINISTRATION OF JUSTICE.

The powers assigned to the Dominion and the provinces are as follows :

	Dominion.	*Provinces.*
Court of Appeal.	"The constitution, maintenance and organisation of a General Court of Appeal for Canada and for the establishment of any additional courts for the better administration of the laws of Canada." s. 101.	
Criminal Law.	Criminal Law except the constitution of courts of jurisdiction, but including procedure in criminal matters. s. 91 (27).	The administration of justice in the province, including the constitution, maintenance and organisation of provincial courts both of civil and criminal jurisdiction, including procedure in civil matters in those courts. s. 92 (14)

Establishment, maintenance and management of penitentiaries. s. 91 (28).

The establishment, maintenance and management of public reformatory prisons in and for the province. s. 92 (6). **Prisons.**

The imposition of punishment by fine, penalty or imprisonment for enforcing any law of the province made in relation to any matter coming within any of the classes of subjects enumerated in section 92. s. 92 (15). **Enforcing provincial laws.**

The trial of controverted elections and proceedings incident thereto. s. 41. **Election petitions.**

Courts of Appeal. By the 38 Vic. c. 2, passed in the year 1875, a Supreme and an Exchequer Court were established for the Dominion[1], and in 1877 a Court of Maritime Jurisdiction was created for Ontario. **Court of Appeal.**

Administration of justice in the province. The power of the Governor-General under s. 96 to appoint judges is limited to judges of the Superior, District and County Courts in each province. For inferior courts the right of appointing belongs under s. 92 (14) to the province[2]; but the Lieutenant-Governor as such and without legislative authority cannot appoint justices of the peace, since he is not authorized as is the Governor-General to exercise that prerogative of the Crown[3]. The taking of evidence to be used in an action pending in a foreign tribunal is a matter of Dominion and not of provincial regulation[4]. **Administration of Justice.**

Criminal Law. The 15th clause of s. 92 confers a limited jurisdiction in criminal matters on the local Legislatures, and the right of the Dominion to legislate on Criminal Law under s. 91 (27) is subject to this provincial right. **Criminal Law.**

[1] See *ante* p. 216.   [2] *R.* v. *Bennett*, 1 Ont. Rep. 445 ; 2 Cart. 634 : *Wilson* v. *McGuire*, 2 Ont. Rep. 118 ; 2 Cart. 605.   [3] Doutre, p. 54.
[4] *Re Wetherell & Jones*, 4 Ont. Rep. 713.

This limited power of criminal jurisdiction does not authorize a provincial Legislature to enforce a law of the province, made in relation to matters within the exclusive jurisdiction of a provincial Legislature, by declaring acts to be offences which are criminal offences at common law. When therefore the Ontario Legislature provided that tampering with a witness in the case of prosecutions under the Liquor License Act should involve a penalty, the Ontario Court of Queen's Bench held the proviso *ultra vires*, inasmuch as tampering with a witness was an offence at common law[1]. In this case an attempt was made, similar to that in English cases[2], to distinguish between acts that are *offences*, viz. those punishable by magistrates, and acts that are *crimes*, viz. those punishable on indictment, and it was suggested that the former were within the jurisdiction of the local Legislatures; but the decision was ultimately based on the principle that the act in question was a crime by common law and therefore not within provincial jurisdiction.

Enforcement of Temperance Laws.

The validity of clauses in provincial laws relating to temperance has been questioned.

In some cases[3] it has been held that the method adopted for enforcing the Act in question was *ultra vires,* and in other cases that it was valid[4].

A provincial law forbidding the compromise of offences against a law regulating tavern and shop licenses, and enacting that any party to such a compromise should on conviction be liable to imprisonment, was held not to be *ultra vires*[5].

---

[1] *R.* v. *Lawrence*, 43 U. C. Q. B. 164.

[2] See remarks of Martin B. in *A. G.* v. *Radloff*, 10 Ex. p. 96.

[3] *R.* v. *Prittie*, 42 U. C. Q. B. 612; 2 Cart. 606; *R.* v. *Lake*, 43 U. C. Q. B. 515; 2 Cart. 616.

[4] *License Commissioners of Prince Edward* v. *County of Prince Edward,* O. 26 Grant, 452; 2 Cart. 678.

[5] *Regina* v. *Boardman*, 30 U. C. Q. B. 553; 1 Cart. 676.

This limited power of criminal jurisdiction does not Rules of evidence. extend to the alteration of the rules of evidence existing for the protection of persons accused of offences; a man therefore cannot be compelled to criminate himself, even though the offence be one created by a provincial Legislature[1].

In so far as a province has power to enact penal laws, it Procedure. has an implied power to regulate the procedure requisite for enforcing such laws[2].

The point has been raised in Quebec, whether a provincial Punishment. Legislature has power to punish by *both* fine and imprisonment or by one only of these modes. In one case[3] the latter view was taken, but in a subsequent case[4] it was held that the word *or* in s. 92 (15) is not used in a disjunctive sense[5].

A province it has been held may enforce its penal laws by hard labour in addition to imprisonment[6].

Though this power of making criminal laws is vested in the Dominion, the Attorney-General of the province is the proper officer to prosecute in the courts of justice in the province[7].

Election Petitions. By section 41 of the Act it was pro- Election petitions. vided that until the Parliament of the Dominion should otherwise determine, the old mode of hearing Election Petitions was to continue, and it was held[8] that this gave jurisdiction to the Dominion Parliament.

By an Act passed in 1874[9] the existing provincial courts were constituted courts for the trial of Election Petitions,

[1] *Regina* v. *Roddy*, 41 U. C. Q. B. 291; 1 Cart. 709.

[2] *Pope* v. *Griffith*, 16 L. C. Jurist 169; 2 Cart. 291. *Ex parte Duncan* 16 L. C. Jurist 188; 2 Cart. 297. *Page* v. *Griffith*, 17 L. C. Jurist 302; 2 Cart. 308.

[3] *Ex parte Papin*, 15 L. C. Jurist 334; 16 L. C. Jurist 319; 2 Cart. pp. 320–323. [4] *Paige* v. *Griffith*, 18 L. C. Jurist 119; 2 Cart. 324.

[5] See the English Cases of *Fowler* v. *Padget*, 7 T. R. 514 and *Ditcher* v. *Denison*, 11 Moore's P. C. 338 where "or" in an Act of Parliament was held to mean "and." [6] *Regina* v. *Frawley*, O. 7 App. Rep. 246.

[7] *A. G.* v. *Niagara Falls Inter. Bridge Co.*, 20 Grant 34; 1 Cart. 813.

[8] *Valin* v. *Langlois*, 5 App. Cas. 115; 1 Cart. p. 158.

[9] 37 Vic. c. 10.

but it was objected that this was an interference "with the administration of justice in the provinces" committed to the Provincial Legislatures; it was however held that the Act was valid, as it created a new jurisdiction, and though it adopted the machinery of the courts it did not merely add to the old jurisdiction[1].

Procedure in civil suits. *Procedure.* An Act of N. B. abolishing imprisonment for debt was held valid as respects a person not a trader or subject to the Dominion Insolvent Acts, inasmuch as the Act regulates procedure in civil suits in relation to civil rights[2].

8. STATUS.

The Dominion has sole jurisdiction regarding

Status. 1. Naturalisation and Aliens. s. 91 (25).

Indians. 2. Indians and lands reserved for Indians. s. 91 (24). By "lands reserved for Indians" is meant lands reserved for the use of Indians and not surrendered by them. Such lands are sometimes described as "Indian Reserves." Lands surrendered by them and to which their title is extinguished come within the jurisdiction of the province[3].

Marriage. 3. Marriage and Divorce, except the solemnization of marriage within a province, which falls under provincial legislation. s. 92 (12); s. 91 (26).

9. EDUCATION.

In and for each province the Legislature may exclusively make laws in relation to education, subject to the following conditions:—

(1) All rights and privileges which any class of persons had at the time of the Union in denominational schools are not to be affected prejudicially.

(2) Privileges enjoyed by Roman Catholic schools in

[1] *Valin* v. *Langlois,* supra.
[2] *Armstrong* v. *McCutchin,* N. B. 2 Pugsley, 381 ; 2 Cart. 494.
[3] *Church* v. *Fenton,* 28 U. C. C. P. 384 ; 1 Cart. 831.

Upper Canada are extended to the dissentient schools of Protestants and of Roman Catholics in Quebec.

(3) An appeal to the Governor-General in Council is allowed against any provincial Act or decision affecting any right of the Protestant or Roman Catholic minority of the Queen's subjects in the province.   s. 93.

A province has, subject to the above powers, a right of Denomilegislating in regard to denominational schools, so long as national Schools. such legislation is not "prejudicial" to any right or privilege existing at the time of the Union. (An Ontario Act providing for the election of trustees of certain Roman Catholic schools was on this ground held valid[1].)

The rights and privileges protected are only those which at the time of the Union existed in each province by virtue of positive legal enactment, and not privileges enjoyed under exceptional and accidental circumstances and without legal rights[2].

The right of appeal referred to in subsection (3) only refers to legislative Acts or their equivalents, and not to the every-day details of the working of the school.

In case any provincial law requisite for carrying out the Dominion above provisions is not made, or in case the decision of the powers. Governor-General in Council in an appeal under this section is not duly executed, power is given to the Parliament of Canada to make remedial laws for carrying out the above provisions and for executing the said decision.   s. 93 (4).

10.   PROPERTY.

To the Dominion is given jurisdiction in
    Bankruptcy and Insolvency.   s. 91 (21).
To the province is given jurisdiction in
    Property and civil rights in the province.   s. 92 (13).
    Procedure in civil matters in the province.   s. 92 (14).

---

[1] *Separate School Trustees of Belleville* v. *Grainger*, O. 25 Grant 570; 1 Cart. 816.   [2] *Ex parte Renaud*, N. B. 1 Pugsley 273; 2 Cart. 445.

Property and civil rights. Property and civil rights are assigned to the provinces : bankruptcy and insolvency to the Dominion. The right to legislate on property and civil rights is restricted to property in the province, and to rights existing in the province. Within such limits a local Legislature has unrestricted power. The Legislature of Ontario was therefore held to be within its power in passing a private Act dividing, at the request of the children, a testator's property in a way different to that prescribed by the will[1].

Fisheries.

Toll bridges.

Property includes property in fisheries and the transfer or transmission of rights in fisheries[2], as well as toll bridges belonging to a municipality in the province[3].

Debts belonging to persons domiciled abroad.

In 1881 the important question arose whether a " debt " belonging to a person domiciled elsewhere could be said to come under the head of property or civil rights within the province in view of the acknowledged rule that the locality of a debt is determined by the domicile of the creditor. The Ontario Court of Queen's Bench on the ground that the rule was not of universal application[4] refused to limit the clause in this way, and held, that where debts or other obligations arose out of, or were authorized to be contracted under, a local Act passed in relation to a matter within the powers of a local Legislature, such debts or obligations may be dealt with by subsequent Acts of the same Legislature, notwithstanding that by a fiction of law such debts may be domiciled out of the province.

Legislation limited by express powers of the Dominion.

The power of the provinces to legislate on property and civil rights is limited by several of the rights given to the Dominion, as for instance by the right to legislate on bankruptcy and insolvency, since, to use the words of the

[1] *Re Goodhue*, 19 Grant 366 ; 1 Cart. 560.

[2] *Queen* v. *Robertson*, 6 Can. S. C. R. 52, 2 Cart. 65.

[3] *Municipality of Cleveland* v. *Municipality of Melbourne*, Q. 4 Legal News, 277 ; 2 Cart. 241.

[4] See *Nickle* v. *Douglas*, 35 U. C. Q. B. 126, 37 U. C. Q. B. 51.

Judicial Committee, "it is impossible to advance a step in the construction of a scheme for the administration of insolvent estates without interfering with and modifying some of the ordinary rights of property and other civil rights[1]."

Patents, copyrights, lands reserved for Indians as well as other specific subjects enumerated in the 91st section, relate to property and civil rights, and therefore it is only as regards property and civil rights other than the property and civil rights assigned to the Dominion Parliament that fall within the jurisdiction of the provincial Legislatures.

In some cases a province may avoid any conflict by inserting a special clause in the provincial Act. A grant of shore or of land extending into the water, with a proviso that the grant was not to give any right to interfere with "commerce and navigation," was held valid, inasmuch as this proviso reserved all Dominion rights[2]. *Saving clause.*

The provincial rights are limited also by the implied power of the Dominion to legislate on property and civil rights so far as that is necessary to exercise jurisdiction over the subjects assigned to it. *Implied powers of Dominion.*

On this ground the Dominion Act, 34 Vic. c. 5, s. 46, authorizing the transfer of warehouse receipts to banks by direct endorsement was held valid, inasmuch as such legislative power was implied in the right to regulate trade, commerce and banking[3].

The validity of the Canadian Temperance Act 1878, which authorized the inhabitants of a city or county under certain restrictions to prohibit the sale of intoxicating liquors, was challenged on this ground amongst others, that it affected "property and civil rights" in the provinces, but the Judicial

[1] *Cushing* v. *Dupuy*, 5 App. Cas. 409; 1 Cart. 252: and see *Kinney* v. *Dudman*, N. S. 2 Russell & Chesley 19; 2 Cart. 412.

[2] *Normand* v. *St Lawrence Navigation Co.* Q. 5 L. R. 215; 2 Cart. 231.

[3] *Smith* v. *the Merchants' Bank*, O. 28 Grant, 629; 1 Cart. 828, and see *Crombie* v. *Jackson*, 34 U. C. Q. B. 575; 1 Cart. 685.

Committee held that the Act could not properly be said to be a law in relation to property and civil rights in the sense in which the words are used in section 92, but related to the public order and safety, and therefore fell within the authority of the Dominion Parliament to make laws for the order and good government of Canada[1].

Police Regulations.

This power of the Dominion Legislature does not prevent a province from making regulations in the nature of police or municipal regulations of a local character for the good government of taverns licensed for the sale of liquors by retail, and such as are calculated to preserve in the municipality peace and public decency and repress drunkenness and disorderly and riotous conduct, nor are such regulations any interference with the general regulations of trade and commerce[2].

As an example of a Dominion Act held invalid as affecting civil rights reference may be made to the 42 Vic. c. 48 applying to all building societies, whether solvent or not[3].

Bankruptcy and Insolvency. The effect of these words was considered in *L'Union St Jacques* v. *Belisle.*

Bankruptcy.

The scheme of enumeration in section 91 is "to mention various categories of general subjects which may be dealt with by legislation. There is no indication in any instance of anything being contemplated except what may be properly described as general legislation: such legislation as is well expressed by Mr Justice Cawn when he speaks of the general laws governing faillite, bankruptcy and insolvency, all which are well-known legal terms expressing systems of legislation with which the subjects of this country and probably of most other civilized countries, are perfectly

---

[1] *Russell* v. *Regina*, L. R. 7 App. Cas. 829; 2 Cart. 12.   *Griffith* v. *Rioux*, Q. 6 Legal News, 211.

[2] *Hodge* v. *The Queen*, L. R. 9 App. Cas. 117, see also *Ex parte Pillow*, 27 L. C. Jurist 216.

[3] *McClanaghan* v. *St Ann's Mutual Building Society*, 21 L. C. Jurist 162; 2 Cart. 237.

familiar. The words describe in their known legal sense provisions made by law for the administration of the estates of persons who may become bankrupt or insolvent according to rules and definitions prescribed by law, including of course the conditions in which that law is to be brought into operation, the manner in which it is to be brought into operation and the effect of its operation[1]." Hence an Act of the Dominion providing for the liquidation of building societies in the province of Quebec only was held *ultra vires*[2].

A provision that claims by and against assignees in insolvency may be disposed of by a County Court Judge on petition is within the jurisdiction of the Dominion Government[3], and the clause in the Insolvent Act of 1875 which enacted that a person who purchased goods on credit knowing himself unable to meet his engagements and concealing the fact with intent to defraud should be liable to two years' imprisonment, was held valid by the Ontario Court of Appeal, though such enactment was connected with property and civil rights as well as with the administration of justice[4].

The following provincial Acts have been held invalid, as infringing on the Dominion rights regarding bankruptcy and insolvency :— *Acts held invalid.*

An Act of New Brunswick providing for the examination of a debtor before a judge and authorizing the judge to grant the debtor a discharge from gaol on proof that he is unable to pay his debts and had made no fraudulent transfer or undue preference[5].

The Quebec License Act 1870 in so far as it imposed a tax on the sum realized from the sale of an insolvent's effects[6].

[1] *L'Union St Jacques* v. *Belisle*, L. R. 6 P. C. 31 ; 1 Cart. p. 63.
[2] *McClanaghan* v. *St Ann's Society*, Q. 24 L. C. J. 162.
[3] *Crombie* v. *Jackson*, 34 U. C. Q. B. 575 ; 1 Cart. 685.
[4] *Peek* v. *Shields*, 6 Ont. App. Rep. 639.
[5] *R.* v. *Chandler*, N. B. 1 Hannay 556 ; 2 Cart. 421.
[6] *Coté* v. *Watson*, 3 Quebec, L. R. 157 ; 2 Cart. 343.

A portion of an Act of Nova Scotia, 1874, to facilitate arrangements between Railway Companies and their auditors[1].

The power to legislate on bankruptcy and insolvency is not only a limitation of the provincial power of legislating on "property and civil rights" but also of provincial powers relating to "procedure in civil matters."

Cushing v. Dupuy.

In *Cushing* v. *Dupuy*[2] it was contended that an Act of the Dominion Parliament which made the judgment of the Court of Queen's Bench in Quebec final in matters of insolvency was *ultra vires*, as interfering with property and civil rights and as dealing with procedure in a civil matter.

"The answer to these objections," said Sir Montague Smith in delivering the judgment of the Privy Council, "is obvious. It would be impossible to advance a step in the construction of a scheme for the administration of insolvent estates without interfering with and modifying some of the ordinary rights of property and other civil rights nor without providing some mode of special procedure for the vesting, realisation and distribution of the estate and the settlement of the liabilities of the insolvent. Procedure must necessarily form an essential part of any law dealing with insolvency. It is therefore to be presumed, indeed it is a necessary implication, that the Imperial Statute in assigning to the Dominion Parliament the subjects of bankruptcy and insolvency intended to confer on it legislative power to interfere with property, civil rights and procedure within the provinces so far as a general law relating to these subjects might affect them. Their Lordships therefore think that the Parliament of Canada would not infringe the exclusive powers given to the Provincial Legislatures by enacting that the judgment of the Court of Queen's Bench in matters of insolvency

---

[1] *Murdoch* v. *Windsor & Annapolis Ry. Co.*, Russell's Eq. Rep. 137, and *Re Windsor & Annapolis Ry.*; 4 Russell & Geldert 312.

[2] L. R. 5 App. Cas. 409.

should be final and not subject to the Appeal as of right to Her Majesty in Council allowed by Art. 1178 of the Code of Civil Procedure[1]."

The following provincial Acts have been held valid :—

An Act of N. B. providing that as against the assignee of the grantor under any law relating to insolvency, a bill of sale should take effect only from the time of filing thereof[2].

An Act of New Brunswick abolishing imprisonment for debt as respects a person not shewn to be a trader or subject to the Dominion Insolvent Act[3].

An Act of N. B. for the imprisonment of a person making default in payment of a sum due on a judgment in certain cases[4].

11. Trade and Commerce.

To the Dominion are assigned

The regulation of Trade and Commerce.   s. 91 (2).

Bankruptcy and Insolvency.   s. 91 (21).

Trade and Commerce.

The words 'regulation of trade and commerce' in their unlimited sense are sufficiently wide if uncontrolled by the context and other parts of the Act, to include every regulation of trade ranging from political arrangements in regard to trade with foreign Governments requiring the sanction of Parliament down to minute rules for regulating particular trades. But a consideration of the Act shews that the words were not used in this unlimited sense. In the first place the collocation of No. 2 with classes of subjects of national and general concern affords an indication that regulations relating to general trade and commerce were in the mind of the Legislature when conferring this power on the

---

[1] It was also held that the Statute did not affect the right of Her Majesty to allow an appeal as of Grace.

[2] *In re De Veber*, 21 N. B. R. 401 ; 2 Cart. 552.

[3] *Armstrong* v. *McCutchin*, N. B. 2 Pugsley, 381 ; 2 Cart. 494.

[4] *Ex parte Ellis*, N. B., 1 Pugsley & Burbidge, 593 ; 2 Cart. 527.

Dominion Parliament. If the words had been intended to have the full scope of which in their literal meaning they are susceptible, the specific mention of several of the other classes of subjects enumerated in section 91 would have been unnecessary, as 15, banking; 17, weights and measures; 18, bills of exchange and promissory notes; 19, interest; and even 21, bankruptcy and insolvency."

"'Regulation of trade and commerce' may have been used in some such sense as the words 'regulations of trade,' in the Act of Union between England and Scotland (6 Anne c. 11), and as these words have been used in Acts of state relating to trade and commerce. Article V. of the Act of Union enacted that all the subjects of the United Kingdom should have "full freedom and intercourse of trade and navigation" to and from all places in the United Kingdom and the Colonies, and Article VI. enacted that all parts of the United Kingdom from and after the Union should be under the *same* prohibitions, restrictions and *regulations of trade*. Parliament has at various times since the Union passed laws affecting and regulating specific trades in one part of the United Kingdom only without its being supposed that it thereby infringed the Articles of Union. Thus the Acts for regulating the Sale of Intoxicating Liquors notoriously vary in the two kingdoms. So with regard to Acts relating to bankruptcy and various other matters."

"Construing therefore the words 'regulations of trade and commerce' by the various aids to their interpretation above suggested, they would include political arrangements in regard to trade requiring the sanction of Parliament, regulations of trade in matters of inter-provincial concern, and it may be that they would include general regulations of trade affecting the whole Dominion."

The above remarks of Sir Montague Smith in the important case of *Citizens' Insurance Co.* v. *Parsons*[1] indicate the

---

[1] L. R. 7 App. Cas. p. 112.

view taken by the Judicial Committee, as to the meaning of the words "regulation of trade and commerce," though it is expressly stated that " their Lordships abstain on the present occasion from any attempt to define the limits of the authority of the Dominion Parliament in this direction." They held however that the authority to legislate for the regulation of trade and commerce did not comprehend the power to regulate by legislation the contracts of a particular trade, such as the business of a fire insurance in a single province.

The subsection in question is limited in its operation by the effect of some of the provisions in section 92. To prohibit the sale of certain articles in the public street is an interference with trade, but it was held that a by-law of a municipal body to this effect was not *ultra vires* of a provincial Legislature, inasmuch as it related to police or municipal matters which are within provincial control[1]. *Limita-tions.*

The power of the Dominion Parliament to legislate on trade and commerce is limited by the implied or incidental power the provinces have of passing laws necessary to give effect to the express powers of legislation committed to them.

On this ground the Quebec Pharmacy Act 1875, requiring qualifications on the part of persons exercising the business of selling drugs and medicines, was held valid[2] as falling within " local " matters in the province.

12. MONOPOLIES.

The Dominion has also sole jurisdiction in

1. Patents of Invention and Discovery. s. 91 (22).
2. Copyrights. s. 91 (23).
3. Incorporation of Banks. s. 91 (15).

[1] *Re Harris & the Corporation of City of Hamilton*, 44 U. C. Q. B. 641 ; 1 Cart. 756 ; see also *Hodge* v. *The Queen*, L. R. 9 App. Cas. 117, and the cases in Cartwright, vol. ii.

[2] *Bennett* v. *Pharmaceutical Association of Quebec*, 1 Dorion's Quebec Appeals, 336 ; 2 Cart. 250.

But with the exception of banks the provinces have full power as regards "the incorporation of companies with provincial objects," s. 92 (11). This however implies that the incorporation of companies to carry on business throughout the Dominion belongs to the Dominion, and the fact that a company confines the exercise of its powers to one province will not render its incorporation *ultra vires*[1].

13. MONEY AND BANKING.

The following matters are solely within Dominion legislation :—

  1. Currency and Coinage.   s. 91 (14).
  2. Issue of Paper Money.   s. 91 (15).
  3. Legal Tender.   s. 91 (20).
  4. Bills of Exchange and Promissory Notes.   s. 91 (18).
  5. Banking and Incorporation of Banks.   s. 91 (15).
  6. Savings Banks.   s. 91 (16).
  7. Interest.   s. 91 (19).

A province may authorize a corporation or other body to borrow money at a rate of interest legalised by the Dominion Parliament, but it cannot alter the legal rate of interest[2].

14. AGRICULTURE AND IMMIGRATION.

On two subjects, viz.

  1. Agriculture in the province,
  2. Immigration into the province,

concurrent powers of legislation are given to the Dominion and the provinces, subject to the proviso that a provincial law is only to be of force in so far as it is not repugnant to the Dominion Act.   s. 95.

---

[1] *A. G. for Quebec* v. *Colonial Building and Investment Association*, 9 App. Cas. 157.

[2] *Royal Canadian Insurance Co.* v. *Montreal Warehousing Co.* Q. 3 Legal News, 155; 2 Cart. 361; *Ross* v. *Torrance*, Q. 2 Legal News, 186; 2 Cart. 352.

15. LOCAL MATTERS.

Each province has jurisdiction in

(1) Municipal institutions in the province. s. 92 (8). Municipal institutions.

(2) Generally all matters of a merely local or private nature in the province. s. 92 (16).

This last sub-section must be read in connection with the following provision in section 91 :—

"Any matter coming within any of the classes of subjects enumerated in this section [s. 91] shall not be deemed to come within the class of matters of a local or private nature comprised in the enumeration of the classes of subjects by this Act assigned exclusively to the Legislatures of the provinces."

In the case of *L'Union St Jacques* v. *Belisle*[1] the Judicial What are local matters. Committee of the Privy Council was called upon to consider the meaning of the words "matters of a merely local or private nature." A benefit society called L'Union St Jacques de Montreal, incorporated in the city of Montreal, and consisting of members living within the Province of Quebec, had owing to improvident regulations become embarrassed. The local Legislature passed an Act imposing a forced commutation of existing rights upon two widows who were annuitants of the society, but reserving the rights so cut down in the possible event of an improvement in the affairs of the association. "Clearly this matter is private," said Lord Selborne in delivering the judgment of the Court ; "clearly it is local, so far as locality is to be considered, because it is in the province and in the city of Montreal." A majority of the judges of the Quebec Court of Queen's Bench had held that the subject-matter of the Act came within the class of "insolvency," which under the 91st section belonged exclusively to the authority of the Dominion Parliament ; a view not followed by the Judicial Committee. The fact that the

[1] L. R. 6, P. C. 31 ; 1 Cart. 63.

society was embarrassed did not make it "insolvent," and the
object of the Act was to prevent insolvency and enable the
society to continue.

Dow v. Black.

This case was followed in *Dow* v. *Black*[1], where an Act of
the Legislature of New Brunswick to enable the majority of
the inhabitants of a parish within the province to raise, by
local taxation, a subsidy to promote the construction of a
railway extending beyond the province, but already duly
authorized to be made, was held to be a "local or private
matter" resembling an Act authorizing trustees or guardians
of a minor to let a warehouse to the company.

Liquor traffic.

Municipal Institutions. The right of a province to
regulate the liquor traffic has been held in several cases[2]
to be valid as an exercise of the power to make police or
municipal regulations. The validity of such laws has been
attacked, chiefly on the ground that they are an interference
with trade, but the case of *Hodge* v. *The Queen* has finally
determined that such laws so long as they relate to police or
to municipal or local matters are not *ultra vires*. A province
may therefore enforce a Sunday Closing Act[3].

This power to deal with municipal institutions impliedly
gives power to alter and amend the laws relating to such
institutions as existed at the time the Act passed[4]. And
where a by-law of a municipal body forbade the sale by
retail in public streets of certain articles, it was held not
to be an interference with "the regulation of trade and
commerce[5]."

[1] L. R. 6, P. C. 272; 1 Cart. p. 95.
[2] See *Hodge* v. *The Queen*, 9 App. Cas. 117; *Sulte* v. *Corporation of City of Three Rivers*, 12 C. S. C. R. 25.
[3] *Poulin* v. *Corporation of Quebec*, 9 Can. S. C. R. 185.
[4] *Re Harris and the Corporation of the City of Hamilton*, 44 U. C. Q. B. 641; 1 Cart. 756.
[5] *Ib.*

16.   ALTERATION OF LAWS EXISTING AT TIME OF THE UNION.

By section 129, the laws in force in each province were to continue in force, subject (except as regards Imperial Acts) to being altered by the Dominion or province, according as their subject-matter was within the jurisdiction of the Dominion or the province under the provisions of the Act of Union.

The powers possessed by a provincial Legislature to repeal and alter old statutes are co-extensive with the powers of direct legislation which the province possesses under other clauses of the Act[1].

---

[1] *Dobie* v. *The Temporalities Board*, L. R. 7 App. Cas. 136; 1 Cart. 351.

CHAPTER XX.

DOMINION CONTROL OF THE PROVINCES.

THE Dominion Executive has, within very definite limits, a certain degree of control over the provincial Legislatures and Administrations.

Veto of Governor-General.

As regards the provincial Legislatures, every Act passed has to be transmitted to the Governor-General, who, within one year, may disallow the same. An account has already been given of the course followed by the Governor-General on receipt of a provincial Act[1]. As a rule it is referred to the Minister of Justice, who reports thereon to the Governor-General. The power of disallowance is in practice exercised only on the advice of the Dominion Ministry. Up to the present time it has been but seldom used. From 1867 to 1882 out of 6000 Acts only 31 were disallowed. Since 1883 the following Acts have been disallowed[2]:—

Acts disallowed.

1883 An Act of New Brunswick to incorporate a Bridge Company.

Two Acts of British Columbia incorporating Railway Companies.

1884 An Act of Ontario respecting Licence duties.

1885 An Act of British Columbia restricting the immigration of Chinese.

[1] *Ante*, p. 175.

[2] On the Disallowance of Provincial Acts, see Can. Sess. Pap. 1882, No. 141; Ib. 1885, No. 29, and Ib., Report of Minister of Justice, 1st April, 1886.

An Ordinance of the North West Territories ex- Acts dis-
allowed.
empting certain property from seizure and sale.

An Act of Manitoba respecting escheats and forfeitures and estates of intestates.

1886   An Act of British Columbia to prevent the immigration of Chinese.

An Act of British Columbia to amend the Land
Act 1884.

An Act of British Columbia to amend the Sumas
Dyking Act 1878.

Two Acts of Manitoba to incorporate certain Railway Companies.

1887   A Manitoba Act respecting the Lieutenant-Governor
and his Deputies.

A Manitoba Act to incorporate the Rock Lake,
Louis Valley and Brandon Railway Company.

A Nova Scotia Act concerning the collection of
freight and wharfage and warehouse charges.

In the majority of cases in which an Act has been Reasons.
disallowed it has been on the ground that the Act in
question was clearly beyond the competency of the provincial
Legislature.   Where there is a reasonable doubt as to the
power of the Legislature to pass the Act, it is usually allowed
to come into operation, and the persons affected thereby are
left to pursue their remedy in the Courts.

The British Columbia, Manitoba, and Nova Scotia Rail- Railway
Acts.
way Acts have been disallowed on another ground, viz., that
they were contrary to the railway policy of the Dominion.   By
a clause of the contract between the Government of Canada
and the Canadian Pacific Railway Company it is provided :—

"That for twenty years from the date hereof, no line of
railway shall be authorized by the Dominion Parliament to
be constructed south of the Canadian Pacific Railway from
any point at or near the Canadian Pacific Railway, except
such line as shall run south-west or to the westward of south-

west; nor to within fifteen miles of Latitude 49, and in the establishment of any New Province in the North West Territory provision shall be made for continuing such prohibition after such establishment until the expiration of the said period."

The Dominion Government up to the present year has maintained the policy embodied in this contract and has disallowed all provincial Acts incorporating railways forbidden to be constructed by the above clause.

Manitoba dispute.

Notwithstanding the disallowing of a recent Railway Act the Government of Manitoba proceeded with the construction of a railway, and thereupon the Minister of Justice obtained an injunction against the contractor and the Railway Company practically prohibiting the construction of the line. During the dispute the Manitoba Government petitioned the Queen in Council, urging that a provincial bill ought not to be vetoed so long as it was within the competence of the provincial Legislature. It may be pointed out, that any interference by the Crown with the veto of the Governor-General, exercised on the advice of his responsible advisers, would be distinctly " unconstitutional" and at variance with the principle of ministerial responsibility.

Negotiations, not yet completed, have resulted in an understanding between the Dominion, the Province, and the Pacific Railway Company, by which the Company are to surrender the monopoly in consideration of a money payment.

Provincial administration.

As regards the provincial administration the appointment of the Lieutenant-Governor and the Judges is in the hands of the Governor-General in Council. The Lieutenant-Governor is therefore a Dominion and not a provincial officer and that he is responsible to the Dominion Government for his acts was clearly shewn in the *Letellier case*[1], when the

---

[1] *Ante*, p. 173.

Lieutenant-Governor was removed from his office on the advice of the Canadian Privy Council. The sections of the B. N. A. Act 1867[1] relating to the appointment and tenure of office by a Lieutenant-Governor, provide that the appointment shall be by the " Governor-General in Council," and that he shall hold office during the pleasure of the " Governor-General." Much stress was laid on this distinction in the *Letellier case* as the then Governor-General was adverse to acting on the advice of his Ministers to remove M. Letellier de St Just. The Colonial Secretary in his despatch pointed out, " that other powers vested in a similar way by the statute in the Governor-General were clearly intended to be, and in practice are, exercised by and with the advice of his Ministers: and though the position of a Governor-General would entitle his views on such a subject as that under consideration to peculiar weight, yet Her Majesty's Government do not find anything in the circumstances which would justify him in departing in this instance from the general rule, and declining to follow the decided and sustained opinion of his Ministers."

Advice of Ministers.

The enforcement of the judgments and orders of the Supreme Court of Canada in the provinces, is a matter of the greatest importance in view of the fact that the Supreme Court may be called upon to decide on the legality of a provincial Act. It is therefore necessary that in all the provinces the Supreme Court should be represented by its officers, but in order to avoid the cost of maintaining Dominion officers, as well as provincial officers, the plan has been adopted of making the officers of the provincial Courts *ex officio* officers of the Supreme Court. By section 105 of the Revised Statutes of Canada, 1886, it is enacted that " the process of the Supreme Court and the process of the Exchequer Court shall run throughout Canada and shall be tested in the name of the Chief Justice, or in the case of a

Enforcing judgments of Supreme Court.

---

[1] ss. 58, 59.

vacancy in the office of Chief Justice, in the name of the senior puisne Judge of the Court, and shall be directed to the Sheriff of any County or other Judicial division into which any province is divided: and the sheriffs of the second respective counties or divisions shall be deemed and taken to be *ex officio* officers of the Supreme and Exchequer Courts respectively, and shall perform the duties and functions of Sheriffs in connection with the said Courts, and in any case where the Sheriff is disqualified such process shall be directed to any of the coroners of the county or district."

CHAPTER XXI.

IMPERIAL CONTROL OVER THE DOMINION.

THE legislative powers conferred on the Dominion Parliament and the provincial Legislatures, though of a very wide character, are limited in several ways: (1) they do not exhaust the whole sphere of legislation, (2) they are concurrent with and are not exclusive of the legislative powers of the Imperial Parliament, (3) where an Imperial and a Colonial Statute conflict, the former is to prevail, and (4) the Crown may veto any Act of the Dominion Parliament. Limitations.

1. *Limitations on Dominion Legislation.*

Though power is given, in general terms, to the Dominion by section 91 of the B. N. A. Act 1867 "to make laws for the peace, order, and good government of Canada in relation to all matters not coming within the classes of subjects by this Act assigned exclusively to the Legislatures of the Provinces," yet other sections of this Act and at least one other Act of Parliament, apart from the clauses defining the legislative powers of the Provinces, restrict the powers of the Dominion Parliament. General Powers.

The most important limitations are as follow :—

1. The Dominion has but a limited power of altering its constitution. It may prescribe the qualification of voters and regulate the method of election, but it cannot abolish either House of Parliament, or alter the constitution of the Senate, or affect the veto of the Crown. Even its power of Altering Constitution.

altering the number of members of the House of Commons
has to be exercised in accordance with certain principles
laid down in the Act. A province has greater power to alter
its constitution than has the Dominion.

Provincial Constitutions. 2. After the Dominion grants a constitution to a new Province it cannot alter such constitution[1].

Protective duties. 3. The Dominion cannot impose any protective duties as between provinces[2].

Public lands. 4. The Dominion cannot tax any lands or property belonging to Canada or any Province[3].

Acts of English Parliament. 5. Acts of the Parliament of Great Britain or of the Parliament of Great Britain and Ireland which were in force in any of the provinces at the time of the Union, can be repealed, abolished or altered only by Imperial legislation[4].

Seat of Government. 6. The seat of the Government can be altered only by the Crown[5].

2. *Concurrent Power of Legislation.*

Imperial Legislation. The Imperial Parliament has concurrent legislative power on all matters within the legislative jurisdiction of Canada and its Provinces.

It is true that in *Holmes* v. *Temple*[6], the Judge of the Quebec Sessions held that "exclusive" meant exclusive of the Imperial Parliament, and dismissed a prosecution for persuading a soldier to desert, brought under the Imperial Army Act of 1881, on the ground that the Dominion Parliament had "exclusive" jurisdiction in matters relating to "militia, military and naval service and defence[7];" but the Ontario Court of Queen's Bench in another case[8] laid down the true principle, viz. that the word "exclusive" as

---

[1] 34 Vic. (i.) c. 28, s. 2.   [2] B. N. A. Act 1867, s. 121.
[3] Ib. s. 125.   [4] Ib. s. 129.   [5] Ib. s. 16.
[6] 8 Quebec Law Reports, 357 ; 2 Cart. 396.
[7] B. N. A. Act, s. 91 (7).
[8] *R.* v. *College of Physicians and Surgeons of Ontario*, 44 U. C. Q. B. 564 ; 1 Cart. 761.

applied to Dominion powers of legislation in the Act meant exclusive of provincial Legislatures. The facts of the case were as follows:—

By section 93 of the British North America Act 1867, "Exclusive" power is given to Provincial Legislatures to "exclusively Legislation. make laws in relation to Education," and in 1874 the Ontario Legislature under this clause amended and consolidated the laws relating to the Medical profession in the Province. The year after the passing of the Act of 1867, the Imperial Parliament by the 31 & 32 Vic. c. 79, enacted, that any person registered under the Medical Act of 1858 should upon payment of the fees required, and upon proof of his registration, be entitled to be registered in any Colony of the Crown. In 1879 a medical practitioner duly registered under the Imperial Act applied to the College of Physicians and Surgeons of Ontario to be registered in the Province. The College refused to do so, and in the subsequent legal proceedings it was urged, that by the 93rd section of the Act 1867 the registration of doctors was within the exclusive jurisdiction of the provinces, and that the Imperial Act could only be taken to apply where there was no provincial legislation. In giving the judgment of the Court, Hagarty, C. J., remarked, "The case of the defendants was argued in a very fair and candid spirit admitting, as of course was necessary with the Federation Act before us, that if the Imperial Parliament distinctly legislate for us they can do so notwithstanding any previous enactment or alleged surrender of the power of exclusive legislation on any subject. But it was ably urged that as the subject of Education was one in which the exclusive right was given to the Province, we should read the Imperial Act as not interfering with the right so granted. To this it may be argued that where the Federation Act speaks of any such exclusive right, it means exclusive as opposed to any attempt to legislate by the Dominion Parliament."

A similar view was expressed in *Smiles* v. *Belford*[1] in regard to the Dominion power of legislating on copyright, which by section 91 of the Act of 1867 is placed within the "exclusive" jurisdiction of the Dominion Parliament and yet was affected by Imperial Acts passed after the Union.

Imperial Acts passed since Union.

The following are some of the chief Acts passed since the Union by the Imperial Parliament relating to Canada.

Merchant Shipping Acts, 32 & 33 Vic. c. 11; 34 & 35 Vic. c. 110; 39 & 40 Vic. c. 80; 43 & 44 Vic. c. 16; Ib. c. 18; Ib. c. 22; Ib. c. 43; 45 & 46 Vic. c. 76; 46 & 47 Vic. c. 41.

Naturalisation Acts, 33 & 34 Vic. c. 14; 33 & 34 Vic. c. 102.

Extradition Act, 33 & 34 Vic. c. 52.

Foreign Enlistment Act, 33 & 34 Vic. c. 90.

Act relating to Treaty of Washington, 35 & 36 Vic. c. 45.

The Courts Colonial Jurisdiction Act, 37 & 38 Vic. c. 27.

Canada Copyright Act, 38 & 39 Vic. c. 53.

Unseaworthy Ships Act, 38 & 39 Vic. c. 88.

Confirmation of Marriages on Her Majesty's Ships Act, 42 & 43 Vic. c. 29.

Shipping Casualties Investigations Act, 42 & 43 Vic. c. 72.

Fugitive Offenders Act, 44 & 45 Vic. c. 69.

Companies Colonial Registers Act, 46 & 47 Vic. c. 30.

Colonial Prisoners' Removal Act, 47 & 48 Vic. c. 31.

Submarine Telegraph Act, 48 & 49 Vic. c. 49.

Evidence by Commission Act, 48 & 49 Vic. c. 74.

Copyright Act, 49 & 50 Vic. c. 33.

Medical Act 1886, 49 & 50 Vic. c. 48.

Submarine Telegraphs Act, 50 Vic. c. 3.

3. *Powers of the Crown.*

(a). PROVINCIAL BILLS.

Veto of Crown.

The Crown has no power of vetoing a provincial bill. Power is given to a Lieutenant-Governor, when a bill is

---

[1] 1 Ont. App. Rep. 436; 1 Cart. 576.

presented to him for his assent, to reserve the same for the signification of the pleasure of his Excellency the Governor-General[1]. If within one year from the date of such reservation the Governor-General does not issue a proclamation intimating that it has received his assent, the bill never comes into force[2].

Instead of reserving the bill the Lieutenant-Governor may assent to it, but the Governor-General has the power to disallow the bill at any time within one year from its passing[3].

Reservation.

If the Governor-General does not disallow the Act within such year then it can be questioned only in an action in which it is alleged that the subject-matter was not within the legislative powers of the province.

It is however open to the Governor-General to communicate with the Imperial Government in regard to the disallowance of a provincial law. For instance, when the Ontario Legislature passed an Act conferring upon the Legislative Assembly the same privileges as those enjoyed by the Dominion House of Commons, the competency of the Legislature to pass this Act was doubted, and on the recommendation of the Dominion Minister of Justice, the question was referred to the English law officers of the Crown. They were of opinion that the Act was *ultra vires,* and it was therefore disallowed by the Governor-General in Council[4].

Consulting Home Government.

Attempts have been made in several cases by the Dominion House of Commons, and by parties interested in provincial legislation, to persuade the Imperial Government to interfere with provincial legislation. When New Brunswick in 1871 passed an Act relating to common schools, not only did the Dominion House of Commons ask the Governor-General to take the opinion of the law officers of the Crown

Attempts to obtain Imperial interference.

---

[1] B. N. A. Act, s. 90.   [2] Ib.   [3] See *ante,* 165.
[4] Todd, p. 305.

on the validity of the Act, but they applied through the Governor-General to the Privy Council for its opinion. The law officers reported in favour of the Act, and on the ground that the power of confirming or disallowing provincial Acts was vested by law absolutely and exclusively in the Governor-General[1], the Lord President of the Council declined to interfere.

Governor-General may consult Home Government.

The legality of the Act was upheld by the Supreme Court of New Brunswick, but notwithstanding this, the Dominion House of Commons asked the Governor-General to disallow certain other statutes amending the Act in question. At the request of his Ministers the Governor-General laid the whole matter before the Imperial Government, and the Secretary of State for the Colonies replied, that as the Acts in question were within the powers of the local legislature, they ought to be allowed to remain in force and could not be interfered with by the Dominion House of Commons[2].

Petitions sent direct to Imperial Government.

It is a standing rule of the Colonial service that all communications from a Colony should be transmitted to the Imperial Government through the Governor, and when a petition against an Act of Ontario granting special privileges to an Orange Society was presented to the Colonial Secretary, it was forwarded to the Governor-General. The Colonial Secretary in acknowledging the petition laid down the principle, "that it is contrary to established constitutional procedure for Her Majesty's Government to interfere unless in very special circumstances with such legislation as is within the competency of a provincial Legislature[3]."

The rule may be taken as established—that, except in very special or extraordinary circumstances, the Home Government will not recommend the Governor-General to disallow a provincial Act that falls within the matters over which the Provinces have full jurisdiction.

---

[1] Todd, p. 347; Can. Sess. Pap. 1877, No. 89, p. 343.

[2] Todd, p. 348; Can. Sess. Pap. 1874, No. 25, p. 8.   [3] Todd, p. 357.

(b). DOMINION BILLS.

When a bill has passed the Dominion Parliament it is presented to the Governor-General for the Queen's assent.

Instead of assenting to the bill, he may reserve the bill for the signification of Her Majesty's pleasure. If he assents to the bill, he is required to transmit a copy to one of her Majesty's Secretaries of State, and if the Queen in Council within two years after the receipt thereof by the Secretary of State disallows the Act, it is annulled from the date of such signification. The Imperial Government has therefore full control over Dominion legislation.

The power of the Governor-General to assent to bills is, Reserved by the B. N. A. Act, s. 55, limited by his instructions. Bills. Previous to 1878 the instructions required him, in the case of certain bills, not to assent to the bill except in case of urgent necessity, unless there was a clause suspending the operation of the bill, until Her Majesty's pleasure could be signified. In accordance with these instructions the Governor-General reserved twenty-one bills between the years 1867 and 1878. Eleven of these related to divorce and received the royal assent. In 1872 a Copyright Bill was not approved, as it conflicted with imperial legislation. Two Extradition Bills were not allowed in 1873 and 1874. A Merchant Shipping Bill was disallowed in 1878, as it contained provisions in excess of Dominion powers, whilst a reserved bill that might have prejudiced the rights of subjects not resident in Canada was dropped in 1874, and a modified bill passed in the following year[1].

In the revised instructions issued in 1878 the clauses Modern relating to the reservation of bills were omitted, "because practice. her Majesty's Government thought it undesirable that they should contain anything which could be interpreted as

---

[1] See Todd, p. 144.

limiting or defining the legislative powers conferred in 1867 on the Dominion Parliament[1]."

Since 1878 it has not been the custom to reserve bills, as it is understood that the statutory power to disallow any bill within two years is sufficient for all purposes.

A reserved bill has no force until the Governor-General signifies by speech or message to the Dominion Parliament or by proclamation that it has received Her Majesty's assent[2].

Disallowance of Bills. The B. N. A. Act, s. 56, requires the Governor-General to send to a Secretary of State by the first convenient opportunity an authentic copy of every Act to which he assents; and a Dominion Act[3] requires the Clerk of Parliaments to certify and deliver to the Governor-General a bound copy of the Statutes for transmission to one of the Secretaries of State, together with certified copies of all reserved bills.

---

[1] Can. Sess. Pap. 1877, No. 3; Burinot, p. 573.

[2] B. N. A. Act, s. 57.   [3] 35 Vic. c. 1, s. 4.

APPENDIX.

18

GOVERNORS-GENERAL AND LIEUTENANT-GOVERNORS.

GOVERNORS-GENERAL.

Up to 1791.

1765 Gen. James Murray.
1766 Gen. Sir Guy Carleton.
1785 Gen. Frederick Haldemand.

From 1797.

LOWER CANADA.		UPPER CANADA.	
1797	Major Gen. Prescott.	1792	G. Simcoe.
1808	Sir James Craig.	1796	P. Russel (Ad.).
1811	Sir George Prevost.	1799	Gen. P. Hunter.
1813	Sir George Drummond.	1806	Francis Gore.
1816	Sir John Cope Sherbrooke.	1812	Gen. Brock (Ad.).
1818	Duke of Richmond.	1812	Gen. Sheafe (Ad.).
1819	Sir Peregrine Maitland.		Gen. Murray (Ad.).
1820	Earl of Dalhousie.		Gen. Robinson (Ad.).
1828	Sir James Kempt.	1815	Francis Gore.
1830	Lord Aylmer.	1818	Sir Peregrine Maitland.
1835	Lord Gosford.	1828	Sir John Colborne.
1838	Earl of Durham.	1836	Sir Francis Bond Head.
1838	Sir James Colborne.	1838	Sir George Arthur.
1839	Lord Sydenham.		

Since 1840.

1842 Sir Chas. Bagot.
1843 Sir Chas. Metcalfe.
1845 Earl Cathcart.
1847 Earl of Elgin.
1855 Sir Edmund Walker Head.
1861 Lord Monck.

Since 1867.

1867 Viscount Monck.
1868 Lord Lisgar.
1872 Earl of Dufferin.
1878 Marquis of Lorne.
1883 Marquis of Lansdowne.
1888 Lord Stanley of Preston.

LIEUTENANT-GOVERNORS OF QUEBEC. *Since* 1867.	LIEUTENANT-GOVERNORS OF ONTARIO. *Since* 1867.
1867 Sir N. F. Belleau.	1867 Gen. Stisted (Ad.).
1873 R. E. Caron.	1868 W. P. Howland.
1876 Letellier de St Just.	1873 John Crawford.
1879 Dr T. Robitaille.	1875 D. A. MacDonald.
1884 L. F. R. Masson.	1880 J. B. Robinson.
1887 A. R. Angers.	1887 Sir A. Campbell.

NOVA SCOTIA.

1710	Col. Vetch.	1819	Earl of Dalhousie.
1714	Gen. Nicholson.	1820	Sir J. Kempt.
1719	Gen. Philips.	1826	M. Wallace.
1725	Col. L. Armstrong.	1836	Sir G. Campbell.
1740	Cap. P. Mascarene.	1840	Lord Falkland.
1749	Lord Cornwallis.	1846	Sir J. Harvey.
1752	V. Hopson.	1852	Sir G. L. Marchant.
1754	Major Lawrence.	1858	Earl of Mulgrave.
1756	A. Moulton.	1864	Sir R. G. MacDonnell.
1760	J. Belcher.	1865	Gen. Sir W. F. Williams.
1764	Col. M. Wilmot.		
1783	P. Fanning.	1867	Gen. Williams (Ad.).
1791	R. Bulkeley.	1867	Gen. Doyle.
1792	J. Wentworth.	1870	Sir E. Kenny (acting).
1808	Sir G. Prevost.	1873	J. Howe.
1811	Sir J. Sherbrooke.	1873	A. G. Archibald, Q.C.
1811	Gen. Daroch.	1883	M. H. Richey.
1816	Gen. Smyth.	1888	A. W. McLean.

NEW BRUNSWICK.

1786	Guy Carleton.	1848	Sir E. Head.
1787	E. Winslow.	1854	Hon. J. H. Sutton.
1788	Lt. Col. Johnston.	1861	Hon. A. H. Gordon.
1809	Gen. M. Hunter.	1866	Major-Gen. H. Doyle.
1811	Gen. W. Balfour.		
1812	Gen. Geo. S. Smyth.	1867	Lieut-Gen. Sir H. Doyle.
1823	Ward Chapman.	1867	Col. F. P. Harding.
1824	J. M. Bliss.	1868	L. A. Wilmot.
1825	Gen. Sir H. Douglass.	1873	S. L. Tilley.
1831	Gen. Sir A. Campbell (Ad.).	1878	E. B. Chandler, Q.C.
1837	Gen. Sir J. Harvey.	1880	R. D. Wilmot.
1841	Col. Sir W. Colbrooke.	1885	Sir S. L. Tilley.

MANITOBA.

1870	A. G. Archibald.	1882	J. Cox Aikins.
1873	A. Morris.	1888	J. C. Schultz.
1879	J. E. Cauchon.		

BRITISH COLUMBIA.

VANCOUVER ISLAND.

1849	R. Blanshard.		
1851 1864	} James Douglass.		
1864	Captain Kennedy.		

BRITISH COLUMBIA.

1859	James Douglass.

BRITISH COLUMBIA AND VANCOUVER ISLAND.

1866	H. Seymour.	1881	C. F. Cornwall.
1871	J. W. Trutch.	1887	Hugh Nelson.
1876	A. N. Richards.		

PRINCE EDWARD ISLAND.

1770	Walter Patterson.	1847	Sir Donald Campbell.
1786	Lieut.-Gen. Edmund Fanning.	1851	Sir Alex. Bannerman.
		1854	Sir Dominick Daly.
1805	Col. J. F. W. DesBarres.	1859	George Dundas.
1813	Charles Douglas Smith.	1870	Sir Wm. F. C. Robinson.
1824	Col. John Ready.	1874	Sir Robert Hodgson (administrator).
1831	Sir Aretes W. Young.		
1836	Sir John Harvey.	1879	Hon. Thomas Heath Haviland, Q.C.
1837	Sir Chas. Augustus Fitzroy.		
1841	Sir Henry Vere Huntley.	1884	A. A. Macdonald.

NORTH-WEST TERRITORIES.

1870	A. G. Archibald.	1876	D. Laird.
1872	F. G. Johnston.	1881	Edgar Dewdney.
	A. Morris.	1888	Joseph Royal.

THE BRITISH NORTH AMERICA ACT, 1867.

30 and 31 Vic. c. 3.

An Act for the Union of Canada, Nova Scotia, and New Brunswick, and the Government thereof; and for purposes connected therewith.

[29 *March*, 1867.]

WHEREAS the Provinces of Canada, Nova Scotia, and New Brunswick, have expressed their desire to be federally united into one Dominion under the Crown of the United Kingdom of Great Britain and Ireland, with a Constitution similar in principle to that of the United Kingdom :

And whereas such a Union would conduce to the welfare of the Provinces and promote the Interests of the British Empire:

And whereas on the establishment of the Union by authority of Parliament it is expedient, not only that the Constitution of the Legislative authority in the Dominion be provided for, but also that the nature of the Executive Government therein be declared:

And whereas it is expedient that provision be made for the eventual admission into the Union of other parts of British North America:

Be it therefore enacted and declared by the Queen's most Excellent Majesty, by and with the advice and consent of the Lords Spiritual and Temporal, and Commons, in this present Parliament assembled, and by the authority of the same, as follows :—

I.—PRELIMINARY.

Short Title.
1. This Act may be cited as "The British North America Act, 1867."

Application of Provisions referring to the Queen.
2. The provisions of this Act referring to Her Majesty the Queen, extend also to the heirs and successors of Her Majesty, Kings and Queens of the United Kingdom of Great Britain and Ireland.

II.—UNION.

3. It shall be lawful for the Queen, by and with the advice Declara-of Her Majesty's Most Honourable Privy Council, to declare $\begin{smallmatrix}\text{tion of}\\\text{Union,}\end{smallmatrix}$ by Proclamation that, on and after a day therein appointed, not being more than six months after the passing of this Act, the Provinces of Canada, Nova Scotia, and New Brunswick, shall form and be one Dominion under the name of Canada; and on and after that day, those three provinces shall form and be one Dominion under that name accordingly.

4. The subsequent provisions of this Act shall, unless it is Construc-otherwise expressed or implied, commence and have effect on and $\begin{smallmatrix}\text{tion of}\\\text{subse-}\end{smallmatrix}$ after the Union, that is to say, on and after the day appointed quent pro-for the Union taking effect in the Queen's Proclamation; and in $\begin{smallmatrix}\text{visions of}\\\text{Act.}\end{smallmatrix}$ the same provisions, unless it is otherwise expressed or implied, the name Canada shall be taken to mean Canada as constituted under this Act.

5. Canada shall be divided into four Provinces, named On- Four Pro-tario, Quebec, Nova Scotia, and New Brunswick. vinces.

6. The parts of the Province of Canada (as it exists at the Provinces passing of this Act) which formerly constituted respectively the $\begin{smallmatrix}\text{of Ontario}\\\text{and Que-}\end{smallmatrix}$ Provinces of Upper Canada and Lower Canada shall be deemed bec. to be severed, and shall form two separate Provinces. The part which formerly constituted the Province of Upper Canada shall constitute the Province of Ontario; and the part which formerly constituted the Province of Lower Canada shall constitute the Province of Quebec.

Provinces
7. The Provinces of Nova Scotia and New Brunswick shall of Nova have the same limits as at the passing of this Act. $\begin{smallmatrix}\text{Scotia and}\\\text{New}\\\text{Bruns-}\end{smallmatrix}$

8. In the general census of the population of Canada which wick. is hereby required to be taken in the year One thousand eight Decennial hundred and seventy-one, and in every tenth year thereafter, the Census. respective populations of the four Provinces shall be distinguished.

III.   EXECUTIVE POWER.

Declara-
9. The Executive Government and authority of and over tion of Canada is hereby declared to continue and be vested in the Queen. $\begin{smallmatrix}\text{Executive}\\\text{power in}\\\text{the Queen.}\end{smallmatrix}$

Applica-
tion of
provisic ns
refer-
ring to
Governor-
General.

10.   The provisions of this Act referring to the Governor-General extend and apply to the Governor-General for the time being of Canada, or other the Chief Executive Officer or Administrator for the time being carrying on the Government of Canada on behalf and in the name of the Queen, by whatever title he is designated.

Constitu-
tion of
Privy
Council
for
Canada.

11.   There shall be a Council to aid and advise in the Government of Canada, to be styled the Queen's Privy Council for Canada ; and the persons who are to be Members of that Council shall be from time to time chosen and summoned by the Governor-General and sworn in as Privy Councillors, and Members thereof may be from time to time removed by the Governor-General.

All powers
under Acts
to be exer-
cised by
Governor-
General
with
advice of
Privy
Council or
alone.

12.   All powers, authorities, and functions which under any Act of the Parliament of Great Britain, or of the Parliament of the United Kingdom of Great Britain and Ireland, or of the Legislature of Upper Canada, Lower Canada, Canada, Nova Scotia, or New Brunswick, are at the Union vested in or exercisable by the respective Governors or Lieutenant Governors of those Provinces, with the advice, or with the advice and consent, of the respective Executive Councils thereof, or in conjunction with those Councils, or with any number of Members thereof, or by those Governors or Lieutenant-Governors individually, shall, as far as the same continue in existence and capable of being exercised after the Union in relation to the Government of Canada, be vested in and exercisable by the Governor-General with the advice or with the advice and consent of or in conjunction with the Queen's Privy Council for Canada, or any Members thereof, or by the Governor-General individually, as the case requires, subject nevertheless (except with respect to such as exist under Acts of the Parliament of Great Britain or of the Parliament of the United Kingdom of Great Britain and Ireland) to be abolished or altered by the Parliament of Canada.

Applica-
tion of
provisions
refer-
ring to
Governor-
General in
Council.

13.   The provisions of this Act referring to the Governor-General in Council shall be construed as referring to the Governor-General acting by and with the advice of the Queen's Privy Council for Canada.

14.   It shall be lawful for the Queen, if Her Majesty thinks fit, to authorize the Governor General from time to time to appoint any person or any persons, jointly or severally, to be his deputy or deputies within any part or parts of Canada, and in that capacity to exercise, during the pleasure of the Governor-General, such of the powers, authorities, and functions of the Governor-General, as the Governor-General deems it necessary or expedient to assign to him or them, subject to any limitations or directions expressed or given by the Queen ; but the appointment of such a deputy or deputies shall not affect the exercise by the Governor-General himself of any power, authority, or function.

Power to Her Majesty to authorize Governor-General to appoint Deputies.

15.   The Command-in-Chief of the Land and Naval Militia, and of all Naval and Military Forces, of and in Canada, is hereby declared to continue and be vested in the Queen.

Command of Armed Forces to continue to be vested in the Queen.

16.   Until the Queen otherwise directs, the Seat of Government of Canada shall be Ottawa.

Seat of Government of Canada.

IV.   LEGISLATIVE POWER.

17.   There shall be one Parliament for Canada, consisting of the Queen, an Upper House styled the Senate, and the House of Commons.

Constitution of Parliament of Canada.

18.   The privileges, immunities, and powers to be held, enjoyed, and exercised by the Senate and by the House of Commons, and by the Members thereof respectively, shall be such as are from time to time defined by Act of the Parliament of Canada, but so that the same shall never exceed those at the passing of this Act held, enjoyed, and exercised by the Commons House of Parliament of the United Kingdom of Great Britain and Ireland and by the Members thereof.   (*Repealed by* 30 *&* 31 *Vic. c.* 3.)

Privileges, &c., of Houses.

19.   The Parliament of Canada shall be called together not later than six months after the Union.

First Session of the Parliament of Canada.

20.   There shall be a Session of the Parliament of Canada once at least in every year, so that twelve months shall not intervene between the last sitting of the Parliament in one Session and its first sitting in the next Session.

Yearly Session of the Parliament of Canada.

The Senate.

Number of Senators. 21. The Senate shall, subject to the provisions of this Act, consist of seventy-two Members, who shall be styled Senators.

Representation of Provinces in Senate. 22. In relation to the constitution of the Senate, Canada shall be deemed to consist of three divisions,—

1. Ontario :
2. Quebec :
3. The Maritime Provinces, Nova Scotia and New Brunswick; which three divisions shall (subject to the provisions of this Act) be equally represented in the Senate as follows :— Ontario by Twenty-four Senators; Quebec by Twenty-four Senators : and the Maritime Provinces by Twenty-four Senators, Twelve thereof representing Nova Scotia, and Twelve thereof representing New Brunswick.

In the case of Quebec each of the twenty-four Senators representing that Province shall be appointed for one of the twenty-four Electoral Divisions of Lower Canada specified in Schedule A to Chapter One of the Consolidated Statutes of Canada.

Qualifications of Senators. 23. The qualification of a Senator shall be as follows :—

(1) He shall be of the full age of Thirty years ;

(2) He shall be either a natural-born subject of the Queen, or a subject of the Queen naturalized by an Act of the Parliament of Great Britain, or of the Parliament of the United Kingdom of Great Britain and Ireland, or of the Legislature of one of the Provinces of Upper Canada, Lower Canada, Canada, Nova Scotia, or New Brunswick, before the Union, or of the Parliament of Canada after the Union :

(3) He shall be legally or equitably seised as of freehold for his own use and benefit of lands or tenements held in free and common socage, or seised or possessed for his own use and benefit of lands or tenements held in franc-alleu or in roture, within the Province for which he is appointed, of the value of Four thousand dollars, over and above all rents, dues, debts, charges, mortgages, and incumbrances due or payable out of or charged on or affecting the same :

(4)   His real and personal property shall be together worth Four thousand dollars over and above his debts and liabilities :

(5)   He shall be resident in the Province for which he is appointed :

(6)   In the case of Quebec he shall have his real property qualification in the Electoral Division for which he is appointed, or shall be resident in that Division.

24.   The Governor-General shall from time to time, in the Queen's name by Instrument under the Great Seal of Canada, summon qualified persons to the Senate; and, subject to the provisions of this Act, every person so summoned shall become and be a member of the Senate and a Senator.

Summons of Senator.

25.   Such persons shall be first summoned to the Senate as the Queen by Warrant under Her Majesty's Royal Sign Manual thinks fit to approve, and their names shall be inserted in the Queen's Proclamation of Union.

Summons of First body of Senators.

26.   If at any time, on the recommendation of the Governor-General, the Queen thinks fit to direct that three or six Members be added to the Senate, the Governor-General may by summons to three or six qualified persons (as the case may be), representing equally the three divisions of Canada, add to the Senate accordingly.

Addition of Senators in certain cases.

27.   In case of such addition being at any time made the Governor-General shall not summon any person to the Senate, except on a further like direction by the Queen on the like recommendation, until each of the three divisions of Canada is represented by twenty-four Senators and no more.

Reduction of Senate to normal number.

28.   The number of Senators shall not at any time exceed seventy-eight.

Maximum number of Senators.

29.   A Senator shall, subject to the provisions of this Act, hold his place in the Senate for life.

Tenure of place in Senate.

30.   A Senator may by writing under his hand, addressed to the Governor-General, resign his place in the Senate, and thereupon the same shall be vacant.

Resignation of place in Senate.

Disqualifi-
cation of
Senators.

31.　The place of a Senator shall become vacant in any of the following cases :—

(1)　If for two consecutive Sessions of the Parliament he fails to give his attendance in the Senate :

(2)　If he takes an oath or makes a declaration or acknowledgment of allegiance, obedience, or adherence to a Foreign Power, or does an act whereby he becomes a Subject or Citizen, or entitled to the rights or privileges of a Subject or Citizen of a Foreign Power :

(3)　If he is adjudged bankrupt or insolvent, or applies for the benefit of any law relating to insolvent debtors, or becomes a public defaulter :

(4)　If he is attainted of treason or convicted of felony or of any infamous crime :

(5)　If he ceases to be qualified in respect of property or of residence ; provided that a Senator shall not be deemed to have ceased to be qualified in respect of residence by reason only of his residing at the Seat of the Government of Canada while holding an office under that Government requiring his presence there.

Summons
on Va-
cancy in
Senate.

32.　When a vacancy happens in the Senate by resignation, death, or otherwise, the Governor-General shall by summons to a fit and qualified person fill the vacancy.

Questions
as to
Qualifica-
tions and
Vacancies
in Senate.

33.　If any question arises respecting the qualification of a Senator, or a vacancy in the Senate, the same shall be heard and determined by the Senate.

Appoint-
ment of
Speaker of
Senate.

34.　The Governor-General may from time to time, by instrument under the Great Seal of Canada, appoint a Senator to be Speaker of the Senate, and may remove him and appoint another in his stead.

Quorum of
Senate.

35.　Until the Parliament of Canada otherwise provides, the presence of at least fifteen Senators, including the Speaker, shall be necessary to constitute a meeting of the Senate for the exercise of its powers.

Voting in
Senate.

36.　Questions arising in the Senate shall be decided by a majority of voices, and the Speaker shall in all cases have a vote, and when the voices are equal the decision shall be deemed to be in the negative.

The House of Commons.

37. The House of Commons shall, subject to the provisions of this Act, consist of One hundred and eighty-one Members, of whom eighty-two shall be elected for Ontario, Sixty-five for Quebec, Nineteen for Nova Scotia, and Fifteen for New Brunswick.

Constitution of House of Commons in Canada.

38. The Governor-General shall from time to time, in the Queen's name, by Instrument under the Great Seal of Canada, summon and call together the House of Commons.

Summoning of House of Commons.

39. A Senator shall not be capable of being elected or of sitting or voting as a Member of the House of Commons.

Senators not to sit in House of Commons.

40. Until the Parliament of Canada otherwise provides, Ontario, Quebec, Nova Scotia and New Brunswick, shall, for the purposes of the Election of Members to serve in the House of Commons, be divided into Electoral Districts as follows :—

Electoral Districts of the four Provinces.

1. *ONTARIO.*

Ontario shall be divided into the Counties, Ridings of Counties, Cities, Parts of Cities, and Towns enumerated in the First Schedule to this Act, each whereof shall be an Electoral District, each such District as numbered in that Schedule being entitled to return one Member.

2. *QUEBEC.*

Quebec shall be divided into Sixty-five Electoral Districts, composed of the Sixty-five Electoral Divisions into which Lower Canada is, at the passing of this Act, divided under Chapter Two of the Consolidated Statutes of Canada, Chapter Seventy-five of the Consolidated Statutes for Lower Canada, and the Act of the Province of Canada of the Twenty-third Year of the Queen, Chapter One, or any other Act amending the same in force at the Union, so that each such Electoral Division shall be for the purposes of this Act an Electoral District entitled to return One Member.

3. *NOVA SCOTIA.*

Each of the Eighteen Counties of Nova Scotia shall be an Electoral District. The County of Halifax shall be entitled to return Two Members, and each of the other Counties One Member.

4. NEW BRUNSWICK.

Each of the Fourteen Counties into which New Brunswick is divided, including the City and County of St John, shall be an Electoral District. The City of St John shall also be a separate Electoral District. Each of those Fifteen Electoral Districts shall be entitled to return One Member.

Continuance of existing Election Laws until Parliament of Canada otherwise provides.

41. Until the Parliament of Canada otherwise provides, all laws in force in the several Provinces at the Union relative to the following matters or any of them, namely:—The qualifications and disqualifications of persons to be elected or to sit or vote as Members of the House of Assembly or Legislative Assembly in the several Provinces; the Voters at Elections of such Members; the oaths to be taken by Voters; the Returning Officers, their powers and duties; the proceedings at Elections; the periods during which Elections may be continued; the trial of controverted Elections, and proceedings incident thereto; the vacating of seats of Members, and the execution of new Writs in case of seats vacated otherwise than by dissolution,—shall respectively apply to Elections of Members to serve in the House of Commons for the same several Provinces. Provided that, until the Parliament of Canada otherwise provides, at any Election for a Member of the House of Commons for the District of Algoma, in addition to persons qualified by the law of the Province of Canada to vote, every male British Subject, aged Twenty-one years or upwards, being a householder, shall have a vote.

Writs for first Election.

42. For the first Election of Members to serve in the House of Commons, the Governor-General shall cause Writs to be issued by such person, in such form, and addressed to such Returning Officers as he thinks fit.

The person issuing Writs under this Section shall have the like powers as are possessed at the Union by the Officers charged with the issuing of Writs for the Election of Members to serve in the respective House of Assembly or Legislative Assembly of the Province of Canada, Nova Scotia, or New Brunswick; and the Returning Officers to whom Writs are directed under this Section shall have the like powers as are possessed at the Union by the Officers charged with the Returning of Writs for the Election of

Members to serve in the same respective House of Assembly or Legislative Assembly.

43.   In case a vacancy in the representation in the House of Commons of any Electoral District happens before the meeting of the Parliament, or after the meeting of the Parliament before provision is made by the Parliament in this behalf, the provisions of the last foregoing Section of this Act shall extend and apply to the issuing and returning of a Writ in respect of such vacant District.

As to Casual Vacancies.

44.   The House of Commons on its first assembling after a General Election shall proceed with all practicable speed, to elect one of its members to be Speaker.

As to Election of Speaker of House of Commons.

45.   In case of a vacancy happening in the office of Speaker by death, resignation, or otherwise, the House of Commons shall, with all practicable speed, proceed to elect another of its members to be Speaker.

As to filling up Vacancy in office of Speaker.

46.   The Speaker shall preside at all meetings of the House of Commons.

Speaker to preside.

47.   Until the Parliament of Canada otherwise provides, in case of the absence for any reason of the Speaker from the chair of the House of Commons for a period of forty-eight consecutive hours, the House may elect another of its members to act as Speaker, and the Member so elected shall, during the continuance of such absence of the Speaker, have and execute all the powers, privileges, and duties of Speaker.

Provision in case of absence of Speaker.

48.   The presence of at least Twenty Members of the House of Commons shall be necessary to constitute a meeting of the House for the exercise of its powers; and for that purpose the Speaker shall be reckoned as a Member.

Quorum of House of Commons.

49.   Questions arising in the House of Commons shall be decided by a majority of voices other than that of the Speaker, and when the voices are equal, but not otherwise, the Speaker shall have a vote.

Voting in House of Commons.

50.   Every House of Commons shall continue for Five Years from the day of the return of the Writs for choosing the House (subject to be sooner dissolved by the Governor-General), and no longer.

Duration of House of Commons.

Decennial Re-adjustment of Representation.

51. On the completion of the census in the year One thousand eight hundred and seventy-one, and of each subsequent decennial census, the representation of the four Provinces shall be re-adjusted by such authority, in such manner, and for such time, as the Parliament of Canada from time to time provides, subject and according to the following rules :—

(1) Quebec shall have the fixed number of Sixty-five members :

(2) There shall be assigned to each of the other Provinces such a number of Members as will bear the same proportion to the number of its population (ascertained at such census) as the number sixty-five bears to the number of the population of Quebec (so ascertained) :

(3) In the computation of the number of Members for a Province a fractional part not exceeding one-half of the whole number requisite for entitling the Province to a Member shall be disregarded ; but a fractional part exceeding one-half of that number shall be equivalent to the whole number :

(4) On any such re-adjustment the number of Members for a Province shall not be reduced unless the proportion which the number of the population of the Province bore to the number of the aggregate population of Canada at the then last preceding re-adjustment of the number of Members for the Province is ascertained at the then latest census to be diminished by one-twentieth part or upwards :

(5) Such re-adjustment shall not take effect until the termination of the then existing Parliament.

Increase of number of House of Commons.

52. The number of Members of the House of Commons may be from time to time increased by the Parliament of Canada, provided the proportionate representation of the Provinces prescribed by this Act is not thereby disturbed.

Money Votes ; Royal Assent.

Appropriation and Tax Bills.

53. Bills for appropriating any part of the Public Revenue, or for imposing any tax or impost, shall originate in the House of Commons.

54. It shall not be lawful for the House of Commons to adopt or pass any Vote, Resolution, Address, or Bill for the appropriation of any part of the Public Revenue, or of any Tax or Impost, to any purpose that has not been first recommended to that house by Message of the Governor-General in the Session in which such Vote, Resolution, Address or Bill is proposed. *Recommendation of money votes.*

55. Where a Bill passed by the Houses of Parliament is presented to the Governor-General for the Queen's assent, he shall declare, according to his discretion, but subject to the provisions of this Act and to Her Majesty's Instructions, either that he assents thereto in the Queen's name, or that he withholds the Queen's assent, or that he reserves the Bill for the signification of the Queen's pleasure. *Royal Assent to Bills, &c.*

56. Where the Governor-General assents to a Bill in the Queen's name, he shall by the first convenient opportunity, send an authentic copy of the Act to one of Her Majesty's Principal Secretaries of State, and if the Queen in Council within two years after receipt thereof by the Secretary of State thinks fit to disallow the Act, such disallowance (with a certificate of the Secretary of State of the day on which the Act was received by him) being signified by the Governor-General, by Speech or Message to each of the Houses of Parliament, or by Proclamation, shall annul the Act from and after the day of such signification. *Disallowance by Order in Council of Act assented to by Governor-General.*

57. A Bill reserved for the signification of the Queen's pleasure shall not have any force unless and until within two years from the day on which it was presented to the Governor-General for the Queen's Assent, the Governor-General signifies, by Speech or Message to each of the Houses of Parliament, or by Proclamation, that it has received the Assent of the Queen in Council. *Signification of Queen's pleasure on Bill reserved.*

An entry of every such Speech, Message, or Proclamation shall be made in the Journal of each House, and a duplicate thereof duly attested shall be delivered to the proper Officer to be kept among the Records of Canada.

V. PROVINCIAL CONSTITUTIONS.

Executive Power.

58. For each Province there shall be an officer, styled the Lieutenant-Governor, appointed by the Governor-General in Council by Instrument under the Great Seal of Canada. *Appointment of Lieutenant-Governors.*

Tenure of office of Lieutenant-Governor. 59. A Lieutenant-Governor shall hold office during the pleasure of the Governor-General; but any Lieutenant-Governor appointed after the commencement of the first Session of the Parliament of Canada shall not be removable within five years from his appointment, except for cause assigned, which shall be communicated to him in writing within one month after the order for his removal is made, and shall be communicated by Message to the Senate and to the House of Commons within one week thereafter if the Parliament is then sitting, and if not, then within one week after the commencement of the next Session of the Parliament.

Salaries of Lieutenant-Governors. 60. The Salaries of the Lieutenant-Governors shall be fixed and provided by the Parliament of Canada.

Oaths, &c., of Lieutenant-Governor. 61. Every Lieutenant-Governor shall, before assuming the duties of his office, make and subscribe before the Governor-General, or some person authorized by him, Oaths of Allegiance and Office similar to those taken by the Governor-General.

Application of provisions referring to Lieutenant-Governor. 62. The provisions of this Act referring to the Lieutenant-Governor extend and apply to the Lieutenant-Governor for the time being of each Province, or other the Chief Executive Officer or Administrator for the time being carrying on the Government of the Province, by whatever title he is designated.

Appointment of Executive Officers for Ontario and Quebec. 63. The Executive Council of Ontario and of Quebec shall be composed of such persons as the Lieutenant-Governor from time to time thinks fit, and in the first instance of the following Officers, namely: the Attorney-General, the Secretary and Registrar of the Province, the Treasurer of the Province, the Commissioner of Crown Lands, and the Commissioner of Agriculture and Public Works, with in Quebec, the Speaker of the Legislative Council, and Solicitor-General.

Executive Government of Nova Scotia and New Brunswick. 64. The Constitution of the Executive Authority in each of the Provinces of Nova Scotia and New Brunswick shall, subject to the provisions of this Act, continue as it exists at the Union until altered under the authority of this Act.

65. All powers, authorities, and functions which under any Act of the Parliament of Great Britain, or of the Parliament of the United Kingdom of Great Britain and Ireland, or of the Legislature of Upper Canada, Lower Canada, or Canada, were or are before or at the Union vested in or exercisable by the respective Governors or Lieutenant-Governors of those Provinces, with the advice, or with the advice and consent, of the respective Executive Councils thereof, or in conjunction with those Councils, or with any number of Members thereof, or by those Governors or Lieutenant-Governors individually, shall, as far as the same are capable of being exercised after the Union in relation to the Government of Ontario and Quebec respectively, be vested in and shall or may be exercised by the Lieutenant-Governor of Ontario and Quebec respectively, with the advice, or with the advice and consent of, or in conjunction with the respective Executive Councils or any Members thereof, or by the Lieutenant-Governor individually, as the case requires, subject nevertheless (except with respect to such as exist under Acts of the Parliament of Great Britain, or of the Parliament of the United Kingdom of Great Britain and Ireland,) to be abolished or altered by the respective Legislatures of Ontario and Quebec.

Powers to be exercised by Lieutenant-Governor of Ontario or Quebec with advice or alone.

66. The provisions of this Act referring to the Lieutenant-Governor in Council shall be construed as referring to the Lieutenant-Governor of the Province acting by and with the advice of the Executive Council thereof.

Application of provisions referring to Lieutenant-Governor in Council.

67. The Governor-General in Council may from time to time appoint an Administrator to execute the office and functions of Lieutenant-Governor during his absence, illness, or other inability.

Administration in absence, &c., of Lieutenant-Governor.

68. Unless and until the Executive Government of any Province otherwise directs with respect to that Province, the seats of Government of the Provinces shall be as follows, namely,—of Ontario, the City of Toronto; of Quebec, the City of Quebec; of Nova Scotia, the City of Halifax; and of New Brunswick, the City of Fredericton.

Seats of Provincial Governments.

Legislative Power.

1. ONTARIO.

Legisla-
ture for
Ontario.   69.   There shall be a Legislature for Ontario consisting of
the Lieutenant-Governor and of one House, styled the Legislative
Assembly of Ontario.

Electoral
Districts.   70.   The Legislative Assembly of Ontario shall be composed
of Eighty-two Members, to be elected to represent the Eighty-
two Electoral Districts set forth in the First Schedule to this
Act.

2. QUEBEC.

Legisla-
ture for
Quebec.   71.   There shall be a Legislature for Quebec consisting of
the Lieutenant-Governor and two Houses, styled the Legislative
Council of Quebec and the Legislative Assembly of Quebec.

Constitu-
tion of
Legislative
Council.   72.   The Legislative Council of Quebec shall be composed of
Twenty-four Members, to be appointed by the Lieutenant-Governor in the Queen's name by Instrument under the Great Seal of
Quebec, one being appointed to represent each of the Twenty-
four Electoral Divisions of Lower Canada in this Act referred to,
and each holding office for the term of his life, unless the Legislature of Quebec otherwise provides under the provisions of this Act.

Qualifica-
tion of
Legisla-
tive Coun-
cillors.   73.   The qualifications of the Legislative Councillors of
Quebec shall be the same as those of the Senators for Quebec.

Resigna-
tion, dis-
qualifica-
tion, &c.   74.   The place of a Legislative Councillor of Quebec shall
become vacant in the cases, *mutatis mutandis*, in which the place
of Senator becomes vacant.

Vacancies.   75.   When a vacancy happens in the Legislative Council of
Quebec by resignation, death, or otherwise, the Lieutenant-
Governor in the Queen's name, by Instrument under the Great
Seal of Quebec, shall appoint a fit and qualified person to fill the
vacancy.

Questions
as to
Vacancies,
&c.   76.   If any question arises respecting the qualification of a
Legislative Councillor of Quebec, or a vacany in the Legislative
Council of Quebec, the same shall be heard and determined by
the Legislative Council.

77. The Lieutenant-Governor may from time to time, by Speaker of Legislative Council. Instrument under the Great Seal of Quebec, appoint a Member of the Legislative Council of Quebec to be Speaker thereof, and may remove him and appoint another in his stead.

78. Until the Legislature of Quebec otherwise provides, the Quorum of Legislative Council. presence of at least ten Members of the Legislative Council, including the Speaker, shall be necessary to constitute a meeting for the exercise of its powers.

79. Questions arising in the Legislative Council of Quebec Voting in Legislative Council. shall be decided by a majority of voices, and the Speaker shall in all cases have a vote, and when the voices are equal, the decision shall be deemed to be in the negative.

80. The Legislative Assembly of Quebec shall be composed Constitution of Legislative Assembly of Quebec. of Sixty-five Members, to be elected to represent the Sixty-five Electoral Divisions or Districts of Lower Canada in this Act referred to, subject to alteration thereof by the Legislature of Quebec : Provided that it shall not be lawful to present to the Lieutenant-Governor of Quebec for assent any Bill for altering the limits of any of the Electoral Divisions or Districts mentioned in the Second Schedule to this Act, unless the second and third readings of such Bill have been passed in the Legislative Assembly with the concurrence of the majority of the Members representing all those Electoral Divisions or Districts, and the assent shall not be given to such Bill unless an address has been presented by the Legislative Assembly to the Lieutenant-Governor stating that it has been so passed.

3. *ONTARIO AND QUEBEC.*

81. The Legislatures of Ontario and Quebec respectively First Session of Legislatures. shall be called together not later than six months after the Union.

82. The Lieutenant-Governor of Ontario and of Quebec Summoning of Legislative Assembly. shall, from time to time, in the Queen's name, by Instrument under the Great Seal of the Province, summon and call together the Legislative Assembly of the Province.

83. Until the Legislature of Ontario or of Quebec otherwise Restriction on election of holders of offices. provides, a person accepting or holding in Ontario or in Quebec any office, commission or employment, permanent or temporary,

at the nomination of the Lieutenant-Governor, to which an annual salary, or any fee, allowance, emolument, or profit of any kind or amount whatever from the Province is attached, shall not be eligible as a Member of the Legislative Assembly of the respective Province, nor shall he sit or vote as such ; but nothing in this Section shall make ineligible any person being a Member of the Executive Council of the respective Provinces, or holding any of the following Offices, that is to say :—the Offices of Attorney-General, Secretary and Registrar of the Province, Treasurer of the Province, Commissioner of Crown Lands, and Commissioner of Agriculture and Public Works, and in Quebec Solicitor-General, or shall disqualify him to sit or vote in the House for which he is elected, provided he is elected while holding such Office.

Continuance of existing election Laws.

84. Until the Legislatures of Ontario and Quebec respectively otherwise provide, all laws which at the Union are in force in those Provinces respectively, relative to the following matters, or any of them, namely,—the qualifications and disqualifications of persons to be elected or to sit or vote as Members of the Assembly of Canada, the qualifications or disqualifications of voters, the oaths to be taken by voters, the Returning Officers, their powers and duties, the proceedings at Elections, the periods during which such Elections may be continued, and the trial of controverted Elections and the proceedings incident thereto, the vacating of the seats of Members and the issuing and execution of new Writs in case of seats vacated otherwise than by dissolution, shall respectively apply to Elections of Members to serve in the respective Legislative Assemblies of Ontario and Quebec.

Provided that until the Legislature of Ontario otherwise provides, at any Election for a Member of the Legislative Assembly of Ontario for the District of Algoma, in addition to persons qualified by the law of the Province of Canada to vote, every male British Subject, aged Twenty-one years or upwards, being a householder shall have a vote.

Duration of Legislative Assemblies.

85. Every Legislative Assembly of Ontario and every Legislative Assembly of Quebec shall continue for Four Years from the day of the return of the Writs for choosing the same (subject nevertheless to either the Legislative Assembly of Ontario or the

Legislative Assembly of Quebec being sooner dissolved by the Lieutenant-Governor of the Province), and no longer.

86. There shall be a Session of the Legislature of Ontario and of that of Quebec once at least in every year, so that twelve months shall not intervene between the last sitting of the Legislature in each Province in one Session and its first sitting in the next Session.

Yearly Session of Legislature.

87. The following provisions of this Act respecting the House of Commons of Canada shall extend and apply to the Legislative Assemblies of Ontario and Quebec, that is to say,— the provisions relating to the Election of a Speaker originally and on vacancies, the duties of the Speaker, the absence of the Speaker, the quorum, and the mode of voting, as if those provisions were here re-enacted and made applicable in terms to each such Legislative Assembly.

Speaker, quorum, &c.

4. NOVA SCOTIA AND NEW BRUNSWICK.

88. The Constitution of the Legislature of each of the Provinces of Nova Scotia and New Brunswick shall, subject to the provisions of this Act, continue as it exists at the Union until altered under the authority of this Act; and the House of Assembly of New Brunswick existing at the passing of this Act shall, unless sooner dissolved, continue for the period for which it was elected.

Constitutions of Legislatures of Nova Scotia and New Brunswick.

5. ONTARIO, QUEBEC, AND NOVA SCOTIA.

89. Each of the Lieutenant-Governors of Ontario, Quebec, and Nova Scotia, shall cause Writs to be issued for the first Election of Members of the Legislative Assembly thereof in such form and by such person as he thinks fit, and at such time and addressed to such Returning Officer as the Governor-General directs, and so that the first Election of Member of Assembly for any Electoral District or any sub-division thereof shall be held at the same time and at the same places as the Election for a Member to serve in the House of Commons of Canada for that Electoral District.

First Elections.

6. *THE FOUR PROVINCES.*

Application to Legislatures of provisions respecting money votes, &c.

90. The following provisions of this Act respecting the Parliament of Canada, namely,—the provisions relating to appropriation and tax Bills, the recommendation of money votes, the assent to Bills, the disallowance of Acts, and the signification of pleasure on Bills reserved,—shall extend and apply to the Legislatures of the several Provinces as if those provisions were here re-enacted and made applicable in terms to the respective Provinces and the Legislatures thereof, with the substitution of the Lieutenant-Governor of the Province for the Governor-General, of the Governor-General for the Queen and for a Secretary of State, of one year for two years, and of the Province for Canada.

VI. DISTRIBUTION OF LEGISLATIVE POWERS.

Powers of the Parliament.

Legislative Authority of Parliament of Canada.

91. It shall be lawful for the Queen, by and with the advice and consent of the Senate and House of Commons, to make laws for the peace, order, and good government of Canada, in relation to all matters not coming within the classes of subjects by this Act assigned exclusively to the Legislatures of the Provinces; and for greater certainty, but not so as to restrict the generality of the foregoing terms of this Section, it is hereby declared that (notwithstanding anything in this Act) the exclusive Legislative Authority of the Parliament of Canada extends to all matters coming within the classes of subjects next hereinafter enumerated, that is to say :—

1. The Public Debt and Property :
2. The regulation of Trade and Commerce :
3. The raising of money by any mode or system of Taxation :
4. The borrowing of money on the Public Credit :
5. Postal Service :
6. The Census and Statistics :
7. Militia, Military and Naval Service, and Defence :
8. The fixing of and providing for the Salaries and Allowances of Civil and other Officers of the Government of Canada :
9. Beacons, Buoys, Lighthouses, and Sable Island :
10. Navigation and Shipping :

11. Quarantine and the establishment and maintenance of Marine Hospitals :
12. Sea Coast and Inland Fisheries :
13. Ferries between a Province and any British or Foreign Country or between two Provinces :
14. Currency and Coinage :
15. Banking, Incorporation of Banks, and the issue of Paper Money :
16. Savings Banks :
17. Weights and Measures :
18. Bills of Exchange and Promissory Notes :
19. Interest :
20. Legal Tender :
21. Bankruptcy and Insolvency :
22. Patents of Invention and Discovery :
23. Copyrights :
24. Indians, and Lands reserved for the Indians :
25. Naturalization and Aliens :
26. Marriage and Divorce :
27. The Criminal Law, except the constitution of Courts of Criminal Jurisdiction, but including the Procedure in Criminal matters :
28. The Establishment, Maintenance, and Management of Penitentiaries :
29. Such classes of subjects as are expressly excepted in the enumeration of the classes of subjects by this Act assigned exclusively to the Legislatures of the Provinces.

And any matter coming within any of the classes of subjects enumerated in this Section shall not be deemed to come within the class of matters of a local or private nature comprised in the enumeration of the classes of subjects by this Act assigned exclusively to the Legislatures of the Provinces.

Exclusive Powers of Provincial Legislatures.

92. In each Province the Legislature may exclusively make laws in relation to matters coming within the classes of subjects next hereinafter enumerated, that is to say :—

Subjects of exclusive Provincial Legislation.

1. The amendment from time to time, notwithstanding anything in this Act, of the Constitution of the Province, except as regards the Office of Lieutenant-Governor :

2. Direct Taxation within the Province in order to the raising of a Revenue for Provincial purposes :

3. The borrowing of money on the sole credit of the Province :

4. The establishment and tenure of Provincial Offices, and the appointment and payment of Provincial officers :

5. The management and sale of the Public Lands belonging to the Province, and of the timber and wood thereon :

6. The establishment, maintenance, and management of Public and Reformatory Prisons in and for the Province :

7. The establishment, maintenance, and management of Hospitals, Asylums, Charities, and Eleemosynary Institutions in and for the Provinces, other than Marine Hospitals :

8. Municipal Institutions in the Province :

9. Shop, Saloon, Tavern, Auctioneer, and other Licences, in order to the raising of a Revenue for Provincial, Local, or Municipal purposes :

10. Local works and undertakings other than such as are of the following classes :

 a. Lines of Steam or other Ships, Railways, Canals, Telegraphs, and other works and undertakings connecting the Province with any other or others of the Provinces, or extending beyond the limits of the Province :

 b. Lines of Steam Ships between the Province and any British or Foreign Country :

 c. Such works as, although wholly situate within the Province, are before or after their execution declared by the Parliament of Canada to be for the general advantage of Canada or for the advantage of two or more of the Provinces :

11. The Incorporation of Companies with Provincial objects :

12. The Solemnization of Marriage in the Province :

13. Property and civil rights in the Province :

14. The Administration of Justice in the Province, including the constitution, maintenance, and organization of Provincial Courts, both of Civil and of Criminal Jurisdiction, and including procedure in civil matters in those Courts :

15. The imposition of punishment by fine, penalty, or imprisonment for enforcing any Law of the Province

made in relation to any matter coming within any of the classes of subjects enumerated in this Section :

16. Generally all matters of a merely local or private nature in the Province.

Education.

93. In and for each Province the Legislature may exclusively make laws in relation to education, subject and according to the following provisions :

Legislation respecting Education.

1. Nothing in any such law shall prejudicially affect any right or privilege with respect to Denominational Schools which any class of persons have by law in the Province at the Union :

2. All the powers, privileges, and duties at the Union by law conferred and imposed in Upper Canada on the separate Schools and School Trustees of the Queen's Roman Catholic Subjects shall be and the same are hereby extended to the Dissentient Schools of the Queen's Protestant and Roman Catholic Subjects in Quebec :

3. Where in any Province a system of separate or Dissentient Schools exists by law at the Union or is thereafter established by the Legislature of the Province, an appeal shall lie to the Governor-General in Council from any act or decision of any Provincial authority affecting any right or privilege of the Protestant or Roman Catholic minority of the Queen's Subjects in relation to Education :

4. In case any such Provincial law as from time to time seems to the Governor-General in Council requisite for the due execution of the provisions of this Section is not made, or in case any decision of the Governor-General in Council on any appeal under this Section is not duly executed by the proper Provincial authority in that behalf, then and in every such case, and as far only as the circumstances of each case require, the Parliament of Canada may make remedial laws for the due execution of the provisions of this Section and of any decision of the Governor-General in Council under this Section.

Uniformity of Laws in Ontario, Nova Scotia, and New Brunswick.

Legislation for uniformity of Laws in three Provinces. 94. Notwithstanding anything in this Act, the Parliament of Canada may make provision for the uniformity of all or any of the laws relative to property and civil rights in Ontario, Nova Scotia and New Brunswick, and of the procedure of all or any of the Courts in those three Provinces, and from and after the passing of any Act in that behalf, the power of the Parliament of Canada to make laws in relation to any matter comprised in any such Act shall, notwithstanding anything in this Act, be unrestricted; but any Act of the Parliament of Canada making provision for such uniformity shall not have effect in any Province unless and until it is adopted and enacted as law by the Legislature thereof.

Agriculture and Immigration.

Concurrent powers of Legislation respecting Agriculture, &c. 95. In each Province the Legislature may make laws in relation to Agriculture in the Province, and to Immigration into the Province; and it is hereby declared that the Parliament of Canada may from time to time make laws in relation to Agriculture in all or any of the Provinces, and to Immigration into all or any of the Provinces; and any law of the Legislature of a Province relative to Agriculture or to Immigration shall have effect in and for the Province as long and as far only as it is not repugnant to any Act of the Parliament of Canada.

VII. JUDICATURE.

Appointment of Judges. 96. The Governor-General shall appoint the Judges of the Superior, District, and County Courts in each Province, except those of the Courts of Probate in Nova Scotia and New Brunswick.

Selection of Judges in Ontario, &c. 97. Until the laws relative to property and civil rights in Ontario, Nova Scotia and New Brunswick, and the procedure of the Courts in those Provinces, are made uniform, the Judges of the Courts of those Provinces appointed by the Governor-General shall be selected from the respective Bars of those Provinces.

Selection of Judges in Quebec. 98. The Judges of the Courts of Quebec shall be selected from the Bar of that Province.

99. The Judges of the Superior Courts shall hold office Tenure of office of during good behaviour, but shall be removable by the Governor- Judges of General on address of the Senate and House of Commons. Superior Courts.

100. The salaries, allowances, and pensions of the Judges of Salaries, the Superior, District, and County Courts (except the Courts of &c., of Judges. Probate in Nova Scotia and New Brunswick), and of the Admiralty Courts in cases where the Judges thereof are for the time being paid by salary, shall be fixed and provided by the Parliament of Canada.

101. The Parliament of Canada may, notwithstanding any- General thing in this Act, from time to time, provide for the constitution, Court of Appeal, maintenance, and organization of a General Court of Appeal for &c. Canada, and for the establishment of any additional Courts for the better administration of the Laws of Canada.

VIII. REVENUES; DEBTS; ASSETS; TAXATION.

102. All Duties and Revenues over which the respective Creation Legislatures of Canada, Nova Scotia, and New Brunswick before of Consolidated and at the Union had and have power of appropriation, except Revenue such portions thereof as are by this Act reserved to the respective Fund. Legislatures of the Provinces, or are raised by them in accordance with the special powers conferred on them by this Act, shall form one Consolidated Revenue Fund, to be appropriated for the public service of Canada in the manner and subject to the charges in this Act provided.

103. The Consolidated Revenue Fund of Canada shall be Expenses permanently charged with the costs, charges, and expenses of collection, &c. incident to the collection, management, and receipt thereof, and the same shall form the first charge thereon, subject to be reviewed and audited in such manner as shall be ordered by the Governor-General in Council until the Parliament otherwise provides.

104. The annual interest of the public debts of the several Interest of Provinces of Canada, Nova Scotia, and New Brunswick at the Provincial Public Union shall form the second charge on the Consolidated Revenue Debts. Fund of Canada.

105. Unless altered by the Parliament of Canada, the salary Salary of Governor- of the Governor-General shall be Ten Thousand Pounds sterling General.

money of the United Kingdom of Great Britain and Ireland, payable out of the Consolidated Revenue Fund of Canada, and the same shall form the third charge thereon.

Appropriation from time to time. 106. Subject to the several payments by this Act charged on the Consolidated Revenue Fund of Canada, the same shall be appropriated by the Parliament of Canada for the public service.

Transfer of stocks, &c. 107. All Stocks, Bankers' Balances, and Securities for money belonging to each Province at the time of the Union, except as in this Act mentioned, shall be the property of Canada, and shall be taken in reduction of the amount of the respective debts of the Provinces at the Union.

Transfer of property in schedule. 108. The Public Works and Property of each Province, enumerated in the Third Schedule to this Act, shall be the property of Canada.

Property in Lands, Mines, &c. 109. All Lands, Mines, Minerals, and Royalties belonging to the several Provinces of Canada, Nova Scotia, and New Brunswick at the Union, and all sums then due or payable for such Lands, Mines, Minerals, or Royalties, shall belong to the several Provinces of Ontario, Quebec, Nova Scotia, and New Brunswick in which the same are situate or arise, subject to any trusts existing in respect thereof, and to any interest other than that of the Province in the same.

Assets connected with Provincial debts. 110. All Assets connected with such portions of the Public Debt of each Province as are assumed by that Province shall belong to that Province.

Canada to be liable for Provincial debts. 111. Canada shall be liable for the Debts and Liabilities of each Province existing at the Union.

Debts of Ontario and Quebec. 112. Ontario and Quebec conjointly shall be liable to Canada for the amount (if any) by which the debt of the Province of Canada exceeds at the Union Sixty-two million five hundred thousand Dollars, and shall be charged with interest at the rate of five per centum per annum thereon.

Assets of Ontario and Quebec. 113. The Assets enumerated in the Fourth Schedule to this Act, belonging at the Union to the Province of Canada shall be the property of Ontario and Quebec conjointly.

114.   Nova Scotia shall be liable to Canada for the amount Debt of (if any) by which its public debt exceeds at the Union Eight Nova Scotia. million Dollars, and shall be charged with interest at the rate of five per centum per annum thereon.

115.   New Brunswick shall be liable to Canada for the Debt of amount (if any) by which its public debt exceeds at the Union New Bruns- Seven million Dollars, and shall be charged with interest at the wick. rate of five per centum per annum thereon.

116.   In case the public debts of Nova Scotia and New Payment Brunswick do not at the Union amount to Eight million and of interest to Nova Seven million Dollars respectively, they shall respectively receive, Scotia and by half-yearly payments in advance from the Government of New Bruns- Canada, interest at five per centum per annum on the difference wick. between the actual amounts of their respective debts and such stipulated amounts.

117.   The several Provinces shall retain all their respective Provincial public property not otherwise disposed of in this Act, subject to Public property. the right of Canada to assume any lands or public property required for Fortifications or for the Defence of the Country.

118.   The following sums shall be paid yearly by Canada to Grants to the several Provinces for the support of their Governments and Provinces. Legislatures :—

	Dollars.
Ontario	Eighty Thousand.
Quebec	Seventy Thousand.
Nova Scotia	Sixty Thousand.
New Brunswick	Fifty Thousand.

Two Hundred and Sixty Thousand ;

and an annual grant in aid of each Province shall be made, equal to Eighty Cents per head of the population as ascertained by the census of One thousand eight hundred and sixty-one, and in the case of Nova Scotia and New Brunswick, by each subsequent decennial census until the population of each of those two Pro- vinces amounts to Four hundred thousand souls, at which rate such grant shall thereafter remain.   Such grants shall be in full settlement of all future demands on Canada, and shall be paid half-yearly in advance to each Province ; but the Government of Canada shall deduct from such grants, as against any Province, all sums chargeable as interest on the public debt of that Province in excess of the several amounts stipulated in this Act.

Further Grant to New Brunswick.   119.   New Brunswick shall receive by half-yearly payments in advance from Canada for the period of ten years from the Union an additional allowance of Sixty-three thousand Dollars per annum; but as long as the public debt of that Province remains under Seven million Dollars, a deduction equal to the interest at five per centum per annum on such deficiency shall be made from that allowance of Sixty-three thousand Dollars.

Form of payments.   120.   All payments to be made under this Act, or in discharge of liabilities created under any Act of the Provinces of Canada, Nova Scotia, and New Brunswick respectively, and assumed by Canada, shall, until the Parliament of Canada otherwise directs, be made in such form and manner as may from time to time be ordered by the Governor-General in Council.

Canadian manufactures, &c.   121.   All articles of the growth, produce, or manufacture of any one of the Provinces shall, from and after the Union, be admitted free into each of the other Provinces.

Continuance of Customs and Excise Laws.   122.   The Customs and Excise Laws of each Province shall, subject to the provisions of this Act, continue in force until altered by the Parliament of Canada.

Exportation and importation as between two Provinces.   123.   Where Customs Duties are, at the Union, leviable on any goods, wares, or merchandizes in any two Provinces, those goods, wares, and merchandizes may, from and after the Union, be imported from one of those Provinces into the other of them on proof of payment of the Customs Duty leviable thereon in the Province of exportation, and on payment of such further amount (if any) of Customs Duty as is leviable thereon in the Province of importation.

Lumber Dues in New Brunswick.   124.   Nothing in this Act shall affect the right of New Brunswick to levy the lumber dues provided in Chapter Fifteen of Title Three of the Revised Statutes of New Brunswick, or in any Act amending that Act before or after the Union, and not increasing the amount of such dues; but the lumber of any of the Provinces other than New Brunswick shall not be subject to such dues.

Exemption of Public Lands, &c.   125.   No Lands or Property belonging to Canada or any Province shall be liable to taxation.

126. Such portions of the Duties and Revenues over which the respective Legislatures of Canada, Nova Scotia, and New Brunswick had before the Union power of appropriation as are by this Act reserved to the respective Governments or Legislatures of the Provinces, and all Duties and Revenues raised by them in accordance with the special powers conferred upon them by this Act, shall in each Province form one Consolidated Revenue Fund to be appropriated for the Public Service of the Province. *Provincial Consolidated Revenue Fund.*

IX. MISCELLANEOUS PROVISIONS.

General.

127. If any person being, at the passing of this Act, a Member of the Legislative Council of Canada, Nova Scotia, or New Brunswick, to whom a place in the Senate is offered, does not within thirty days thereafter, by writing under his hand addressed to the Governor-General of the Province of Canada, or to the Lieutenant-Governor of Nova Scotia or New Brunswick (as the case may be), accept the same, he shall be deemed to have declined the same ; and any person who, being at the passing of this Act a Member of the Legislative Council of Nova Scotia or New Brunswick, accepts a place in the Senate shall thereby vacate his Seat in such Legislative Council. *As to Legislative Councillors of Provinces becoming Senators.*

128. Every Member of the Senate or House of Commons of Canada shall, before taking his Seat therein, take and subscribe before the Governor-General or some person authorized by him, and every Member of a Legislative Council or Legislative Assembly of any Province shall, before taking his Seat therein, take and subscribe before the Lieutenant-Governor of the Province or some person authorized by him, the Oath of Allegiance contained in the Fifth Schedule to this Act; and every Member of the Senate of Canada and every Member of the Legislative Council of Quebec shall also, before taking his Seat therein, take and subscribe before the Governor-General or some person authorized by him, the Declaration of Qualification contained in the same Schedule. *Oath of Allegiance, &c.*

129. Except as otherwise provided by this Act, all Laws in force in Canada, Nova Scotia, or New Brunswick at the Union, and all Courts of Civil and Criminal Jurisdiction, and all legal *Continuance of existing Laws, Courts, Officers, &c.*

Commissions, Powers, and Authorities, and all Officers, Judicial, Administrative, and Ministerial, existing therein at the Union, shall continue in Ontario, Quebec, Nova Scotia, and New Brunswick respectively, as if the Union had not been made; subject nevertheless (except with respect to such as are enacted by or exist under Acts of the Parliament of Great Britain or of the Parliament of the United Kingdom of Great Britain and Ireland,) to be repealed, abolished, or altered by the Parliament of Canada, or by the Legislature of the respective Provinces, according to the authority of the Parliament or of that Legislature under this Act.

Transfer of Officers to Canada. 130. Until the Parliament of Canada otherwise provides, all Officers of the several Provinces having duties to discharge in relation to matters other than those coming within the classes of subjects by this Act assigned exclusively to the Legislatures of the Provinces shall be Officers of Canada, and shall continue to discharge the duties of their respective offices under the same liabilities, responsibilities, and penalties as if the Union had not been made.

Appointment of new Officers. 131. Until the Parliament of Canada otherwise provides, the Governor-General in Council may from time to time appoint such Officers as the Governor-General in Council deems necessary or proper for the effectual execution of this Act.

Treaty obligations. 132. The Parliament and Government of Canada shall have all powers necessary or proper for performing the obligations of Canada or of any Province thereof, as part of the British Empire, towards Foreign Countries, arising under Treaties between the Empire and such Foreign Countries.

Use of English and French languages. 133. Either the English or French language may be used by any person in the debates of the Houses of the Parliament of Canada and of the Houses of the Legislature of Quebec; and both those Languages shall be used in the respective Records and Journals of those Houses; and either of those Languages may be used by any person or in any pleading or process in or issuing from any Court of Canada established under this Act, and in or from all or any of the Courts of Quebec.

The Acts of the Parliament of Canada and of the Legislature of Quebec shall be printed and published in both those Languages.

Ontario and Quebec.

134.   Until the Legislature of Ontario or of Quebec otherwise Appoint- provides, the Lieutenant-Governors of Ontario and Quebec may ment of Executive each appoint, under the Great Seal of the Province, the following Officers for Officers, to hold Office during pleasure, that is to say,—the Ontario and Attorney-General, the Secretary and Registrar of the Province, Quebec. the Treasurer of the Province, the Commissioner of Crown Lands, and the Commissioner of Agriculture and Public Works, and in the case of Quebec the Solicitor-General ; and may, by order of the Lieutenant-Governor in Council, from time to time prescribe the duties of those Officers and of the several Departments over which they shall preside or to which they shall belong, and of the Officers and Clerks thereof; and may also appoint other and additional Officers to hold office during pleasure, and may from time to time prescribe the duties of those Officers, and of the several Departments over which they shall preside or to which they shall belong, and of the Officers and Clerks thereof.

135.   Until the Legislature of Ontario or Quebec otherwise Powers, provides, all rights, powers, duties, functions, responsibilities, or duties,&c., of Execu- authorities at the passing of this Act vested in or imposed on the tive Attorney-General, Solicitor-General, Secretary and Registrar of Officers. the Province of Canada, Minister of Finance, Commissioner of Crown Lands, Commissioner of Public Works, and Minister of Agriculture and Receiver-General, by any Law, Statute, or Ordinance of Upper Canada, Lower Canada, or Canada, and not repugnant to this Act, shall be vested in or imposed on any Officer to be appointed by the Lieutenant-Governor for the discharge of the same or any of them ; and the Commissioner of Agriculture and Public Works shall perform the duties and functions of the office of Minister of Agriculture at the passing of this Act imposed by the law of the Province of Canada, as well as those of the Commissioner of Public Works.

136.   Until altered by the Lieutenant-Governor in Council, Great Seals. the Great Seals of Ontario and Quebec respectively shall be the same, or of the same design as those used in the Provinces of Upper Canada and Lower Canada respectively before their Union as the Province of Canada.

Construction of temporary Acts. 137. The words "and from thence to the end of the then "next ensuing Session of the Legislature," or words to the same effect, used in any temporary Act of the Province of Canada not expired before the Union, shall be construed to extend and apply to the next Session of the Parliament of Canada, if the subject matter of the Act is within the powers of the same, as defined by this Act, or to the next Sessions of the Legislatures of Ontario and Quebec respectively, if the subject matter of the Act is within the powers of the same as defined by this Act.

As to errors in names. 138. From and after the Union the use of the words "Upper Canada" instead of "Ontario," or "Lower Canada" instead of "Quebec," in any Deed, Writ, Process, Pleading, Document, Matter, or Thing, shall not invalidate the same.

As to issue of Proclamations before Union, to commence after Union. 139. Any Proclamation under the Great Seal of the Province of Canada issued before the Union to take effect at a time which is subsequent to the Union, whether relating to that Province, or to Upper Canada, or to Lower Canada, and the several matters and things therein proclaimed shall be and continue of like force and effect as if the Union had not been made.

As to issue of Proclamations after Union. 140. Any Proclamation which is authorized by any Act of the Legislature of the Province of Canada to be issued under the Great Seal of the Province of Canada, whether relating to that Province, or to Upper Canada, or to Lower Canada and which is not issued before the Union, may be issued by the Lieutenant-Governor of Ontario or of Quebec, as its subject matter requires, under the Great Seal thereof; and from and after the issue of such Proclamation the same and the several matters and things therein proclaimed shall be and continue of the like force and effect in Ontario or Quebec as if the Union had not been made.

Penitentiary. 141. The Penitentiary of the Province of Canada shall, until the Parliament of Canada otherwise provides, be and continue the Penitentiary of Ontario and of Quebec.

Arbitration respecting Debts, &c. 142. The division and adjustment of the Debts, Credits, Liabilities, Properties, and Assets of Upper Canada and Lower Canada shall be referred to the arbitrament of three arbitrators, one chosen by the Government of Ontario, one by the Government of Quebec, and one by the Government of Canada; and the selection of the arbitrators shall not be made until the Parliament of Canada and the Legislatures of Ontario and Quebec have met; and the arbitrator chosen by the Government of Canada shall not be a resident either in Ontario or in Quebec.

143.   The Governor-General in Council may from time to time Division of order that such and so many of the records, books, and documents Records. of the Province of Canada as he thinks fit shall be appropriated and delivered either to Ontario or to Quebec, and the same shall thenceforth be the property of that Province; and any copy thereof or extract therefrom, duly certified by the Officer having charge of the original thereof, shall be admitted as evidence.

144.   The Lieutenant-Governor of Quebec may from time to Constitu-time, by Proclamation under the Great Seal of the Province, to tion of townships take effect from a day to be appointed therein, constitute Town- in Quebec ships in those parts of the Province of Quebec in which Town-ships are not then already constituted, and fix the metes and bounds thereof.

X.   Intercolonial Railway.

145.   Inasmuch as the Provinces of Canada, Nova Scotia, and Duty of New Brunswick have joined in a declaration that the construction Govern-ment and of the Intercolonial Railway is essential to the consolidation of Parlia-the Union of British North America, and to the assent thereto ment of Canada to of Nova Scotia and New Brunswick, and have consequently agreed make rail-that provision should be made for its immediate construction by way herein described. the Government of Canada: Therefore, in order to give effect to that agreement, it shall be the duty of the Government and Parliament of Canada to provide for the commencement, within Six Months after the Union, of a Railway connecting the River St Lawrence with the City of Halifax in Nova Scotia, and for the construction thereof without intermission, and the completion thereof with all practicable speed.

XI.   Admission of other Colonies.

146.   It shall be lawful for the Queen, by and with the Power to admit advice of Her Majesty's Most Honourable Privy Council, on Newfound-Addresses from the Houses of the Parliament of Canada, and land, &c., into the from the Houses of the respective Legislatures of the Colonies Union. or Provinces of Newfoundland, Prince Edward Island, and

British Columbia, to admit those Colonies or Provinces, or any of them, into the Union, and on Address from the Houses of the Parliament of Canada to admit Rupert's Land and the North-Western Territory, or either of them, into the Union, on such terms and conditions in each case as are in the Addresses expressed and as the Queen thinks fit to approve, subject to the provisions of this Act; and the provisions of any Order in Council in that behalf shall have effect as if they had been enacted by the Parliament of the United Kingdom of Great Britain and Ireland.

As to representation of Newfoundland and Prince Edward Island in Senate.

147. In case of the admission of Newfoundland and Prince Edward Island, or either of them, each shall be entitled to a representation in the Senate of Canada of Four Members, and (notwithstanding anything in this Act) in case of the admission of Newfoundland the normal number of Senators shall be Seventy-six and their maximum number shall be Eighty-two; but Prince Edward Island when admitted shall be deemed to be comprised in the third of the Three Divisions into which Canada is, in relation to the constitution of the Senate, divided by this Act, and accordingly, after the admission of Prince Edward Island, whether Newfoundland is admitted or not, the representation of Nova Scotia and New Brunswick in the Senate shall, as vacancies occur, be reduced from Twelve to Ten Members respectively, and the representation of each of those Provinces shall not be increased at any time beyond Ten, except under the provisions of this Act for the appointment of Three or Six additional Senators under the direction of the Queen.

SCHEDULES.

THE FIRST SCHEDULE.

Electoral Districts of Ontario.

[Omitted.]

THE SECOND SCHEDULE.

Electoral Districts of Quebec specially fixed.

[Omitted.]

THE THIRD SCHEDULE.

Provincial Public Works and Property to be the Property of Canada.

1. Canals, with lands and water power connected therewith.
2. Public Harbours.
3. Lighthouses and Piers, and Sable Island.
4. Steamboats, Dredges, and Public Vessels.
5. Rivers and Lake Improvements.
6. Railways and Railway Stocks, Mortgages, and other Debts due by Railway Companies.
7. Military Roads.
8. Custom Houses, Post Offices, and all other Public Buildings, except such as the Government of Canada appropriate for the use of the Provincial Legislatures and Governments.
9. Property transferred by the Imperial Government, and known as Ordnance Property.
10. Armouries, Drill Sheds, Military Clothing, and Munitions of War, and Lands set apart for general Public Purposes.

THE FOURTH SCHEDULE.

Assets to be the Property of Ontario and Quebec conjointly.

[Omitted.]

THE FIFTH SCHEDULE.

Oath of Allegiance.

I, *A. B.*, do swear, that I will be faithful and bear true Allegiance to Her Majesty Queen Victoria.

Note.—*The name of the King or Queen of the United Kingdom of Great Britain and Ireland for the time being is to be substituted from time to time, with proper terms of reference thereto.*

Declaration of Qualification.

I, *A. B.*, do declare and testify, that I am by law duly qualified to be appointed a Member of the Senate of Canada [*or as the case may be*], and that I am legally or equitably seised as of Freehold for my own use and benefit of Lands or Tenements held in free and Common Socage [*or* seised or possessed for my own use and benefit of Lands or Tenements held in Franc-alleu or in Roture (*as the case may be,*)] in the Province of Nova Scotia [*or as the case may be*] of the value of Four Thousand Dollars over and above all Rents, Dues, Debts, Mortgages, Charges, and Incumbrances due or payable out of or charged on or affecting the same, and that I have not collusively or colourably obtained a title to or become possessed of the said Lands and Tenements, or any part thereof, for the purpose of enabling me to become a Member of the Senate of Canada [*or as the case may be*], and that my Real and Personal Property are together worth Four Thousand Dollars over and above my Debts and Liabilities.

TERMS OF UNION OF BRITISH COLUMBIA.

ORDER IN COUNCIL DATED 16 *May*, 1871.

1. Canada shall be liable for the debts and liabilities of British Columbia existing at the time of the Union.

2. British Columbia not having incurred debts equal to those of the other Provinces now constituting the Dominion, shall be entitled to receive, by half-yearly payments, in advance, from the General Government, interest at the rate of five per cent. per annum on the difference between the actual amount of its indebtedness at the date of the Union and the indebtedness per head of the population of Nova Scotia and New Brunswick (27·77 dollars), the population of British Columbia being taken at 60,000.

3. The following sums shall be paid by Canada to British Columbia for the support of its Government and Legislature, to wit, an annual subsidy of 35,000 dollars, and an annual grant equal to 80 cents per head of the said population of 60,000, both half-yearly in advance; such grant of 80 cents per head to be augmented in proportion to the increase of population, as may be shown by each subsequent decennial census, until the population amounts to 400,000, at which rate such grant shall thereafter remain, it being understood that the first census be taken in the year 1881.

4. The Dominion will provide an efficient mail service, fortnightly, by steam communication, between Victoria and San Francisco, and twice a week between Victoria and Olympia; the vessels to be adapted for the conveyance of freight and passengers.

5. Canada will assume and defray the charges for the following services:

A. Salary of the Lieutenant-Governor;

B. Salaries and allowances of the Judges of the Superior Courts and the County or District Courts;

C. The charges in respect to the Department of Customs;
D. The Postal and Telegraphic Services;
E. Protection and encouragement of Fisheries;
F. Provision for the Militia;
G. Lighthouses, Buoys, and Beacons, Shipwrecked crews, Quarantine and Marine Hospitals, including a Marine Hospital at Victoria;
H. The Geological Survey;
I. The Penitentiary.

And such further charges as may be incident to and connected with the services which, by the "British North America Act of 1867," appertain to the General Government, and as are or may be allowed to the other Provinces.

6. Suitable pensions, such as shall be approved of by Her Majesty's Government, shall be provided by the Government of the Dominion for those of Her Majesty's servants in the Colony whose position and emoluments derived therefrom would be affected by political changes on the admission of British Columbia into the Dominion of Canada.

7. It is agreed that the existing Customs Tariff and Excise Duties shall continue in force in British Columbia until the Railway from the Pacific Coast and the system of Railways in Canada are connected, unless the Legislature of British Columbia should sooner decide to accept the tariff and excise laws of Canada. When customs and excise duties are, at the time of the union of British Columbia with Canada, leviable on any goods, wares, or merchandizes in British Columbia, or in the other Provinces of the Dominion, those goods, wares, and merchandizes may, from and after the Union, be imported into British Columbia from the Provinces now composing the Dominion, or from either of those Provinces into British Columbia, on proof of payment of the customs or excise duties leviable thereon in the Province of exportation, and on payment of such further amount (if any) of customs or excise duties as are leviable thereon in the Province of importation. This arrangement to have no force or effect after the assimilation of the tariff and excise duties of British Columbia with those of the Dominion.

8. British Columbia shall be entitled to be represented in the Senate by three members, and by six members in the House

of Commons. The representation to be increased under the provisions of the " British North America Act, 1867."

9. The influence of the Dominion Government will be used to secure the continued maintenance of the Naval Station at Esquimalt.

10. The provisions of the "British North America Act, 1867," shall (except those parts thereof which are in terms made, or by reasonable intendment may be held to be specially applicable to and only affect one and not the whole of the Provinces now comprising the Dominion, and except so far as the same may be varied by this Minute) be applicable to British Columbia, in the same way and to the like extent as they apply to the other Provinces of the Dominion, and as if the Colony of British Columbia had been one of the Provinces originally united by the said Act.

11. The Government of the Dominion undertake to secure the commencement simultaneously, within two years from the date of Union, of the construction of a Railway from the Pacific towards the Rocky Mountains, and from such point as may be selected, east of the Rocky Mountains, towards the Pacific, to connect the seaboard of British Columbia with the railway system of Canada ; and further, to secure the completion of such Railway within ten years from the date of the union.

And the Government of British Columbia agree to convey to the Dominion Government, in trust, to be appropriated in such manner as the Dominion Government may deem advisable in furtherance of the construction of the said Railway, a similar extent of public lands along the line of Railway, throughout its entire length in British Columbia, not to exceed, however, Twenty (20) miles on each side of said line, as may be appropriated for the same purpose by the Dominion Government from the public lands in the North-west Territories and the Province of Manitoba. Provided, that the quantity of land which may be held under pre-emption right or by Crown grant within the limits of the tract of land in British Columbia to be so conveyed to the Dominion Government shall be made good to the Dominion from contiguous public lands ; and, provided further, that until the commencement, within two years as aforesaid from the date of the union, of the construction of the said Railway, the Government of British Columbia shall not sell or alienate any further portions of the public lands of British Columbia in any other way than under right of pre emption, requiring actual residence of the pre-emptor on the land claimed by him. In consideration of the land to be so conveyed in aid of the construction of the said Railway, the Dominion Government agree to pay to British Columbia, from the date of the union, the sum of 100,000 Dollars per annum, in half-yearly payments in advance.

12. The Dominion Government shall guarantee the interest for ten years from the date of the completion of the works, at the rate of five per centum per annum, on such sum, not exceeding £100,000 sterling, as may be required for the construction of a first class Graving Dock at Esquimalt.

13. The charge of the Indians, and the trusteeship and management of the lands reserved for their use and benefit, shall be assumed by the Dominion Government, and a policy as liberal as that hitherto pursued by the British Columbia Government shall be continued by the Dominion Government after the union.

To carry out such policy, tracts of land of such extent as it has hitherto been the practice of the British Columbia Government to appropriate for that purpose, shall from time to time be conveyed by the Local Government to the Dominion Government in trust for the use and benefit of the Indians, on application of the Dominion Government; and in case of disagreement between the two Governments respecting the quantity of such tracts of land to be so granted, the matter shall be referred for the decision of the Secretary of State for the Colonies.

14. The constitution of the Executive Authority and of the Legislature of British Columbia shall, subject to the provisions of the "British North America Act, 1867," continue as existing at the time of the union until altered under the authority of the said Act, it being at the same time understood that the Government of the Dominion will readily consent to the introduction of Responsible Government when desired by the inhabitants of British Columbia, and it being likewise understood that it is the intention of the Governor of British Columbia, under the authority of the Secretary of State for the Colonies, to amend the existing constitution of the Legislature by providing that a majority of its members shall be elective.

The union shall take effect according to the foregoing terms and conditions on such day as Her Majesty by and with the advice of Her Most Honourable Privy Council may appoint on Addresses from the Legislature of the Colony of British Columbia and of the Houses of Parliament of Canada, in the terms of the 146th Section of the " British North America Act, 1867," and British Columbia may in its Address specify the Electoral Districts for which the first election of members to serve in the House of Commons shall take place.

TERMS OF UNION OF PRINCE EDWARD ISLAND.

Order in Council dated 26*th June,* 1873.

1. Canada shall be liable for the debts and liabilities of Prince Edward Island at the time of the Union.

2. That in consideration of the larger expenditure authorized by the Parliament of Canada for the construction of railways and canals and in view of the possibility of a re-adjustment of the financial arrangements between Canada and the several provinces now embraced in the Dominion as well as the isolated and exceptional condition of Prince Edward Island that. Colony shall on entering the Union be entitled to incur a debt equal to 50 dollars per head of its population as shown by the census returns of 1871 that is to say 4,701,050 dollars.

3. That Prince Edward Island not having incurred debts equal to the sum mentioned in the next preceding resolution shall be entitled to receive by half-yearly payments in advance from the general government interest at the rate of five per cent. per annum on the difference from time to time between the actual amount of its indebtedness and the amount of indebtedness authorized as aforesaid, viz. 4,701,050 dollars.

4. That Prince Edward Island shall be liable to Canada for the amount (if any) by which its public debt and liabilities at the date of the Union may exceed 4,701,050 dollars and shall be chargeable with interest at the rate of five per cent. per annum.

5. That as the Government of Prince Edward Island holds no lands from the Crown, and consequently enjoys no revenue from that source for the construction and maintenance of local works the Dominion Government shall pay by half-yearly instalments in advance to the Government of Prince Edward Island 45,000 dollars per annum less interest at five per cent. per annum

upon any sum not exceeding 800,000 dollars which the Dominion Government may advance to the Prince Edward Island Government for the purchase of lands now held by large proprietors.

6. That in consideration of the transfer to the Parliament of Canada of the powers of taxation the following sums shall be paid yearly by Canada to Prince Edward Island for the support of its Government and Legislature that is to say 30,000 dollars and an annual grant equal to 80 cents per head of its population as shown by the census returns of 1871, viz. 94,021, both by half-yearly payments in advance—such grant of eighty cents per head to be augmented in proportion to the increase of population of the Island as may be shown by each subsequent decennial census until the population amounts to 400,000 at which rate such grant shall remain it being understood that the next census shall be taken in the year 1881.

7. That the Dominion Government shall assume and defray all the charges for the following services, viz.

The salary of the Lieutenant-Governor.

The salaries of the Judges of the Superior Court and the District or County Courts when established.

The charges in respect of the Department of Customs.

The Postal Department.

The protection of fisheries.

The provision for the Militia.

The lighthouses, shipwrecked crews, Quarantine and Marine Hospitals.

The geological survey.

The Penitentiary.

Efficient steam service for the conveyance of mails and passengers to be established and maintained between the Island and the mainland of the Dominion winter and summer, thus placing the Island in continuous communication with the intercolonial railway and the railway system of the Dominion.

The maintainance of telegraphic communication between the Island and the mainland of the Dominion.

And such other charges as may be incident to and connected with the services which by the B. N. A. Act 1867 appertain to the General Government and as are or may be allowed to the other provinces.

8. That the new building in which are held the Law Courts, Registry Office &c., shall be transferred to Canada on the payment of 69,000 dollars. The purchase to include the land on which the building now stands and a suitable space of ground in addition for yard room &c.

That the Steam Dredge Boat in course of construction shall be taken by the Dominion at a cost not exceeding 22,000 dollars.

That the Steam Ferry Boat owned by the Government of the Island and used as such shall remain the property of the Island.

9. That the population of Prince Edward Island having been increased by 15,000 or upwards since the year 1861 the Island shall be represented in the House of Commons of Canada by six members; the representation to be adjusted from time to time under the provisions of the B. N. A. Act 1867.

10. That the constitution of the executive authority and of the Legislature of Prince Edward Island shall, subject to the provisions of the B. N. A. Act 1867, continue as at the time of the Union until altered under the authority of the said Act and the House of Assembly of Prince Edward Island existing at the date of the Union shall unless sooner dissolved continue for the period for which it was elected.

11. That the provisions in the B. N. A. Act 1867 shall, except those parts thereof which are in terms made or by reasonable intendment may be held to be especially applicable to and only to affect one and not the whole of the provinces now comprising the Dominion and except so far as the same may be varied by these resolutions be applicable to Prince Edward Island in the same way and to the same extent as they apply to the other Provinces of the Dominion and as if the Colony of Prince Edward Island had been one of the Provinces originally united by the said Act.

12. That the Union shall take place on such day as Her Majesty may direct by Order in Council on addresses to that effect from the Houses of the Parliament of Canada and of the Legislature of the Colony of Prince Edward Island under the 146th section of the B. N. A. Act 1867 and that the Electoral Districts for which, the time within which and the laws and provisions under which the first election of members to serve in the House of Commons of Canada for such Electoral Districts

shall be such as the said House of the Legislature of the said colony of Prince Edward Island shall specify in their said addresses.

In the addresses from Prince Edward Island it was stipulated that the Island should be divided into three districts each returning two members and

"that the 1st election of members to serve in the House of Commons of Canada shall take place within three calendar months after this Island shall be admitted and become part of the Dominion of Canada and that all laws which at the date of the Order in Council by which the said Island of Prince Edward shall be admitted into the Dominion of Canada, relating to the qualification of any person to be elected to sit or vote as a member of the House of Assembly of the said Island, and relating to the qualifications or disqualifications of voters and to the oaths to be taken by voters and to returning officers and poll clerks and their powers and duties, and relating to polling divisions within the said Island, and relating to the proceedings at elections and to the period during which such elections may be continued, and relating to the trial of controverted elections and the proceedings incident thereto, and relating to the vacating of seats of members and to the execution of new writs in case of any seat being vacated otherwise by a dissolution, and all other matters connected with or incidental to elections of members to serve in the House of Assembly of the said Island shall apply to elections of members to serve in the House of Commons for the Electoral Districts, situate in the said Island of Prince Edward."

Extracts from Order in Council, dated **24** *June,* 1870, *surrendering the North-West Territories of Canada.*

"It is hereby ordered and declared by Her Majesty by and with the advice of the Privy Council in pursuance and exercise of the powers vested in Her Majesty by the said Acts of Parliament[1] that from and after the 15th day of July, 1870, the said North-Western Territory shall be admitted into and become part of the Dominion of Canada upon the terms and conditions set forth in the first hereinbefore recited address[2] and that the Parliament of Canada shall have from the day aforesaid full power and authority to legislate for the future welfare and good government of the said Territory. And it is further ordered that without prejudice to any obligations arising from the aforesaid approved report, Rupert's Land shall from and after the said date be admitted into and become part of the Dominion of Canada."

The conditions contained in the Address from the Parliament of Canada regarding the North-West Territory were :—

" That the Government and Parliament of Canada would provide that the legal rights of any corporation, company or individual within the same should be respected and placed under the protection of courts of competent jurisdiction. "

" That the claims of the Indian tribes to compensation for lands required for purposes of settlement should be considered and settled in conformity with the equitable principles that had uniformly governed the British Crown in its dealing with the aborigines."

The conditions relating to Rupert's Land were :—

1. " Canada to pay the Hudson's Bay Company £300,000 when Rupert's Land is transferred to the Dominion."

2. " The Company are to retain the posts they actually occupy in the North-West Territory and may within twelve months of

[1] i.e. B. N. A. Act, 1867 : Rupert's Land Act, 1868.

[2] i.e. from the Canadian Parliament.

the surrender select a block of land adjoining each of its posts within any part of British North America not comprised in Canada and British Columbia in conformity except as regards the Red River Territory with a list made out by the Company and communicated to the Canadian Ministers being the list in the Schedule to the Deed of Surrender. The actual survey is to be proceeded with, with all convenient speed."

3. "The size of each block is not to exceed 10 acres round Upper Fort Garry, 300 acres round Lower Fort Garry ; in the rest of the Red River Territory a number of acres to be settled at once between the Governor in Council and the Company but so that the aggregate extent of the blocks is not to exceed 50,000 acres."

4. "So far as the configuration of the country admits, the blocks shall front the river or road by which means of access are provided and shall be approximately in the shape of parellelograms of which the frontage shall not be more than half the depth."

5. "The Company may for fifty years after the surrender, claim in any township or district, within the Fertile belt, in which land is set out for settlement, grants of land not exceeding one twentieth part of the land so set out. The blocks so granted to be determined by lot and the Company to pay a rateable share of the survey expenses not exceeding eight cents Canadian an acre. The Company may defer the exercise of their right of claiming the proportion of each township for not more than ten years after it is set out : but their claim must be limited to an allotment from the lands remaining unsold at the time they declare their intention to make it."

6. "For the purposes of the last article, the Fertile belt is to be bounded as follows—On the South by the United States boundary : on the West by the Rocky Mountains : on the North by the northern branch of the Saskatchewan : on the East by Lake Winnipeg, the Lake of the woods and the waters connecting them."

7. "If any township shall be formed abutting on the north bank of the northern branch of the Saskatchewan River the Company may take their one twentieth of any such township which for the purpose of this article shall not extend more than

five miles inland from the river, giving to the Canadian Dominion an equal quantity of the portion of lands coming to them of townships established on the southern bank."

8. "In laying out any public roads, canals, &c., through any block of land secured to the Company the Canadian Government may take without compensation such land as is necessary for the purpose not exceeding one twenty fifth of the total acreage of the block : but if the Canadian Government require any land which is actually built upon or which is necessary for giving the Company's servants access to any river or lake, or as a frontage to any river or lake, they shall pay to the Company the fair value of the same and shall make compensation for any injury done to the Company or their servants."

9. "It is understood that the whole of the land to be appropriated within the meaning of the last preceding clause shall be appropriated for public purposes."

10. "All titles to land up to the 8th March, 1869, conferred by the Company are to be confirmed."

11. "The Company is to be at liberty to carry on its trade without hindrance in its corporate capacity and no exceptional tax is to be placed on the Company's land, trade or servants nor any import duty on goods introduced by them previous to the surrender."

12. "Canada is to take over the materials of the electric telegraph at cost price —such price including transport but not including interest for money and subject to a deduction for ascertained deterioration."

13. "The Company's claim to land under agreement of Messrs Vankvughnet and Hopkins is to be withdrawn."

14. "Any claims of Indians to compensation for lands required for the purposes of settlement shall be disposed of by the Canadian Government in connection with the Imperial Government and the Company shall be relieved of all responsibility in respect of them."

An Act respecting the establishment of Provinces in the Dominion of Canada.

[29 *June,* 1871.]

WHEREAS doubts have been entertained respecting the powers of the Parliament of Canada to establish Provinces in territories admitted, or which may hereafter be admitted, into the Dominion of Canada, and to provide for the representation of such Provinces in the said Parliament, and it is expedient to remove such doubts and to vest such powers in the said Parliament :

Be it enacted by the Queen's Most Excellent Majesty, by and with the advice and consent of the Lords spiritual and temporal, and Commons, in this present Parliament assembled and by the authority of the same, as follows :—

1. This Act may be cited for all purposes as "The British North America Act 1871." *Short Title.*

2. The Parliament of Canada may from time to time establish new Provinces in any territories forming for the time being part of the Dominion of Canada, but not included in any Province thereof, and may, at the time of such establishment, make provision for the constitution and administration of any such Province and for the passing of laws for the peace, order and good government of such Province, and for its representation in the said Parliament. *Parliament of Canada may establish new Provinces and provide for the constitution, &c. thereof.*

3. The Parliament of Canada may from time to time, with the consent of the Legislature of any Province of the said Dominion increase, diminish or otherwise alter the limits of such Province upon such terms and conditions as may be agreed to by the said Legislature, and may with the like consent make provision respecting the effect and operation of any such increase or diminution or alteration of territory in relation to any Province affected thereby. *Alteration of limits of Provinces.*

Parliament of Canada may legislate for any territory not included in a Province.

4. The Parliament of Canada may from time to time make provision for the administration, peace, order and good government of any territory not for the time being included in any Province.

Confirmation of Acts of Parliament of Canada 32 & 33 Vict. (Canadian) c. 3, 33 Vict. (Canadian) c. 3.

5. The following Acts passed by the said Parliament of Canada and intituled respectively :—

"An Act for the temporary government of Rupert's Land and the North-Western Territory when united with Canada;" and

"An Act to amend and continue the Act 32 and 33 Vict. c. 3, and to establish and provide for the government of the Province of Manitoba"

shall be and be deemed to have been valid and effectual for all purposes whatsoever from the date at which they respectively received the assent in the Queen's name of the Governor-General of the said Dominion of Canada.

Limitation of powers of Canada to legislate for an established Province.

6. Except as provided by the 3rd section of this Act it shall not be competent for the Parliament of Canada to alter the provisions of the last mentioned Act of the said Parliament in so far as it relates to the Province of Manitoba, or of any other Act hereafter establishing new Provinces in the said Dominion subject always to the right of the Legislature of the Province of Manitoba to alter from time to time the provisions of any law respecting the qualification of electors and members of the Legislative Assembly and to make laws respecting elections in the said Province."

An Act to remove doubts with respect to the powers of the Parliament of Canada under section 18 of the British North America Act 1867.

[19 *July*, 1875.]

WHEREAS by section 18 of the British North America Act 1867 it is provided as follows : 30 & 31 Vic. c. 3.

"The privileges, immunities and powers to be held, enjoyed and exercised by the Senate and by the House of Commons and by the members thereof respectively, shall be such as are from time to time defined by Act of the Parliament of Canada, but so that the same shall never exceed those at the passing of this Act held, enjoyed and exercised by the Commons House of Parliament of the United Kingdom of Great Britain and Ireland and by the members thereof."

And whereas doubts have arisen with regard to the power of defining by an Act of the Parliament of Canada in pursuance of the said section, the said privileges, powers or immunities ; and it is expedient to remove such doubts :

Be it therefore enacted by the Queen's Most Excellent Majesty, by and with the advice and consent of the Lords spiritual and temporal and Commons in this present Parliament assembled, and by the authority of the same as follows :—

1. Section eighteen of the British North America Act 1867 is hereby repealed, without prejudice to anything done under that section, and the following section shall be substituted for the section so repealed. Substitution of new section for section 18 of 30 & 31 Vic. c. 3.

The privileges, immunities and powers to be held, enjoyed and exercised by the Senate and by the House of Commons and by the members thereof respectively, shall be such as are from time to time defined by Act of the Parliament of Canada, but so that any Act of the Parliament of Canada defining such privileges, immunities and powers shall not confer any privileges, immunities or powers exceeding those at the passing of such Act held, enjoyed and exercised by the Commons House of Parliament of the United Kingdom of Great Britain and Ireland and by the members thereof.

Confirmation of Act of Canadian Parliament.
2. The Act of the Parliament of Canada passed in the 31st year of the reign of Her present Majesty, chapter 24, intituled "An Act to provide for oaths to witnesses being administered in certain cases for the purposes of either House of Parliament" shall be deemed to be valid and to have been valid as from the date at which the Royal assent was given thereto by the Governor-General of the Dominion of Canada.

Short title.
3. This Act may be cited as "The Parliament of Canada Act 1875."

49 and 50 Vic. (i) c. 35.

An Act respecting the representation in the Parliament of Canada of Territories which for the time being form part of the Dominion of Canada but are not included in any Province.

[25 *June*, 1886.]

WHEREAS it is expedient to empower the Parliament of Canada to provide for the representation in the Senate and House of Commons of Canada, or either of them, of any territory which for the time being forms part of the Dominion of Canada but is not included in any Province:

Be it therefore enacted by the Queen's Most Excellent Majesty, by and with the advice and consent of the Lords spiritual and temporal and Commons in this present Parliament assembled, and by the authority of the same as follows:—

Provision by Parliament of Canada for representation of territory.
1. The Parliament of Canada may from time to time make provision for the representation in the Senate and House of Commons of Canada or in either of them of any territories which for the time being form part of the Dominion of Canada but are not included in any Province.

2.   Any Act passed by the Parliament of Canada before the passing of this Act for the purpose mentioned in this Act shall if not disallowed by the Queen be and shall be deemed to have been valid and effectual from the date at which it received the assent in Her Majesty's name of the Governor-General of Canada. *Effect of Acts of Parliament of Canada.*

It is hereby declared that any Act passed by the Parliament of Canada whether before or after the passing of this Act for the purposes mentioned in this Act or in the B. N. A. Act 1871 has effect notwithstanding anything in the B. N. A. Act 1867 and the number of Senators or the number of Members of the House of Commons specified in the last mentioned Act is increased by the number of Senators or of Members as the case may be provided by any such Act of the Parliament of Canada for the representation of any provinces or territories of Canada. *34 & 35 Vic. c. 28. 30 & 31 Vic. c. 3.*

3.   This Act may be cited as the British North America Act 1886. *Short title.*

This Act and the British North America Act 1867 and the British North America Act 1871 shall be construed together and may be cited as the British North America Acts 1867 to 1886

DRAFT OF LETTERS-PATENT passed under the Great Seal of the United Kingdom, constituting the Office of Governor-General of the Dominion of *Canada*.

———

Letters Patent,
    Dated 5th October, 1878. }

Victoria, by the Grace of God, of the United Kingdom of *Great Britain and Ireland,* Queen, Defender of the Faith, Empress of *India ;* To all to whom these Presents shall come, Greeting :

WHEREAS We did, by certain Letters-Patent under the Great Seal of Our United Kingdom of *Great Britain* and *Ireland,* bearing date at *Westminster* the Twenty-second day of May, 1872, in the Thirty-fifth year of Our Reign, constitute and appoint Our Right Trusty and Right Well-beloved Cousin and Councillor, *Frederick Temple,* Earl of *Dufferin,* Knight of Our Most Illustrious Order of *Saint Patrick,* Knight Commander of Our Most Honourable Order of the Bath (now Knight Grand Cross of Our Most Distinguished Order of *Saint Michael* and *Saint George*), to be Our Governor-General in and over Our Dominion of *Canada* for and during Our will and pleasure : And whereas by the 12th section of "The *British North America* Act 1867," certain powers, authorities, and functions were declared to be vested in the Governor-General : and whereas we are desirous of making effectual and permanent provision for the office of Governor-General in and over Our said Dominion of *Canada,* without making new Letters-Patent on each demise of the said Office : Now know ye that We have revoked and determined, and by these presents do revoke and determine, the said recited Letters-Patent of the Twenty-second day of May, 1872, and every clause, article and thing therein contained : And further know ye that We, of our special grace, certain knowledge and mere motion, have thought fit to constitute, order, and declare, and do by these presents constitute, order, and declare that there shall be a Governor-General (hereinafter called Our said Governor-General) in and over Our Dominion of *Canada* (hereinafter called our said Dominion) and that the person who shall fill the said Office of the Governor-General shall be from time to time appointed by Commission under our Sign-Manual and Signet. And we do hereby authorize and command Our said Governor-General to do and execute, in due order, all things that shall belong to his said command, and to the trust we have reposed in him, according to the several powers and authorities granted or appointed him by virtue of "The *British North America* Act, 1867", and of these present Letters-Patent and of such Commission as may be issued to him under our Sign-Manual and Signet, and according to such Instructions as may from time to time be given to him, under our Sign-Manual and Signet, or by Our Order in Our Privy Council, or by Us through one of Our Principal Secretaries of State, and to such Laws as are or shall hereafter be in force in Our said Dominion.

II.   And We do hereby authorize and empower Our said Governor-General to keep and use the Great Seal of Our said Dominion for sealing all things whatsoever that shall pass the said Great Seal.

III.   And We do further authorize and empower Our said Governor-General to constitute and appoint, in Our name and on Our behalf, all such Judges, Commissioners, Justices of the Peace, and other necessary Officers and Ministers of Our said Dominion, as may be lawfully constituted or appointed by Us.

IV.   And we do further authorize and empower Our said Governor-General, so far as we lawfully may upon sufficient cause to him appearing, to remove from his office, or to suspend from the exercise of the same, any person exercising any office within Our said Dominion, under or by virtue of any Commission or Warrant granted, or which may be granted, by Us in Our name or under Our authority.

V. And We do further authorize and empower our said Governor-General to exercise all powers lawfully belonging to Us in respect of the summoning, proroguing, or dissolving the Parliament of Our said Dominion.

VI. And whereas by "The *British North America* Act, 1867," it is amongst other things enacted, that it shall be lawful for Us, if We think fit, to authorize the Governor-General of Our Dominion of *Canada* to appoint any person or persons, jointly or severally, to be his Deputy or Deputies within any part or parts of Our said Dominion, and in that capacity to exercise, during the pleasure of our said Governor-General, such of the powers, authorities and functions of Our said Governor-General as he may deem it necessary or expedient to assign to such Deputy or Deputies, subject to any limitations or directions from time to time expressed or given by Us: Now We do hereby authorize and empower Our said Governor-General, subject to such limitations and directions as aforesaid, to appoint any person or persons, jointly or severally, to be his Deputy or Deputies within any part or parts of Our said Dominion of *Canada*, and in that capacity to exercise, during his pleasure, such of his powers, functions and authorities, as he may deem it necessary or expedient to assign to him or them: Provided always, that the appointment of such a Deputy or Deputies shall not affect the exercise of any such power, authority or function by Our said Governor-General in person.

VII. And We do hereby declare Our pleasure to be that, in the event of 'the death, incapacity, removal or absence of Our said Governor-General out of Our said Dominion, all and every the powers and authorities herein granted to him shall, until our further pleasure is signified therein, be vested in such person as may be appointed by Us under Our Sign-Manual and Signet to be Our Lieutenant-Governor of Our said Dominion; or if there shall be no such Lieutenant-Governor in Our said Dominion, then in such person or persons as may be appointed by Us under Our Sign-Manual and Signet to administer the Government of the same; and in case there shall be no person or persons within Our said Dominion so appointed by Us, then in the Senior Officer for the time being in command of Our regular troops in Our said Dominion: Provided that no such powers or authorities shall vest in such Lieutenant-Governor, or such other person or persons, until he or they shall have taken the oaths appointed to be taken by the Governor-General of Our said Dominion, and in the manner provided by the instructions accompanying these Our Letters-Patent.

VIII. And We do hereby require and command all Our Officers and Ministers, Civil and Military, and all other the inhabitants of Our said Dominion, to be obedient, aiding and assisting unto our said Governor-General, or, in the event of his death, incapacity or absence, to such person or persons as may, from time to time, under the provisions of Our Letters Patent, administer the Government of Our said Dominion.

IX. And We do hereby reserve to Ourselves, our heirs and successors, full power and authority from time to time to revoke, alter or amend these Our Letters-Patent as to Us or them shall seem meet.

X. And We do further direct and enjoin that these Our Letters-Patent shall be read and proclaimed at such place or places as Our said Governor-General shall think fit within Our said Dominion of *Canada*.

In Witness whereof We have caused these Our Letters to be made Patent. Witness Ourself at Westminster, the fifth day of October, in the Forty-second Year of Our Reign.

By Warrant under the Queen's Sign-Manual.

C. ROMILLY.

DRAFT OF INSTRUCTIONS passed under the Royal Sign-Manual and Signet to the Governor-General of the Dominion of *Canada*.

Dated 5th October, 1878.
VICTORIA R.

Instructions to our Governor-General in and over our Dominion of *Canada*, or, in his absence, to Our Lieutenant-Governor or the Officer for the time being administering the Government of Our said Dominion.

Given at Our Court at *Balmoral*, this Fifth day of October, 1878, in the Forty-second year of Our Reign.

WHEREAS by certain Letters-Patent bearing even date herewith, We have constituted, ordered and declared that there shall be a Governor-General (hereinafter called Our said Governor-General) in and over Our Dominion of *Canada* (hereinafter called Our said Dominion), And we have thereby authorized and commanded Our said Governor-General to do and execute in due manner all things that shall belong to his said command, and to the trust we have reposed in him, according to the several powers and authorities granted or appointed him by virtue of the said Letters-Patent and of such Commission as may be issued to him under Our Sign-Manual and Signet, and according to such Instructions as may from time to time be given to him, under Our Sign-Manual and Signet, or by Our Order in Our Privy Council, or by Us through One of Our Principal Secretaries of State, and to such Laws as are or shall hereafter be in force in Our said Dominion. Now, therefore, We do, by these Our Instructions under Our Sign-Manual and Signet, declare Our pleasure to be, that Our said Governor-General for the time being shall, with all due solemnity, cause our Commission, under Our Sign-Manual and Signet, appointing Our said Governor-

General for the time being, to be read and published in the presence of the Chief Justice for the time being, or other Judge of the Supreme Court of Our said Dominion, and of the members of the Privy Council in Our said Dominion : And we do further declare Our pleasure to be that Our said Governor-General, and every other officer appointed to administer the Government of Our said Dominion, shall take the Oath of Allegiance in the form provided by an Act passed in the Session holden in the thirty-first and thirty-second years of Our Reign, intituled "An Act to amend the Law relating to Promissory Oaths ;" and likewise that he or they shall take the usual Oath for the due execution of the Office of Our Governor-General in and over Our said Dominion, and for the due and impartial administration of justice; which Oaths the said Chief Justice for the time being, of Our said Dominion, or, in his absence, or in the event of his being otherwise incapacitated, any Judge of the Supreme Court of Our said Dominion shall, and he is hereby required to tender and administer unto him or them.

II.   And We do authorize and require Our said Governor-General from time to time by himself or by any other person to be authorized by him in that behalf, to administer to all and to every person or persons as he shall think fit, who shall hold any office or place of trust or profit in Our said Dominion, the said Oath or Allegiance, together with such other Oath or Oaths as may from time to time be prescribed by any Laws or Statutes in that behalf made and provided.

III.   And We do require Our said Governor-General to communicate forthwith to the Privy Council for Our said Dominion these Our Instructions, and likewise all such others from time to time, as he shall find convenient for Our service to be imparted to them.

IV.   Our said Governor-General is to take care that all laws assented to by him in Our name, or reserved for the signification of Our pleasure thereon, shall, when transmitted by him, be fairly abstracted in the margins, and be accompanied, in such cases as may seem to him necessary, with such explanatory observations as may be required to exhibit the reasons and occasions for proposing such Laws ; and he shall also transmit fair copies of the Journals and Minutes of the proceedings of the

Parliament of Our said Dominion, which he is to require from the clerks, or other proper officers in that behalf, of the said Parliament.

V. And We do further authorize and empower Our said Governor-General, as he shall see occasion, in Our name and on Our behalf, when any crime has been committed for which the offender may be tried within our said Dominion, to grant a pardon to any accomplice, not being the actual perpetrator of such crime, who shall give such information as shall lead to the conviction of the principal offender; and further to grant to any offender convicted of any crime in any Court, or before any Judge, Justice, or Magistrate, within Our said Dominion, a pardon, either free or subject to lawful conditions or any respite of the execution of the sentence of any such offender, for such period as to Our said Governor-General may seem fit, and to remit any fines, penalties, or forfeitures, which may become due and payable to Us. Provided always, that Our said Governor-General shall not in any case, except where the offence has been of a political nature, make it a condition of any pardon or remission of sentence that the offender shall be banished from or shall absent himself from Our said Dominion. And We do hereby direct and enjoin that Our said Governor-General shall not pardon or reprieve any such offender without first receiving in capital cases the advice of the Privy Council for our said Dominion, and in other cases the advice of one, at least, of his Ministers; and in any case in which such pardon or reprieve might directly affect the interests of Our Empire, or of any country or place beyond the jurisdiction of the Government of our said Dominion, Our said Governor-General shall, before deciding as to either pardon or reprieve, take those interests specially into his own personal consideration in conjunction with such advice as aforesaid.

VI. And whereas great prejudice may happen to Our service and to the security of our said Dominion, by the absence of Our said Governor-General, he shall not, upon any pretence whatever, quit Our said Dominion without having first obtained leave from Us for so doing under Our Sign-Manual and Signet, or through one of Our Principal Secretaries of State.

V. R.

DRAFT OF A COMMISSION passed under the Royal Sign-Manual and
  Signet, appointing the Right Honourable the Marquis of
  Lorne, K.T., G.C.M.G., to be Governor-General of the
  Dominion of *Canada*.

Dated 7th October, 1878.
  VICTORIA R.

Victoria, by the Grace of God, of the United Kingdom of *Great
  Britain* and *Ireland*, Queen, Defender of the Faith, Empress
  of *India*, To our Right Trusty and Well-beloved Councillor
  Sir JOHN DOUGLAS SUTHERLAND CAMPBELL (commonly called
  the Marquis of *Lorne*), Knight of Our Most Ancient and Most
  Noble Order of the Thistle, Knight Grand Cross of Our Most
  Distinguished Order of *St Michael* and *St George*, Greeting :

WE do, by this Our Commission under Our Sign-Manual and
Signet, appoint you, the said Sir JOHN DOUGLAS SUTHERLAND
CAMPBELL (commonly called the Marquis of *Lorne*), until Our
further pleasure shall be signified, to be Our Governor-General in
and over Our Dominion of *Canada* during Our will and pleasure,
with all and singular the powers and authorities granted to the
Governor-General of Our said Dominion in Our Letters-Patent
under the Great Seal of Our United Kingdom of *Great Britain*
and *Ireland*, constituting the office of Governor, bearing date at
Westminster the Fifth day of October, 1878, in the Forty-second
year of Our Reign, which said powers and authorities We do
hereby authorize you to exercise and perform, according to such
Orders and Instructions as Our said Governor-General for the
time being hath already or may hereafter receive from Us.   And
for so doing this shall be your Warrant.

M.   22

II. And we do hereby command all and singular Our officers, Ministers, and loving subjects in Our said Dominion, and all others whom it may concern, to take due notice hereof, and to give their ready obedience accordingly.

Given at Our Court at *Balmoral*, this Seventh day of October, 1878, in the Forty-second year of Our Reign.

By Her Majesty's Command,

M. E. HICKS BEACH.

INDEX.

CAMBRIDGE : PRINTED BY C. J. CLAY, M.A. & SONS, AT THE UNIVERSITY PRESS.